Health and India's Economic Development:
Challenges and Opportunities

Health and India's Economic Development:

Challenges and Opportunities

L.N. Dash

Synergy Books India

(A Unit of M/s Bookwell Publication)

New Delhi

First Published, 2013
ISBN:978-93-82059-13-4

Published by:
Synergy Books India
(A Unit of M/s Bookwell Publication)
24/4800 Ansari Road, Darya Ganj
New Delhi-110002
Phone: 011-23268786, 23257264
Fax: 011-23281315
E-Mail: synergybooks@gmail.com
bookwell@vsnl.net
Website: www.synergybooksindia.com

Printed at : DK FINE ART PRESS (P). LTD. Delhi-92

Content

Introduction xi

1. Health Inequality, Poverty and Inclusive Growth in India 1
L.N. Dash

2. Health Manpower and Health Development in India 17
L.N. Dash

3. Health for All: From Firm Promises to New Realism 33
K.Gangadharan

4. Public Expenditure on Health: Global Scenario with Particular Reference to India 60
Harvinder Kaur & Gursimran Kaur

5. Health Financing Reform in India: Lessons from Other Countries 78
S. Sandhya

6. Trends and Determinants of Early Neonatal Mortality in India 125
Binod Bihari Jena &Prakash Chandra Sahoo

7. Differentials in Maternal Health Care Utilisation in Odisha: An Inter-District Analysis 151
Ayusmati Das & Pratap C. Mohanty

8. Health Status of Tribes in Odisha: Reflection on Critical Issues and Problems 169
Sudhakar Patra & Kabita Kumari Sahu

9. Health Status of Tribals in Odisha: A Case for Concern 185
Bijaya Kumar Panda

10. Growth and Pattern of Health Care Expenditure in Odisha 202
Hadibandhu Sahoo, Anuva Choudhury , & Amita Kumari Choudhury

11. Addressing Health Issues in Rajasthan: A Critical Review 232
Alpana Kateja

12. Trends in Health Status in Punjab 248
Bharati Kapur & Vipla Chopra

Acknowledement

In the process of producing this volume I have received support of various kinds, overtly or covertly, from many sources. My teacher late Prof. Bibekananda Das had the fascination of working in new areas of economics, such as economics of education, health, gender etc. On numerous occasions, during my early years of academic career, I had several discussions on certain tricky issues. All those discussions had settled in my mind. When I pursued a career in academics, natural I got inclined to research in those domains of economics. Therefore, all the books that I have authored so far in the areas of economics of gender, education, infrastructure and health are a culmination of the ideas which I had drawn from my teacher late Prof. Bibekananda Das. I am indeed grateful to him for sharing his ideas and thought with me a few decades ago.

Some of my colleagues and well wishers in my University and in other universities have always encouraged and appreciated me for producing such academic output. Their encouragement has been a boon for me. To name a few are Prof. U.B. Mohapatra from North Orissa University, Prof. J.K.Patnaik from Mizoram University, Prof. B.C.Choudhury from Berhampur University, and Prof. S.K.Swain from VSSUT, Burla (Odisha) and so on.

In my family, my wife Dr (Mrs) Jayanti Panda is an all time supporter. My son Soumeet and daughter Sanmeeta, in their childlike manner, appreciate my academic activities. I indeed aknowledge their encouragement.

Finally, I am thankful to Synergy Books India, New Delhi for willing to publish the book.

List of Contributors

Dr. Alpana Kateja, Professor of Economics, University of Rajasthan, Jaipur (Rajasthan)

Dr. K.Gangadharan, Head, Department of Economics, Kannur University, Thelassery Campus, Palayad - 670 661

Dr. Harvinder Kaur, Professor of Economics, Punjabi University, Patiala (Punjab)

Ms. Gursimran Kaur, Research Scholar, Punjabi University, Patiala (Punjab)

Dr. S. Sandhya, Associate Professor, Jimma University, Ethiopia

Mr. Binod Bihari Jena, Research Scholar, JNU, New Delhi- 110 067

Dr. Prakash Chandra Sahoo, Research Scholar, JNU, New Delhi- 110 067

Ms. Ayusmati Das, Senior Research Scholar, Center for the Study of Regional Development, Population Studies School of Social Science, JNU, 110067

Pratap C. Mohanty, Assistant Professor, Indian Institute of Foreign Trade(IIFT), New Delhi - 110 016

Dr. Bijaya Kumar Panda, Professor of Economics, Berhampur University, Berhampur- 760 007, Odisha

Dr. Hadibandhu Sahoo, Research Scholar, Department of Economics, Berhampur University.

Ms. Anuva Choudhury, Research Scholar, Department of IR & PM, Berhampur University.

Dr. Amita Kumari Choudhury, Professor of Economics, Berhampur University, Berhampur- 760 007, Odisha

Ms. Bharati Kapur, Research Scholar, Punjabi University, Patiala (Punjab)

Dr. Vipla Chopra, Professor of Economics, Department of Distance Education, Punjabi University, Patiala (Punjab).

Dr. Sudhakar Patra, Reader in Economics, Ravenshaw University, Cuttack (Odisha)

Dr. Kabita Kumari Sahu, Lecturer in Economics, North Orissa University, Baripada- 757 003, Odisha

Introduction

In the 1940s and 1950s the key problem of development was seen as one of increasing material production. All the theories of growth laid emphasis on material production. Subsequently, development economists realised that enhancement of material production was a necessary but not a sufficient condition for greater welfare. Consequent upon the recognition of this fact the traditional indicators of welfare were supplemented by social factors such as health and education. In the 1970s efforts were made for the development of health so that it could contribute more to development. That health is both a consumption and investment good was well recognised. Health as a productive good produces the output: healthy days. This production function relationship is shown in Fig. 1. The horizontal axis measures health stock in a given period. The greater one's stock of health, the greater the number of healthy days (up to a maximum of 365 days). The bowed shape of the curve illustrates the law of diminishing marginal returns. The maximum health stock is shown as $H_{min.}$ At this point, production of healthy days drops to zero, indicating death. Therefore, increasing attention was paid to health in the development policies. Once seen as a non-productive sector, it is now viewed as a driver to economic growth. Over the last three decades health has received greater attention in the formulation of development policies at the national and international levels. The "Basic Needs" approach developed in the 1970s incorporated health as an important ingredient for accelerating the pace of the goals of redistribution with growth. The UNDP while assessing the Human

Development Index (HDI), the Gender Development Index (GDI), and Human Poverty Index (HPI) of the countries started taking health as a parameter. In course of time many other decisions at the international level have contributed to the importance of health. In 2000, the WHO set up the Commission on Macroeconomics and Health to assess the importance of health in global economic development. The UN Millennium Development Goals (MDGs) were declared to eliminate poverty from the world. Of the eight goals, three directly concern health. The Ministerial Summit on health held in Mexico in 2004 addressed the role of research in the improvement and sustainable development of population health.

Fig. 1

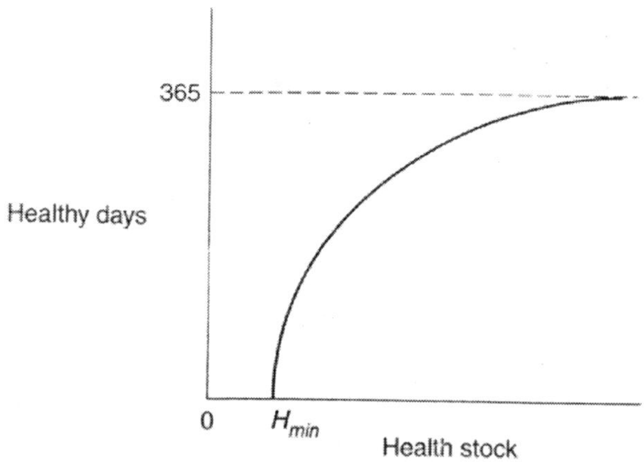

Apart from the international organisations, a number of economists have also highlighted the importance of health. That health is a form of human capital was recognised by Selma J Mushkin in 1962. Grossman (1972) developed a model which explains that ill health has an adverse effect on labour productivity. According to Amartya Sen health like education is among the basic capabilities that gives value to human life. Theodore Schultz and Gary Becker have emphasised that health and education are the two cornerstones of human capital. Health development facilitates economic development of a nation in very many ways. The development experience of different countries has shown that the Great Take-offs in the United Kingdom and the United States, rapid growth of Japan in the early 20th Century, dynamic development of Europe and East Asia in the 1950s and 1960s were supported by important breakthrough in public health, disease control, and improved nutritional intake.

Improvement in health is important for improvement in income. Empirical evidence has shown that high level of population health go hand in hand with high level of national income. This works through a number of mechanisms. Health plays a key role in promoting labour productivity. Healthy workers lose less time from work due to ill health and also are more productive. Secondly, the effect of health on education is profound. Childhood health has direct bearing on cognitive development and the ability to learn as well as on school attendance. Further, as adult mortality and morbidity can lower the prospective returns to investments in schooling, improving adult health can raise the incentive to invest in education. Thirdly, health has significant effect on saving. A longer life span can increase the incentives to save for retirement, increasing the level of saving and wealth. A healthy workforce can also increase the incentives for business investment.

The health seeking behaviour, more particularly in the developing countries has expanded. In India, in the post-liberalisation period, poverty level has declined. The GDP growth rate of India is the second highest in the world. It is now the fifth largest economy in the world. As people's income has gone up, the demand for healthcare has enlarged. Consequently, the issue of demand for and supply of health as a commodity has surfaced prominently in the country. Despite this, public expenditure on health has not increased in commensurate with demand. Public health expenditure as percent of GDP was just 0.22 percent of the GDP in 1950-51 which increased to 0.96 percent in 1990-91. Subsequently, it declined to 0.9 percent in 2000-01 and in 2010-11 it stood at 1.37 percent. (Table 1) The increase in recent years is mostly due to the huge amount of funds allocated through the NRHM. As the public sector has failed to cope up with the health needs of the people the private sector dominates the healthcare expenditure in India. Private sector accounts for nearly 76 percent of a person's expense on health. The last 10 years have seen tremendous growth in the number of private hospitals. Government hospitals have not kept pace due to lack of funds. Rising cost of diagnosis, medicines and hospitalisation push millions of Indians below the poverty line. A majority of Indians spend around 70 percent of their income on medicines and healthcare, compared to 30-40 percent on other Asian countries like Sri Lanka. India has one of the highest proportions of out-of-pocket (OOP) spending on healthcare in the world. The higher proportions of out-of-pocket spend in India has put India in the bracket of such extremely poor countries as Congo, Chad, Burundi, and Ghana. OOP spending is just 13 percent in the US, 12 percent in UK and 33 percent in Brazil. (Table 2) The private sector accounted for about 59 percent of all hospital stays in 2004, and for 82 percent of all outpatient visits. According to the National Sample Survey Organisation report on this subject, per person spending on health was Rs. 242 by the government and Rs. 959 by private means which is called out-of-pocket (OOP) spending. According to a survey by the Indian Institute of Population Sciences and WHO in six states, more than 40 percent of low-income families in India have to borrow money from outside the family to meet their healthcare costs. Those who require hospitalisation are perennially repaying debts. In fact, rural indebtedness caused by illness is far greater than that caused by crop failure. Healthcare has become a foremost reason for impoverishment of people. It is estimated that 39 million people are pushed into poverty every year due to illness and medical bills, although an estimated 20 percent of sicknesses go untreated because people just do not have the money to see a doctor. According to WHO, in India people who pay for their health care services suffer 'catastrophic costs.' While millions suffer and die because they do not have money to pay for healthcare, others suffer because they end up paying through their noses.

Table 1: Expenditure on Health in India

Year	*Percentage of GDP*
1950-51	0.22
1960-61	0.63
1970-71	0.74
1980-81	0.91
1990-91	0.96
2000-01	0.9
2009-10	1.09

Source: Govt.of India. Various reports and documents.

Table 2: Out of Pocket Expenses (As % of total health Expenses)

Country	*Out of Pocket spending (%)*
India	76
Guinea	87
Congo	62
Chad	62
Cameroon	68
United States	13
United Kingdom	12
Russia	30
China	54
Brazil	33

Source: WHO

The *World Health Report 2010* estimated that between 20 – 40 percent of all health expenditures is wasted due to inefficiency. Millions of people miss out on healthcare because they simply cannot afford to pay for it. Studies have shown that even if the government were to provide free healthcare for the poor, accessing it would still be expensive as they would have to spend on travel to the facility, expensive in the absence of affordable public transport in most of the country. Further, duration of treatment would also mean loss of daily earnings, something few families can afford. Medicines in India come far too costly for its people. The WHO points out that 649 million people in India have no regular access to essential medicines. According to the National Sample Survey (55th round), expenditure on medicines accounts for more than two-thirds of outpatient costs. In some places medicine prices are up to 67 times more than the international average price, grossly affecting expenditure for other health services. No one in need of health care should risk financial ruin as a result of this. Therefore, something needs to be done to reduce treatment costs in general and medicine prices in particular. Some states like Kerala and Tamil Nadu supply free medicines and Rajasthan and Bihar are on the verge of implementing such a scheme. In line with the Kerala and Tamil Nadu model, the Government of India is planning to initiate provision of free medicine to all during the 12th Five Year Plan (2012-2017) with a financial outlay of Rs. 28,675 crore. It is indeed a welcome step. If implemented, the Central government will bear 85 percent and the state governments 15 percent of the total cost. This is likely to give a sigh of relief to the poor people in India.

The limited public sector also suffers from unlimited problems. Even with the NRHM boost to the public health infrastructure and enhancement of the health budget, most public facilities continue to be underutilised as they fail to provide basic services. The lack of service stems from inadequate infrastructure, diagnostic and medical facilities and the problem of persistent vacancies in government health setups at all levels from health workers and nurses to laboratory technicians and specialist doctors. The last survey conducted by the Health Ministry reveals that there is a shortfall of over 20,500 Sub-centres, 4500 primary health centres (PHCs) and 2135 community health centres (CHCs). This shortfall means that in many states a CHC meant to cater to a population of about 1.2 lakh might have to cater to as many as 10.6 lakh as in Bihar or 3.3 lakh in Andhra Pradesh or 2.6 lakh in Uttar Pradesh. Similarly, PHCs meant to cater to a population of about 30,000 ends up bearing the burden of over 65,000 in Jharkhand, 62,000 in West Bengal or 41,000 in Bihar. Even as several facilities are stretched due to the size of the population they have to cater to, matters are worsened by the fact that many of these facilities do not have the requisite staff in place as the government finds it difficult to get people willing to work in health setups in rural areas. There is a shortfall of over 12,000 specialists and physicians even at the CHC level. Ten percent of the PHCs have no doctors. Almost a third of the sub-centres and about 10 percent PHCs have no electricity or water. A report of the Central Bureau of Health Intelligence (CBHI) says that in 2009 there were 3.99 lakh government hospital beds for the country's urban population and just 1.49 lakh beds for the rural population. That works out to about 883 persons for each hospital beds in urban areas and 5583 persons per rural hospital beds. With such handicaps, it is hardly surprising that patients are forced to shift to the private sector. More than any pull factor of vastly better care facilities in the private sector, it is the push factor of a non-functional public sector that is forcing a majority of the people in our country to bankrupt themselves seeking healthcare in private facilities.

A country which boosts of its high growth rate also has high disease burden. Chronic underinvestment in health has resulted in the country witnessing an increase in suffering and death from various diseases, accounting for about 20 percent of the world's disease burden. Almost half of the children (46 percent) are malnourished and plagued by ill health. Even sub-Saharan Africa is better off, with 33 percent of children are malnourished. No other country is worse off than India in the case of malnourished children. Over 53 percent of children in India under-five years - that is, 67 million - live without basic healthcare facilities. This means that India alone accounts for about one-third of all children in the world aged below five who do not have basic healthcare. In turn, it also means that poor children are three times more likely to die before their fifth birth days than children in other parts of the world. India ranks 27th along with Ghana and Eritrea when it comes to providing basic healthcare to its children. While the country has been able to reduce its overall child mortality rate by 34 percent since 1990, the survival gap between girls and boys has widened. In absolute numbers the under-five deaths in 2008 declined to 8.8 million from 12.5 million in 1990. While progress is made, it is unacceptable that each year 8.8 million children die before their fifth birthday. From the health profile of India it has been inferred that India might be the fifth largest economy in the world, but its health profile is closer to countries in sub-Saharan Africa.

If this grim scenario persists, India's demographic dividend will not pay off. High growth is now generating the resources needed to enable India to address these problems on a war footing. Like in infrastructure, social sector outlays must be seen as an integral aspect of our push for prosperity. Annual health spending by Centre and states accounts for just 1.37 percent of GDP or about Rs. 57,000 crore. Women and children's health deserves special emphasis and medical education must get urgent attention to address the shortfall of doctors and nurses. The health of the economy must contribute to the health of everyone. Growth alone cannot create well-being, if it is not accompanied by better health. There is an urgent need to provide access to healthcare in a sustainable manner. This should be based on an underlying strategy of preventive rather than curative medical care if we are to improve in India's health indicators. The only viable proposition is an insurance model that will support millions across India's rural areas. Several such initiatives have taken root and many more need to be initiated. There exists a sharp disconnect between urban and rural healthcare in India. If we continue to ignore this deepening divide, we run the risk of destabilizing our socio-economic fabric. The time has come to provide basic healthcare to our 1.21 billion people.

Health Inequality, Poverty and Inclusive Growth in India

L.N.Dash

There is a link between inequality of opportunities and economic growth. Inequality of opportunities prevents the economic agents such as individuals, households, firms etc from fully expressing their economic potential, thereby reducing economic efficiency and slowing growth. When there are fundamental inequalities of opportunities to generate income, this result in income inequality and slow or stagnating growth. Inequality or inequity, therefore, makes the economy less efficient and slows growth. Both the normative and positive views argue against inequality. According to the normative view certain distribution of income and opportunities are morally unacceptable. Amartya Sen is one of the ardent advocates of this view. According to him development is nothing if it is not about enhancing freedoms and the freedom of all people can be realised when all citizens lead a life on an equal footing (Bourguignon and Dessus 2009). The inequality of opportunities includes education, health, credit, infrastructure, public decision making, etc. But the present paper takes into account the inequality of opportunity in health in India in order to discuss the problem of poverty and inclusive growth.

A host of economic literature has come up from the early 1990s which amply explain the relationship between inequality and growth. Some of the pioneering works include Banerjee and Newman (1991), Aghion and Bolton (1992), Bertola (1993), Galor and Zeira (1993), Alesina and Rodrik (1994), Persson and Tabellini (1994). Macroeconomic evidence on the relationship between inequity and growth has been depicted in the *World Development Report 2006*. All these studies emphasise the fact that equity is conducive to growth and inequity hinders it. Recent literature on economic development has also argued that economic inequalities interact with other inequalities, resulting in pernicious consequences for growth (Bebbington *et al* 2008). Bourguignon and Dessus (2009) highlight the fact that inequality acts as brake to growth. Apart from these, a few studies undertaken in recent years have discussed about the inequality in health services, particularly in India. Some of them have also highlighted how health inequity has perpetuated poverty and exclusive growth in the country. Some of them are by Nanda (2009), Yazbeck (2009), Radwan (2005), World Bank (2005, 2011), Gragnolati, et al. (2006), Harris and Kohli (2009). But these few studies do not present an adequate picture on the theme. It is, therefore, felt pertinent to lay bare the link between health inequality, poverty and inclusive growth in India.

Inequality in Health

The importance of health in economic development cannot be overemphasized. For individuals and families health brings the capacity for personal development and economic security in the future. Theodore Shultz and Gary Becker have highlighted that health and education are two cornerstones of human capital. Countries with heavy burden of disease tend to experience severe impediments to economic progress. The great take-offs in Great Britain and in the US, the rapid growth of Japan in the early 20th Century, the dynamic development of southern Europe and East Asia in the 1950s and 1960s were supported by important breakthroughs in public health, disease control, and improved nutritional intake. Individuals with limited access to opportunities in health have limited opportunities to realise their economic potential. On the contrary, poor people all the world over remain poor because they lack opportunities. Good health, nutrition and low fertility help reduce poverty by increasing opportunities to generate income. The costs of illness keep people in poverty. The 1978 Alma Ata Declaration was the first international effort to mobilize global effort to reduce inequalities in health between and within countries. India as a signatory to this took several steps to strengthen its primary health system. The various steps undertaken to improve health system have resulted in substantial improvement in health outcomes. There has been increased access among the rural people. Despite all this, there are differentials in health status of the people in the country. There are high levels of infant mortality, maternal mortality and malnutrition relative to China and Indonesia or even many low-income countries. Within India, inter-and intra-state disparities are large. The poor, rural women, disabled and people belonging to SC and ST stand out as the most vulnerable sections of society. Poverty reduction and realization of inclusive growth in the near future may not be easy without major improvements in spending on and delivery of health in these states.

India is one of the 56 low-and middle-income countries in the world where health inequality is rampant. Reduction in infant and child mortality is one of the important millennium development goals, as children are the most important assets of a country. Infant mortality indeed has declined impressively in India. As is shown in Table 1 the average infant mortality rate (IMR) in all India is 73, but the rate for the infants in the poorest 20 percent of the population is more than 2.6 times than for infants in the wealthiest 20 percent (95.6 versus 36.1). The variation between urban and rural areas is very large, both on average and across wealth quintiles (Fig.1.1). The disparities in selected states are also large on average and across wealth groups. An infant born to a family in the wealthiest quintile in Tamil Nadu is almost five times more likely to survive until age one than an infant born to a family in the poorest quintile in Uttar Pradesh (Yazbeck 2009). From the wide variation in IMR in India it is inferred that Kerala is comparable to Bulgaria, Russia and Ukraine while Odisha is comparable to Lesotho, Cameroon and Tanzania (World Bank 2004).

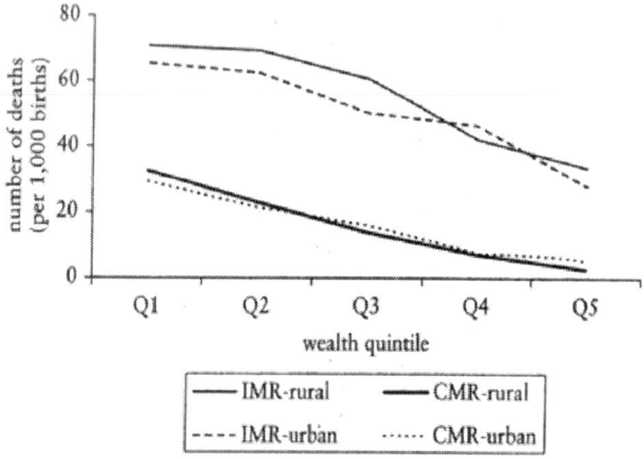

Source: Adapted from World Bank. 2011.

Fig. 1.1: Health Outcomes are Substantially Worse among the Poor

Further, the performance of different Indian states in terms of reducing their IMRs also significantly indicates equity in health performance. For instance, the state of Kerala with the lowest level of infant mortality in 1981 reduced its infant mortality at the fastest rate of 5 percent annually between 1981 and 2000. On the contrary, Bihar and Uttar Pradesh which had among the highest IMRs in the country in 1981 were also among the top performers in IMR reduction over the same period. Andhra Pradesh and Karnataka - the states normally perceived to be good human development performers - had the slowest rate of IMR decline over the two decades. In general there was limited convergence in IMRs in the past decades (World Bank 2004).

A significant feature of infant deaths in India is that they are concentrated in only a few states. Six states - Uttar Pradesh, Bihar, Madhya Pradesh, Rajasthan and Odisha - contribute almost 60 percent of infant deaths. Apart from the interstate variations, there are also region-level disparities in the country. For instance, IMR ranges from a low of 7.8 per 1000 live births to a high of 125.3. The IMR in northern Kerala is more than two times as high as that in southern Kerala. In Karnataka, the IMR ranges from 38.8 in the coastal and Ghats region to 76.5 in the inland southern region. The NFHS-II data show that infant deaths are heavily concentrated in a relatively small number of districts and villages in the country. For instance, a fifth of the country's districts and villages accounted for one-half of all infant deaths in the country. It is also further seen that there is significant association between infant mortality on the one hand and female literacy and per capita GSDP on the other hand. There is also significant gender disparity in the likelihood of children dying in India. While the probability of death is greater for males than females until age one, the reverse is true from ages one to five. Parental neglect towards girls appears to be an important cause of the gender disparity in child mortality. Girls are less likely to receive adequate food allocations and medical treatment for their illness than boys.

Total fertility shows a similar pattern of variation across India. At the national level, the poor have much higher fertility rates. Though the gap between fertility among the urban and rural population is not as large as IMR gap, but the variations are considerable across selected states. In the area of inequality of health services, reproductive health services stand out as the worst of the worst. The wealthy use the maternal and child health services more than the poor. For all the basic health services, the better-off are much more likely to obtain access even though the poor need them more. The size of the gap between the lowest and highest wealth groups varies by service and by region. Table 1.2 presents the use of three reproductive and child health services, such as immunisation, maternal care and use of modern contraceptives among women. All these three variables reveal significant inequalities. It is found that large variations are noticed both in averages and across wealth groups. For example, full immunisation for all children is found to be 89 percent in Tamil Nadu while it is only 16.5 percent in Rajasthan. Similarly, only 5 percent of the poorest women in

Uttar Pradesh get antenatal care while over 80 percent of the poorest in Tamil Nadu get this service.

Table 1.1: Inequality in Health and Fertility Outcomes in Rural and Urban India and by Selected States

Quintiles of wealth	*All India*	*Rural India*	*Urban India*	*Tamil Nadu*	*Maha-rashtra*	*Uttar Pradesh*	*Rajas-than*	*Pun-jab*
Infant Mortality								
st(Poorest)	95.61	94.15	74.17	62.16	68.6	125.57	110.52	83.02
2nd	82.72	92.18	50.85	59.86	65.27	100,26	85.99	62.37
3rd	75.28	77.89	41.32	52.79	60.15	94.90	100.96	54.45
4th	55.90	73.08	41.56	46.26	31.33	87.11	71.00	31.70
5th	36.09	49.46	23.64	27.68	26.06	52.15	59.34	33.80
Average	73.02	79.67	49.22	50.97	53.22	95.36	88.09	56.80
Total fertility								
1st(Poorest)	3.73	3.75	3.04	2.51	3.18	5.07	4.62	3.45
2nd	3.33	3.46	2.60	2.26	2.72	4.57	4.67	2.80
3rd	2.80	3.11	2.26	2.14	2.75	4.18	3.80	2.12
4th	2.56	2.73	1.84	2.02	2.32	3.77	3.53	1.84
5th	1.96	2.39	1.73	2.03	1.73	2.64	2.49	1.56
Average	2.85	3.07	2.27	2.19	2.52	3.99	3.78	2.28

Source: Yazbeck, Abdo S. (2009). *Attacking Inequality in the Health Sector*, Washington, D.C.: World Bank, P.7.

The distribution of inequality in health outcomes is depicted in the concentration curve. The concentration curves capture the burden of health outcomes or the benefit of using a health service, cumulatively for the poorest 20 percent, the poorest 40 percent, the poorest 60 percent, and so on until the full population is represented. Fig. 1.2 and Fig. 1.3 represent the concentration curves of infant mortality (IMR) and full immunisation, respectively. The concentration curves for IMR are above the 45 degree line which means that the poorest quintiles of the population shoulder a higher burden of mortality rate than the wealthiest. Also, the concentration curve for IMR in urban India is above the concentration curve for IMR in rural India, which reflect the fact that while IMR, on average, is lower among the urban population, inequality is lower among the rural population. Fig. 1.3 depicts concentration curve for full immunisation of children in four states in India based on data of Table 1.2.

Table 1.2: Service Use Inequality in (percentage of relevant population who receive service)

Quintiles of wealth	*All India*	*Rural India*	*Urban India*	*Tamil Nadu*	*Maharashtra*	*Uttar Pradesh*	*Rajasthan*	*Punjab*
Full immunisation								
1st(Poorest)	22.19	22.44	39.85	79.91	64.35	10.19	4.53	42.25
2nd	29.27	24.27	53.34	88.42	70.61	16.27	11.87	74.33
3rd	42.92	36.56	58.45	87.37	74.85	18.70	8.66	71.05
4th	54.54	45.10	65.92	90.32	79.66	32.13	23.44	84.89
5th	66.19	59.56	72.81	97.92	79.40	38.06	45.35	100.0
Average	41.13	36.51	56.62	88.65	73.17	22.07	16.51	71.28
Antenatal care, three or more visits								
1st(Poorest)	20.30	20.92	48.64	82.22	38.35	5.29	10.36	30.49
2nd	30.02	25.31	64.72	83.81	56.27	7.20	15.16	50.71
3rd	45.01	35.70	73.84	95.88	69.11	9.67	16.05	57.63
4th	61.55	46.89	82.70	97.14	85.43	15.26	26.79	78.28
5th	81.31	64.34	92.47	97.42	93.99	47.48	62.90	97.44
Average	44.24	36.90	70.13	90.94	66.20	14.86	23.59	58.42
Use of modern contraceptives among women								
1st(Poorest)	28.90	29.48	42.48	48.44	54.66	12.66	25.41	52.45
2nd	34.42	31.12	49.54	45.27	60.95	14.37	29.43	55.70
3rd	45.42	39.42	51.73	51.73	60.31	17.87	39.01	55.09
4th	49.89	46.80	55.18	50.26	61.26	24.22	40.47	53.03
5th	54.91	51.89	56.28	55.33	62.08	40.18	55.08	52.92
Average	42.85	39.89	51.22	50.27	59.88	21.97	38.06	53.83

Source: Yazbeck, Abdo S. (2009). *Attacking Inequality in the Health Sector.* Washington, D.C.: World Bank, P.13.

Two of the curves, those for Rajasthan and Uttar Pradesh, are considerably below the equality line (the diagonal in the figure) and those for other two, Tamil Nadu and Maharashtra are almost the same as the equality line. A concentration curve for health service that is below the equality line means that the poorest populations are consuming less than the wealthiest.

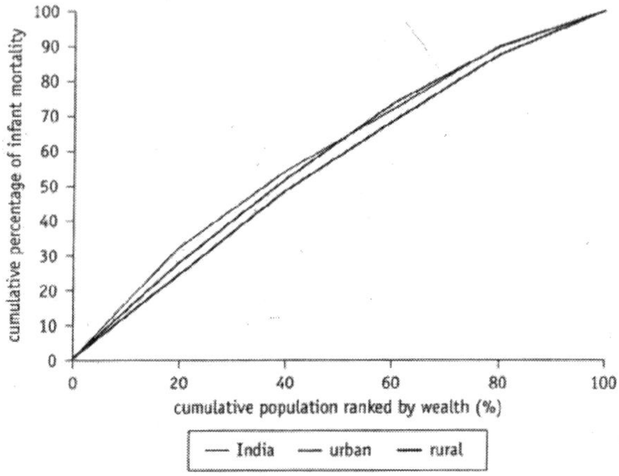

Fig. 1.2: Concentration Curves of Infant Mortality Rates in India

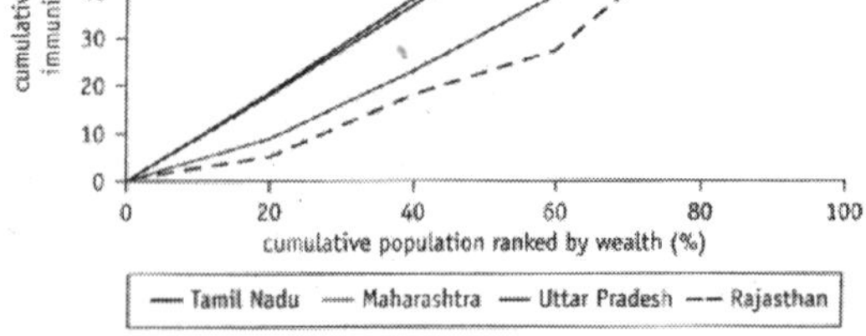

Fig. 1.3: Immunisation Concentration Curves, Selected Indian States

The benefit incidence analysis (BIA) is used to capture the distributional nature of public health spending. It is an indirect method of estimating the allocation of the benefit of public spending across wealth groups. Table 1.3 shows that public spending on health in the majority of states and at the all India level is pro-wealthy. It is pro-poor only in the state of Kerala. The BIA conducted for the whole country indicates that the share of government subsidy of the health sector for curative care that goes to the wealthiest 20 percent is more than three times the size of the subsidy going to the poorest quintile. The poor fare much better in some states like Kerala, Gujarat, Tamil Nadu, and Maharashtra than in others. The finding for the state of Bihar is dire where the share of the public health subsidy received by the rich for curative care is more than 10 times greater than that received by the poor (Table 1.3) The utilisation of public facilities quantified by NCAER show that 10.2 percent of total government investment on health went to the poor while 31 percent went to the rich (Misra 2003).

Table 1.3: Benefit Incidence Analysis in Various States of India

Sl. No.	*State*	*Ratio of curative care subsidy to richest versus poorest quintile*	*Concentration index*
1	Kerala	1.10	- 0.041
2	Gujarat	1.14	0.001
3	Tamil Nadu	1.46	0.059
4	Maharashtra	1.21	0.060
5	Punjab	2.93	0.102
6	Andhra Pradesh	1.85	0.116
7	West Bengal	2.73	0.157
8	Haryana	2.98	0.201
9	Karnataka	3.58	0.208
10	Odisha	4.87	0.282
11	Madhya Pradesh	4.16	0.292
12	Uttar Pradesh	4.09	0.304
13	Rajasthan	4.95	0.334
14	Himachal Pradesh	5.88	0.340
15	Bihar	10.3	0.419
16	All India	3.28	0.214

Source: Yazbeck, Abdo S. (2009). *Attacking Inequality in the Health Sector*, Washington, D.C.: World Bank, P.19.

Health Care and Poverty in India

Although India has made great strides in many fronts since independence, fertility, mortality and morbidity remain unacceptably high. The effect of poverty on healthcare and vice versa is significant. Achieving national health targets and the related Millennium Development Goals (MDGs) will entail addressing challenges to the existing health system. Since independence public financing and provision of health programmes in India have faced well-recognised problems, such as inadequate access by the most vulnerable groups, inadequate focus on maternal and child health and so on. The private sector has filled this gap to some extent. At the time of India's independence the private sector accounted for just 8 percent of health care facilities. The figure has risen to nearly 80 percent. Evidence shows that the private sector provides increasing share of primary health care and large segments of the poor use the private sector.

According to World Bank estimates 29 percent of the people in India lives below poverty line. The poor people in the country have less access to health facilities than the general population. Studies have shown that the poor in India are disproportionately affected by disease and have limited access to adequate medical services. Although the country has made significant strides towards improving the overall health condition of its people, a substantial unmet demand for basic health services remains. Providing healthcare for the poor means focusing on areas that most strongly affect the poor. Coverage levels diverge widely between the richest and poorest segments of society with respect to key interventions, such as antenatal care provision, contraceptive prevalence, and institutional deliveries. The poorest population quintile has fertility rates of 4.1 children per woman, and the richest quintile has fertility rates of 2.1 (World Bank 2003). Increased fertility only increases the level of poverty caused by the increased financial burden that accompanies large family sizes. Almost half of the poor children in India are not immunized. The BIMARU region consisting of Bihar, Madhya Pradesh, Rajasthan and Uttar

Pradesh has the lowest rates of immunisation in the country. Tuberculosis and measles can be easily prevented provided an adequate immunisation is administered. These two diseases are among the top 10 causes of lost DALYs in India. Nearly half of the children in India suffer from malnutrition, and diseases and symptoms resulting from malnutrition such as stunting and wasting. Though undernutrition is endemic in India, it is far more widespread among the poor. Children from the poorest wealth quintile are three times more likely to be underweight or stunted, compared to children in the richest quintile. It has been found that 43 percent of children (age less than five years) were underweight, 48 percent were stunted, and 20 percent were wasted in 2005-06. A large chunk of them were from the poorer sections of the society. Malnutrition is a key risk factor for many childhood illnesses and affects the health status of the poorest women. It is, therefore, vital to improve nutritional outcomes in order to tackle the burden of disease and achieve the MDGs. The level and pace of improvement in undernutrition vary significantly across states. It is found that poorer states tend to have higher prevalence of undernourished women and children (Fig. 1.4). Four states - Bihar, Madhya Pradesh, Rajasthan, and Uttar Pradesh - accounted for 43 percent of India's underweight children (Gragnolati *et al.* 2006). Several factors contribute to these interstate differences. The worrying fact is the widening of these interstate, rural-urban, class and social group disparities during the 1990s (Gragnolati *et al.* 2006, Harris and Kohli 2009). The pace of improvement during the 2000s also varies significantly across states. The current slow pace of improvement is disturbing as preventing children from reaching their developmental potential, undernutrition can itself become a critical factor in perpetuating poverty. Undernutrition in childhood also leads to less schooling which ultimately affects human capital formation and hence lower earnings in adulthood.

Poor health outcomes are not just a loss for the people concerned, health shocks can be a catastrophe for families and a significant cause of impoverishment. For households, ill health implies expenditure on treatment, potential loss of work, and often indebtedness. Though health care spending constitutes about 5 percent of total household expenditure, the expenditure can be huge in case of hospitalisation. The average total expenditure per

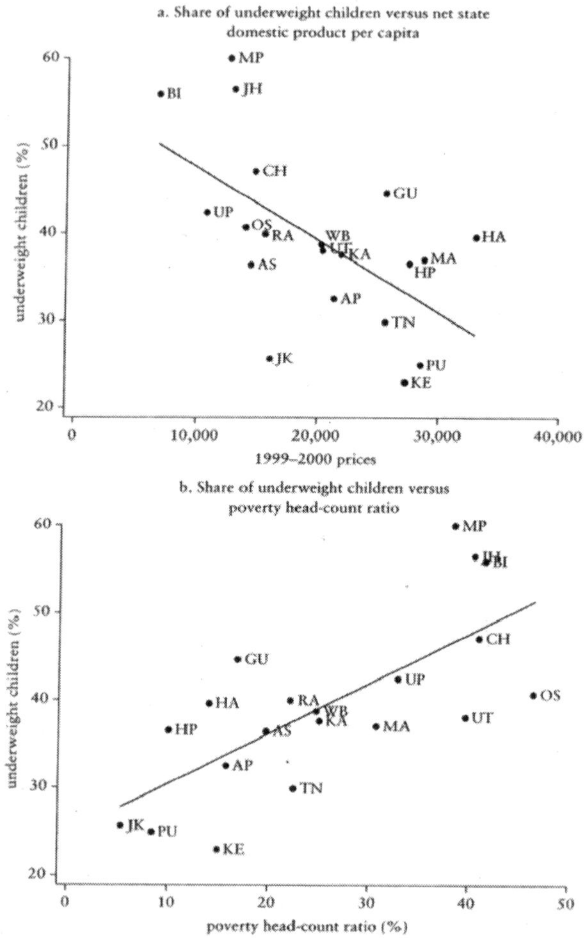

Source: Adapted from World Bank. 2011.

Fig. 1.4: Nutrition is worse in Poorer States

episode of hospitalisation by all quintile groups in the private sector was Rs. 4300 in rural areas and Rs. 5344 in urban areas. This is double the figure for public hospitals, i.e. Rs. 2080 for rural and Rs. 2195 for urban areas. The poor spend a disproportionately higher percentage of their incomes on health services than the rich. In 2005, out-of-pocket expenditure in India was as high as 76 percent of total health expenditures. Because of the huge burden health care entails the poor delay seeking treatment to avoid expenditure and about a fifth do not avail treatment for financial reasons. Borrowing and interest bearing loans are important financial sources for health care for the poor. According to the 52nd NSS data about 45 percent of the country's poor had to borrow or sell assets to meet increasing costs of care. This expenditure improves considerable financial burden on households and may even push households into poverty. Impoverishing effect of out-of-pocket expenditure on health care in India ranges from an overall poverty increase of 3.5 to 6.6 percent in rural areas and 2.5 to 5 percent in urban areas. It is estimated that a total of 39 million people in India are pushed into poverty every year due to expenditure on health.

Conclusion

The health sector has not received adequate attention in tune with the poverty-equity debate that has figured in various plans and policies in recent years. The result has been the low priority accorded to pro-poor interventions in health provision in the country. The inadequate budgetary allocation for areas affecting the poor, insufficient attention paid to the functioning of public facilities, and the disproportionate attention paid to the management of a few city-based hospitals has made it clear that public policy has failed to address the special needs of the poor. Consequently, health inequities are not only exacerbated among the states, but within states and within sub-populations too. This has led to inequitable health development and exclusive economic growth in India.

In order to bring out a solution to the inequities of the Indian health system, a comprehensive review of health system is warranted. There should be a substantial increase in public health spending in line with the Abuja Declaration that at least 15 percent of the government budget spending should be allocated to health. Per capita public health expenditure is the major indicator for measuring the well-being of the population in terms of health status. It has been estimated that low-income countries would need $30 - $ 45 as the minimum per capita amount to introduce essential health interventions. The developing countries, on average, spend $ 47 per capita on health for purchasing essential health services compared to high income countries which spend $ 2841 on health care per capita annually. Despite this the per capita health spending in India is a meagre $24 which is much less than the required level. A vast gap, therefore, exists between required expenditure and the current level of expenditure on health in India.

Public spending on health in India is both inefficient and inequitable. It is inefficient because public funds are allocated across priorities that do not yield significant health benefits for the majority of the population. Public subsidies on health are mostly captured by the richer income groups. In India, share of public subsidy captured by the richest 20 percent of the population is three times that captured by the poorest 20 percent of population. Further, most of the public health services are concentrated in urban areas. In rural areas where there is a higher incidence of infectious diseases, maternal illness and nutritional deficiencies, health care centres are few and far between. In India, 54 percent of the villages are more than 5 km away from the nearest primary health centres. Only 10 percent of the villages have a medicine shop and 20 percent have a private clinic or doctor. Further, an equitable spread of resources among all the three sectors - primary, secondary and tertiary - is necessary.

References

Aghion, P. and P.Bolton. (1992). "Distribution and Growth in Models of Imperfect Capital Markets." *European Economic Review*. 36(2-3), 603-11.

Alesina, A., and D. Rodrik. (1994). "Distributive Politics and Economic Growth," *Quarterly Journal of Economics*, 109(2), 465-90.

Banerjee, A., and A. Newman. (1991). "Risk-Bearing and the Theory of Income Distribution." *Review of Economic Studies*, 58(2), 211-35.

Bebbington, Anthony J. et al. (2008). "Inequalities and Development: Dysfunctions, Traps, and Transition," in Anthony J Bebbington et al. *Institutional Pathways to Equity*. Washington,D.C.: World Bank, PP. 3-41.

Bertola, G. (1993). "Factor Shares and Savings in Endogenous Growth." *American Economic Review*, 83 (5), 1184-98.

Bourguignon, Francois. and Sebastien Dessus. (2009). "Equity and Development: Political Economy Considerations," in Santiago Levy and Michael Walton (eds.). No Growth without Equity? Washington, D. C.: World Bank.

Deaton, A. (2006). 'Global Patterns of Income and Health: Facts, Interpretations and Policies.' NBER Working Paper, Cambridge, M.A.

Galor, O., and J. Zeira. (1993). "Income Distribution and Macro-economics." *Review of Economic Studies*, 60(1), 35-52.

Government of India. (2005). *Report of the National Commission on Macroeconomics and Health*, New Delhi: Government of India, Ministry of Health and Family Welfare.

Gragnolati, M. et al. (2006). *India's Undernourished Children: A Call for Reform and Action*. New Delhi: World Bank.

Gwartkin, D.R., et al. (2007). 'Socioeconomic Differences in Health, Nutrition, and Population: India.' Country Report on HNP and Poverty Series. Washington,D.C.: World Bank.

Harris, J., and N. Kohli. (2009). 'Notes on the Differing States of Child Undernutrition in India.' IDS Research Summary. IDS Bulletin, 40(4), 1-8.

Misra, Rajiv. (2003). *India Health Report*. New Delhi: Oxford University Press.

Nand, Amulya Ratna. (2009). "Access of the Urban Poor to Health and Education Services," in *India Urban Poverty Report*. New Delhi: Govt. of India, Ministry of Housing and Urban Poverty Alleviation.

Persson, T. and G. Tabellini. (1994). "Is Inequality Harmful for Growth? *American Economic Review*, 84(3), 600-21.

Radwan, Ismail. (2005). *India – Private Health Services for the Poor*. Washington,D.C.: World Bank.

World Bank. (2001). *Reducing Poverty, Accelerating Development*. Washington,D.C.: World Bank.

World Bank. (2003). *World Development Indicators*. Washington, D.C.: World Bank.

World Bank. (2004). *Attaining the Millennium Development Goals in India*. Washington, D.C.: World Bank.

World Bank. (2006). *World Development Report*. Washington,D.C.: World Bank.

World Bank. (2011). *Perspectives on Poverty in India*. Washington,D.C.: World Bank.

Yazbeck, Abdo S. (2009). *Attacking Inequality in the Health Sector*. Washington,D.C.: World Bank.

Health Manpower and Health Development in India

L.N.Dash

Health workforce is critical for health development. The health sector as contrast to any other sector depends more on people to attain its objectives. The success of health activities in a country depends on the available human resources. Recent evidence has shown an important link between the number of health workers, and both service delivery and health outcomes. Developing efficient and capable health workers is essential for achieving the health goals at the national and global levels. The only route to attaining the health goals of the Millennium Development Goal (MDGs) and National Health Policy (NHP) - 2002 and the five-year plans is through the health goals. The MDG health objectives also focus on human resources in order to reduce infant and maternal mortality, incidence of TB, HIV/AIDS, and malaria. There is no gainsaying the fact that lack of human resources capacity is a major barrier to the achievement of the MDGs. Added to all this is the rapid growth of the Indian economy in the post-liberalisation period. Due to rapid economic growth poverty level in the country is going down. Consequently, the health seeking behaviour of the people has expanded. At the same time new public health challenges have emerged in the form of changing demographics and environmental conditions. Human resources for health in India are diverse and multifaceted. They include from the rigorously trained biomedicine specialists and super specialists at the end of the community-based healers. But the delivery of health services mainly depends on the trained and qualified doctors of allopathic or modern biomedicine, dentists, radiographers, a range of paramedical professionals, such as nurses, pharmacists, laboratory technicians etc. The paper, therefore, will give emphasis on these types of human resources in the public sector of India.

There has been vast expansion in the public health system in India since independence. It now includes 142,655 sub-centres, 23,109 primary health centres (PHCs) and 3222 community health centres (CHCs). Apart from these, there are a total of 5479 sub-divisional and district hospitals in the public sector. (Satpathy and Venkatesh 2006) The population coverage norms are 3000 to 5000 for sub-centre, 20,000 to 30,000 per PHC and 80,000 to 1,20,000 per CHC respectively depending on the location of the centre in a hilly, tribal, difficult area or in the plains. The sub-centre is the first contact point between the community and public health system. It is manned by an ANM and a male health worker. Nearly 7 percent of the sub-centres lack an ANM which comes to a total shortfall of 11,190 and 50 percent do not have a male health worker. It is estimated that if an additional ANM is provided to each sub-centre as per the NRHM goals and if the 21,983 new sub-centres are established according to the 2001 population norm, the country will need about 200,000 ANMs. In order to fulfill the total requirement of ANMs, there is a need to augment the training capacity of the training schools and open new training schools (Satpathy and Venkatesh 2006). All the 23,109 PHCs are being upgraded to provide round the clock service with the basic objective of improving institutional delivery. In order to fulfill this programme three staff nurses, instead of one are to be provided. Further, about 700 PHCs are currently without doctors. The states have to also establish an additional 4436 PHCs to meet the shortfall of PHCs as per the 2001 population norms. Because of all these an additional 24,000 MBBS/AYUSH doctors and 46,000 staff nurses are needed to provide services in the PHCs.

The type of human resources for health managing the public health system in India is decided by the health situation recommendations of the Bhore Committee of 1946 and other committees of the government. There are 229 medical colleges with an annual intake of 25600, 747 general nursing and midwifery schools, 235 auxiliary nurse midwives (ANMs) training schools, 254 nursing colleges imparting graduation level courses and 40 colleges conducting post-graduate courses and 56 multipurpose worker (MPW) training centres functioning in the country. In addition to all these there are 358 institutions providing degree level education in pharmacy to 11,670 students per annum. The AYUSH system has about 437 colleges with an annual admission capacity of nearly 87,130. About 622,576 doctors were registered in India till 2004. The state institutes of health and family welfare, district training centres provide in-service training to various categories of health personnel.

The rural healthcare system in many states in the country is slowly falling apart. Though a large number of health care centres are present, most remain understaffed. The condition is particularly bad in Uttar Pradesh, Chhattisgarh and the north-eastern parts of the country. Most states suffer from understaffing of health centres. The maximum shortfall in manpower is in case of male health workers. Out of the 146,026 sub-centres in India (as on Sept. 2005), 44,766 or 31 percent do not have a male health worker. A sub-centre is the first contact point with the rural community. Each sub-centre must necessarily be manned by one auxiliary nurse midwife (ANM) and one male health worker for efficient functioning. Primary health centres (PHCs) and CHCs are the other two tiers in the rural healthcare system. Understaffing and vacant positions are seen in these two centres across India. In India as a whole only 48 percent of the PHCs have adequate staff. The percentage of PHCs adequately equipped in staff is more than 97 percent in Tamil Nadu, 96 percent in Maharashtra and 91 percent in Kerala. Their percentage is below the national average in Jharkhand, Punjab, Assam, Madhya Pradesh, Chhattisgarh, Rajasthan, Bihar and Odisha. It is lowest in Odisha. The percentage of PHCs adequately equipped in Staff is more than 60 percent in 130 districts. A well functioning PHC must have staff strength of 15, with at least one medical officer, lab technician and pharmacist.

The situation is even worse in CHCs. While the number of CHCs functioning in all states has improved during the 10th Plan, there remains the problem of acute understaffing. There are 3346 CHCs functioning in rural India, with a requirement of 13,384 specialists. However, only about 7274 specialists are currently working, creating a shortage of nearly 50 percent. In Gujarat, specialists like physicians and paediatricians are not present in the villages.

Table 2.1: Percentage of PHCs Having Adequate Staff

States	
Tamil Nadu	97
Maharashtra	96
Kerala	91
Andhra Pradesh	88
Gujarat	86
Uttaranchal	68
Karnataka	58
Uttar Pradesh	53
Haryana	51
India	48
Jharkhand	38
Punjab	38
Assam	35
Madhya Pradesh	34
Jammu & Kashmir	31
Himachal Pradesh	29
Chhattisgarh	26
Rajasthan	26
Bihar	20
West Bengal	6
Odisha	0

Source: Government of India, *National Family Health Survey- III, 2005-06.*

Despite the fact that the existing manpower is an important prerequisite for the efficient functioning of the rural health infrastructure, the overall shortfall in the posts of HW(F)/ANM was 12.6 percent of the total requirement. In case of Health Assistant (male) was 28.8 percent. There was a shortfall of 7.8

percent of the total requirement in case of doctors. Even out of the sanctioned posts, a significant percentage of posts are vacant at all levels. For example, about 8.8 percent of the sanctioned posts of HW(F)/ANM were vacant as compared to about 32 percent of the sanctioned posts of MPW(male)/male health worker. At PHC, about 13.8 percent of the sanctioned posts of Female Health Assistant/LHV, 22.1 percent of Male Health Assistant and 18 percent of the sanctioned posts of doctors were vacant. At the Sub-centre level the extent of existing manpower can be assessed from the fact that about 5 percent of the sub-centres were without a Female Health Worker/ANM, about 37.2 percent sub-centres were without a male health worker and about 4.7 percent sub-centres were without both Female Health Worker/ANM as well as Male Health Worker. This indicates a large shortfall in Male Health Worker. The current position of specialists manpower at CHCs reveal that out of the sanctioned posts, about 59.2 percent of surgeons, 46.4 percent of obstetricians and gynaecologists, 56.6 percent of physicians and about 51.9 percent of paediatricians were vacant. Overall about 50 percent of the sanctioned posts of specialists at CHCs were vacant. Rural public health facilities across the country are facing the problem of attracting, retaining and ensuring regular presence of highly trained medical professionals. About 80 percent of the district hospitals (DHs) have public health nurse, male health assistants, and pathologists. At least 90 percent of the DHs have obstetrician/ gynaecologists, paediatrician, laboratory technician, female health assistant, multipurpose female worker, staff nurse and pharmacist. The staff at FRUs comprises of multipurpose female worker (91 percent), female health assistant (91 percent), laboratory technician (88 percent), staff nurse.

Table 2.2 : Shortfall of Auxiliary Nurse Midwives (ANMs) and Doctors in Rural India

State	*Shortfall of ANMs**	*Shortfall of doctors**
Kerala	104.60	124.45
Maharashtra	100.00	100.00
Tamil Nadu	114.70	100.00
Andhra Pradesh	117.22	117.22
Odisha	100.82	121.08
Rajasthan	102.18	115.10
Uttar Pradesh	100.48	117.48
Madhya Pradesh	104.24	140.02

Note: * Vacancies plus shortages of posts against population norms.
Source: Mahabub ul Haq Human Development Centre. (2005). *Human Development in South Asia 2004: The Health Challenge,* Oxford: Oxford University Press, P. 167.

India is facing an acute shortage of trained nurses because of mass exodus of qualified nurses to Europe for better pay, shortage of teachers in nursing colleges and low interest and knowledge about nursing as a profession. At present, nearly 9 lakh nurses are registered with various state nursing councils in the country. But only 40 percent of them (3.6 lakh) could be in active duty. According to Health Ministry estimates, by the end of the 11th Plan (2007-2012), India would require 10.43 lakh nurses. But with the existing infrastructure, the number would stand at just 6.84 lakh, short by 3.59 lakh. India which has 1597 nursing schools, 833 B.Sc (nursing) colleges and 97 M.Sc. (nursing) colleges, has a capacity to train 79,850 diploma nurses, 41,650 graduate nurses and 1940 post-graduate nurses a year. However, over 20 percent of this number head to foreign countries in search of better pay. States like Uttar Pradesh, Bihar, Odisha, Madhya Pradesh and Rajasthan are the worst affected by shortage of nurses. Also, for every doctor, there should be three nurses. But at present the doctor nurse ratio in India is 1:1.5. Having allocated Rs. 319 crore for the Eleventh Plan to strengthen nursing education, the Ministry has identified 230 districts where there are no ANM and graduate nurse-midwives institutions and where such colleges will be set up.

Table 2.3: Number of Registered General Nursing Midwives, Auxiliary Nurse and Health Visitors (2005)

States	*General Nursing*	*Midwives Auxiliary Nurse*	*Health Visitors*
Andhra Pradesh	88,457	98,455	2480
Assam (a)	10,540	15,955	-
Bihar	8883	7501	511
Chhattisgarh	462	522	-
Delhi	10,707	1192	-
Gujarat	85,930	35,935	1352
Haryana	17,186	13,172	694
Himachal Pradesh	7920	9087	411
Jharkhand	322	15	-
Karnataka	64,308	47,407	6836
Kerala	77,596	27,712	7797
Madhya Pradesh	93,106	26,138	1017
Maharashtra (b)	86,406	28,190	551
Meghalaya	1524	623	90
Mizoram	1483	1479	-
Odisha	46,311	30,716	172
Punjab ©	45,801	18,152	2584
Rajasthan	37,667	22,239	850
Tamil Nadu (d)	1,59,843	52,909	11,083
Tripura	794	977	144
Uttar Pradesh	17,827	26,956	2763
Uttarakhand	58	-	-
West Bengal (e)	45,831	56,261	11,380

Note: (a) – Data for Assam includes data for Assam, Arunachal Pradesh, Manipur and Nagaland.
(b) - Data for Maharashtra includes data for Maharashtra and Goa.
© - Data for Punjab includes data for Punjab and Jammu & Kashmir.
(d) - Data for Tamil Nadu includes data for Tamil Nadu, A & N Islands and Pondicherry.
(e) – Data for West Bengal includes data for Sikkim.

Source: Government of India. (2007). *Statistical Abstract of India 2007*, New Delhi: Government of India, P. 538.

India is suffering from a doctor deficiency syndrome. The population being serviced per doctor is growing. The country needs to have at least a million doctors. It is being forced to manage with 600,000 doctors, a shortfall of 400,000. The nation may need up to 400 medical colleges in ten years to bridge the gap. There is also disparity in the availability of medical education within states. While Uttar Pradesh and Bihar have just 12 and 8 medical colleges respectively, Maharashtra has 38 and Karnataka has 33. The ratio worth aiming at is 1000 people per doctor, as recommended by a commission appointed by the Government of India. We are far from the goal. At an all India level, there are about 1700 people per doctor. The number is well short of the ratio prevalent in developed countries such as Australia, which has 249 doctors for every 10,000 population. Canada has 209 doctors for every 10,000 people while UK has 166 and US 548. Among the better states, Karnataka, for instance, has adequate number of doctors and each doctor serves 862 people. Maharashtra and Kerala are also very close to the goal of 1000 patients per doctor. However, Uttar Pradesh, Bihar and Odisha have far fewer numbers of doctors. The doctor deficiency in various states translates into very bad medical facility. For example, one doctor has to support more than 4000 people in Uttar Pradesh and 2564 in Odisha and 2500 in Bihar. Andhra Pradesh, Gujarat and West Bengal have serious scarcity of doctors. Scarcity of doctors is a chronic problem in Odisha. And it is likely to adversely affect the implementation of the National Rural Health Mission (NRHM). Because of dearth of doctors, as many as 800 posts of doctors are lying vacant in Odisha, mostly in the rural areas. There are only 2260 doctors left to provide health service to more than 4 crore people. India needs to add 400,000 doctors to reach the acceptable level of adequacy. But the present number of medical colleges (around 235) adds up to 25,000 doctors a year. But considering the growth of population, and retirement and expiry of doctors, this number of doctors is just sufficient to keep the current ratio going. Hence, an additional 400 colleges are required to add the 400,000 doctors so that the gap can be bridged within 10 years. The wide disparity in the number of colleges in different states indicates that the need for new colleges is more in some states such as Uttar Pradesh, Bihar and other regions. Indeed Uttar Pradesh itself could need 100 more medical colleges, or Bihar could need 40 colleges to add to its 8 colleges and West Bengal could use additional 50 colleges to its 9 colleges. Government and private enterprise need to step in to fulfill this need. However, these colleges need to be in states like Uttar Pradesh, Bihar, Odisha, and West Bengal. India also faces an acute shortage of dental surgeons. At present, the number of dental surgeons registered in India stands at just over 73,000 against the requirement of nearly 3 lakh.

Table 2.4: Number of Registered Doctors

States	*1991*	*2001*	*2003*
Andhra Pradesh	19,610	30,687	34,147
Assam	10,499	14,586	15,526
Bihar	26,376	33,070	34,583
Chhattisgarh	- -	101	
Goa	-2030	2236	
Gujarat	22,392	33,653	36,012
Haryana	644	1146	1285
Himachal Pradesh	- -	-	
Jammu & Kashmir	4407	6875	7900
Jharkhand	- -	91	
Karnataka	32,813	61,163	65,789
Maharashtra	49,365	80,764	88,378
Odisha	11,087	14,315	14,707
Punjab	26,636	32,558	33,417
Rajasthan	14,041	20,438	21,885
Tamil Nadu	46,419	65,771	70,357
Uttar Pradesh	33,178	43,492	46,309
West Bengal	41,722	49,941	51,961
Delhi	-468	1514	
Total	3,93,640	5,77,094	6,25,423

Source: Government of India. (2007). *Statistical Abstract of India 2007*, New Delhi: Government of India, P. 587.

Table 2.5: Doctor Deficiency in India

States	*Population/ doctor*	*Medical colleges*	*Colleges required*
Andhra Pradesh	1699	27	10
Assam	1826	8	6
Bihar	2506	8	40
Gujarat	1503	13	15
Haryana	1839	3	6
Odisha	2564	3	17
Uttar Pradesh	4111	12	100
West Bengal	1606	9	50

Source: "This Millennium, India Needs a Million Doctors," *Economic Times*, 4th May 2005.

Table 2.6: Distribution and Annual Intake in the MBBS course in Medical Colleges

Sl no	*State*	*No of colleges*			*Annual intake*
		Govt.	*Other*	*Total*	
1	Andhra Pradesh	9	5	14	1975
2	Assam	3	-	3	391
3	Bihar	6	2	8	510
4	Chandigarh	1	-	1	50
5	Chhattisgarh	1	-	-	100
6	Delhi	4	-	4	460
7	Goa	1	-	1	100
8	Gujarat	8	2	10	1405
9	Haryana	1	-	1	150
10	Himachal Pradesh	2	-	2	115
11	Jammu & Kashmir	2	2	4	350
12	Jharkhand	3	-	3	190

Table contd....

13	Karnataka	4	18	22	2955
14	Kerala	5	1	6	800
15	Madhya Pradesh	5	-	5	620
16	Maharashtra	18	17	35	4010
17	Manipur	-	1	1	100
18	Odisha	3	-	3	364
19	Pondicherry	1	2	3	275
20	Punjab	3	3	6	520
21	Rajasthan	6	-	6	650
22	Tamil Nadu	11	5	16	1865
23	Uttar Pradesh	9	2	11	1212
24	Uttaranchal	-	1	1	100
25	West Bengal	7	-	-	905
	Total	113	61	174	20,172

Source: Government of India, Planning Commission. *Report of the Working Group on Health of Women and Children for the Eleventh Five Year Plan (2007-2012)*, New Delhi: Government of India.

International comparison of data on manpower and facilities suggest that the number of medical personnel and hospital beds in India's public sector is huge in absolute numbers. But in per capita terms it is well below the comparable ratios in many low-income countries. The per capita number of physicians in India is about average the low income countries, where as the ratios for nurses and midwives are well below average.

Health Worker Absenteeism

It is not only that there is manpower shortage in the health sector, but absenteeism among the existing health sector personnel poses serious problem for health delivery in the country. The welfare consequence of health worker absence is enormous (Choudhury et al 2006). It is found that 40 percent of the health workers are absent in primary health centres (PHCs) in India while the figures for Bangladesh is 35 percent, Peru 25 percent, and Uganda 37 percent (Table 2.7). The absenteeism rate in India is also higher than the 35 percent absenteeism rate for the developing countries as a whole. Health workers who are absent from public clinics seem to be providing private medical care. An average of 41 percent of health workers has a private practice. (Choudhury et al 2006) It is also found that for medical providers other than doctors, attendance in CHCs is much higher than in smaller sub-centres where no doctor is assigned.

Table 2.7: Absence Rates in Primary Health Centres by Country

Country	*Absence Rates in Primary Health Centres (%)*
India	40
Bangladesh	35
Indonesia	40
Peru	25
Uganda	37

Source: Chaudhury, Nazmul. *et al.* (2006). "Missing in Action: Teacher and Health Worker Absence in Developing Countries," *Journal of Economic Perspectives*, 20 (1), winter, P.92.

The absence rates are high for medical providers and the problem is found to be worse in case of poorer states (World Bank 2003). It is as high as 58 percent in Bihar and Assam (Table 2.8). The absence rate is 52 percent in Gujarat, 43 percent in Karnataka, 42 percent in Uttar Pradesh, 43 percent in West Bengal and so on. In rural Rajasthan absence is inefficiently high in case of nurses who staff the smaller health sub-centres. On the other hand, 45 percent of the doctors were absent from primary health centres in rural Rajasthan. Absenteeism rate is 45 percent in Sub Centres, 36 percent in PHCs and CHCs in Rajasthan. Further, in case of Sub Centres it was also found that at sub-centres the doors were closed 56 percent of the times visited. Similarly, in Karnataka, absenteeism ranges from 44 percent in Shimoga (a forward district) to 63 percent in Bidar (a backward district). The high rate of absenteeism in Bidar district has contributed to dismal health indicators (iDpms, 2010).

Table 2.8 : Absentee Rates for Primary Health Workers in Selected States, 2003 (in percent).

States	*Primary Health Care Workers*
Andhra Pradesh	n.a.
Assam	58
Bihar	58
Gujarat	52
Haryana	35
Karnataka	43
Kerala	n.a.
Odisha	35
Punjab	n.a.
Rajasthan	39
Tamil Nadu	n.a.
Uttar Pradesh	42
Uttaranchal	45
West Bengal	43

n.a. - data not available

World Bank. (2005). *India: Sustaining Reform, Reducing Poverty*. Washington, D.C.: World Bank, P. 44

Absenteeism is a nebulous issue and serious consideration need to be given for it. As more than a third of health workers absent from their health facilities, India is wasting considerable resources and missing opportunities to improve the health of the populations. Poorly functioning government institutions impair provision of health. Faced with high absence rates policy makers have two challenges. First, how can health policy be adopted to minimise the cost of absence and secondly, how absence can be reduced. Appropriate health policies should be designed to take into account high absence rates. For example, doctor absence may be difficult to prevent, but possible to work around. High salaries combined with effective monitoring may be required to induce well-trained medical personnel to live in rural areas. In order to reduce absence, one approach would be to increase local control. Local level monitoring by the panchayats is likely to give good result. Regular inspection of the hospitals by high level authorities also can minimise absenteeism. Apart from all these priority should be given in building staff quarters and other amenities. This is likely to attract the doctors and other health workers to work in the rural areas.

Conclusion

An acute shortage of trained health care personnel in India continues to be the health sector's greatest curse. To add to that, India holds the top position when it comes to its physicians migrating to developed countries like the UK and US. According to Planning Commission estimates, the country has a shortfall of six lakh doctors, 10 lakh nurses and two lakh dental surgeons. This has led to dismal patient-doctor ratio in the country. For every 10,000 Indians, there is one doctor. In contrast, Australia has 249 doctors for every 10,000 people, Canada has 209, UK has 166 and US has 548. The overriding requirement in the country is for increasing the supply of human resources, from specialists to paramedical personnel. India also has a very low turnout of personnel with post-graduate degrees. The medical education sector needs to be opened up for private sector participation.

References

Ambrose, Soren. (2006). "Preserving Disorder: IMF Policies and Kenya's Health Care Crisis." Global Policy Forum, New York. http://www.globalpolicy.org/socecon/ bwi wto/imf/2006/0601imfhealth.htm.

Bhandari, Laveesh. And Siddhartha Dutta. (2007). "Health Infrastructure in Rural Indioa," in *India Infrastructure Report 2007*, New Delhi: Oxford.

Chaudhury, Nazmul. Et al. (2006). Missing in Action: Teacher and Health Worker Absence in Developing Countries." *Journal of Economic Perspectives*, 20(1), winter, PP. 91-116.

Chaudhury, Nazmul, and Jeffrey S. Hammer. (2004). "Ghost Doctors: Absenteeism in Rural Bangladeshi Health Facilities." *World Bank Economic Review* 18 (3): 423–41.

Das, Jishnu, and Jeffrey S. Hammer. (2004). "Strained Mercy: The Quality of Medical Care in Delhi." Policy Research Working Paper 3228, World Bank, Washington, DC. http://ssrn.com/abstract=610269.

Das, Jishnu, and Paul J. Gertler. (2007). "Variations in Practice Quality in Five Low-Income Countries: A Conceptual Overview." *Health Affairs* 26 (3): 296–309.

Dussault, Gilles, and Maria Cristina Franceschini. (2006). "Not Enough There, Too Many Here: Understanding Geographical Imbalances in the Distribution of the Health Workforce." *Human Resources for Health* 4: 12.

Dussault, Gilles, and Marko Vujicic. (2008). "The Demand and Supply of Human Resources for Health." In *International Encyclopedia of Public Health*, vol. 2, ed. Kris Heggenhougen and Stella Quah, San Diego: Academic Press, 77–84.

Ferrinho, Paulo, Wim Van Lerberghe, Inês Fronteira, Fátima Hipólita, and André Biscaia. (2004). "Dual Practice in the Health Sector: Review of the Evidence." *Human Resources for Health* 2: 14. http://www.human-resources-health.com/ content/2/1/14.

IDpms. (2010). Where Have They Gone? (Draft paper), Bangalore

Kombe, Gilbert, David Galaty, Raj Gadhia, and Catherine Decker. (2005). *The Human and Financial Resource Requirements for Scaling Up HIV/AIDS Services in Ethiopia*. Bethesda, MD: Abt Associates.

Kurowski, Christoph, Kaspar Wyss, Salim Abdulla, and Anne Mills. (2007). "Scaling Up Priority Health Interventions in Tanzania: The Human Resources Challenge." *Health Policy and Planning* 22 (3): 113–27.

OECD (Organisation for Economic Co-operation and Development).(2007). *International Migration Outlook 2007*. Paris: OECD.

Okuonzi, Sam Agatre. (2004). "Dying for Economic Growth? Evidence of a Flawed Economic Policy in Uganda." *Lancet* 364: 1632–37.

Ooms, Gorik, and Ted Schrecker. (2005). "Expenditure Ceilings, Multilateral Financial Institutions, and the Health of Poor Populations." *Lancet* 365 (9473): 1821–23.

Preker, Alexander S., Marko Vujicic, Yohana Dukhan, Caroline Ly, Hortenzia Beciu, and Peter Nicolas Materu. (2008). "Scaling Up Health Professional Education: Opportunities and Challenges for Africa." Paper prepared for the Task Force for Scaling Up Education and Training for Health Workers, Global Health Workforce Alliance, World Bank, Washington, DC.

Ruwoldt, Paul, and Philip Hassett. (2007). "Zanzibar Health Care Worker Productivity Study: Preliminary Study Findings." Capacity Project, Intra-Health International, Chapel Hill, NC. http://www.capacityproject.org/images/stories/files/zanzibar_productivity_study.pdf.

Satpathy, S.K. and S. Venkatesh. (2006). "Human Resources for Health in India's National Rural Health Mission: Dimensions and Challenges," Regional Health Forum, 10(1), PP. 29-37.

Vujicic, Marko, and Robert Evans. (2005). "The Impact of Deficit Reduction on the Nursing Labor Market in Canada: Unintended Consequences of Fiscal Reform." *Applied Health Economics and Health Policy* 4 (2): 99–110.

Vujicic, Marko, Eddie Addai, and Samuel Bosomprah. (2006). "Methodology for Measuring the Productivity of the Health Workforce in Ghana." Ministry of Health, Accra.

Wagstaff, Adam, and Mariam Claeson. (2004). *The Millennium Development Goals for Health: Rising to the Challenges.* Washington, DC: World Bank.

WHO (World Health Organization). (2006). *World Health Report 2006: Working Together for Health.* Geneva: World Health Organization. http://www.who.int/ who/2006/en/index.html.

WHO. (2007). "Task Shifting to Tackle Health Worker Shortages." World Health Organization, Geneva, Switzerland. http://www.who.int/healthsystems/ task_shifting_booklet.pdf.

Health for All: From Firm Promises to New Realism

K. Gangadharan

Over the last 25 years the term health inequalities has become familiar to researchers and among public health and medical practitioners around the world. Health inequalities are generally understood to refer to differences in health between groups of people who are better or worse off socioeconomically, as reflected by their occupational standing, levels of income, expenditure, wealth or education or by economic characteristics of the places where they live. Health inequality (Braveman 2006) is a particular type of difference in health that could potentially be shaped by policies. It is a systematic difference in health according to social advantage meaning one's relative position in a social hierarchy determined by health power and prestige. It is a difference in which disadvantaged social groups systematically experience worse health or greater health risk than more advantaged social group. In the present paper inequality is treated not only on social group division but also on the basis of region and gender. A woman in Panama is 80 times as likely to die from childbirth-related causes as a woman in Sweden (WHO 2004). A baby born in Pakistan is 27 times as likely to die in infancy as a baby born in Singapore (Bellamy 2004). In Indonesia children in the poorest one-fifth of population are 3.5 times as likely to die before reaching the age of 5 as children in the wealthiest fifth (ORC Macro 2003). In Bolivia and Egypt IMR is three times as high among babies born to mothers in the poorest fifth of population as among babies born to mothers of wealthiest one fifth. In the US also babies born to mothers of African American background are twice as likely to die before reaching their first birthday as babies born to mothers of European American background.

The global data on healthcare access and health status is pointing towards some hidden dangers in the years to come. One billion people lack access to health care systems; around 11 million children below the age of 5 die from malnutrition and mostly preventable diseases each year. In 2002, almost 11 million people died of infectious diseases alone, far more than the number killed in the natural or man-made catastrophes that make headlines. AIDS/HIV has spread rapidly. *UN AIDS* estimates for 2007 states that there are roughly 32.8 million living with HIV. There are 8.8 million new cases of Tuberculosis (TB) and 1.75 million deaths from TB, each year 1.6 million people still die from pneumococcal[1] diseases, making it the number one vaccine-preventable cause of death worldwide (http://www.global issues). More than half of the victims are children. Malaria causes more than 300 million acute illnesses and at least one million deaths annually. More than half a million people, mostly children, died from measles in 2003 even though effective immunization costs just 0.30 US dollars per person, and has been available for over 40 years. Social and economic inequality is detrimental to the health of any society. Especially when the society is diverse, multicultural, overpopulated and undergoing rapid but unequal economic growth. The public healthcare centres in India are in a stage of dissatisfaction, discomfort, disability, disease and death. The present paper focuses on the healthcare inequalities that prevails in India in its different dimensions and advocates the need for inclusive healthcare. The paper approaches the problem with caste, class, and gender and also with geographic division.

Theoretical Background

"In the beginning, there was desire which was the first seed of mind," says Rig-Veda, which probably is the earliest piece of literature known to mankind. This desire for a healthy family, healthy society and a healthy country drives individuals and governments alike (Deogaonkar 2004). The government is supposed to create settings that will provide equal opportunity for an individual to fulfill these desires. There is an undisputed association between social equality, social integration and health. The effect of social integration on health is conclusively documented in the theory of 'social support' (Cassel 1976). The effect of social and economic inequality on health is profound too. Poverty, which is a result of social and economic inequality is detrimental to the health of population. The outcome indicators of health (mortality, morbidity and life expectancy) are all directly influenced by the standards of living of a given population. More so, it is not the absolute deprivation of income that matters, but the relative distribution of income (Wilkinson 1992). Various international studies have documented a strong association between income inequality and excess mortality (Shymo *et al.* 1996 and Pamuk *et al* 1996). In a study (Kennedy *et al* 1996) income inequality was shown to directly affect the total mortality in a given population [$p<0.05$]. The same study measures income inequality by 'Robin Hood Index', which is the part of income that needs to be redistributed from the rich to the poor to achieve economic equality. It is stated that one percent rise in this index led to 21.7 excess deaths per 100,000 populations. This shows the profound effect of income inequality on the health of a population. Social order is primarily based on economic consideration. The resource division of the world reveals that 90 percent of population sustains itself on 10 percent of resources of the society, whereas 10 percent population consumes 90 percent of the resources. This is also called '10-90' syndrome. Inequality in all sphere of social determinants cause fault lines in social matrix which brings about its own problem in its wake. The end results are division in the society with unsocial and antisocial activities even to the extent of terrorism. Divide between haves and have-nots is sharp and clear and that causes many unwanted individual and social behavior.

Inequality of Health Care Resources

Inequality in healthcare on the basis of caste, class, gender and geographic dimension is a global healthcare problem, but its severity is more experienced in the developing countries where public healthcare is facing dissatisfaction, discomfort, disability, diseases and death. Table 3.1 presents health inequalities in South Asia. It is revealed that the position of Japan is favourable for better healthcare compared to the situation of Nepal where all the four health indicators shown are deplorable. The position of China is also far better than India.

Table 3.1: Health Inequalities in South Asia.

Country	*IMR per 100 live births*	*Life expectancy M/F years*	*MMR per 100000 live births*	*TFR*
India	58	63.9/66.9	301	2.9
China	32	70.6/74.2	56	1.72
Japan	3	78.9/86.1	10	1.35
Republic of Korea	3	74.2/81.5	20	1.19
Indonesia	36	66.2/69..9	230	2.25
Malaysia	9	71.6/76.2	41	2.71
Vietnam	27	69.5/73.5	130	2.19
Bangladesh	52	63.3/65.1	380	3.04
Nepal	58	62.4/63.4	740	3.40
Pakistan	73	64.0/64.3	500	3.87
Srilanka	15	72.2/77.5	92	1.89

Source: Government of India (2007), *Health information of India*, CBHI; *State of World Population 2006*

Health Indicators by Selected Countries

India is a large country having multicultural society with about 24 percent of land and 16 percent of human population and the density of population in India is rather high. About 72 percent population is in the rural areas where connectivity, availability of portable water, electricity and other basic amenities are scarce. Healthcare professionals are not inclined to work in the rural areas of India. As per the Indian Constitution, provision of healthcare by public sector is shared between the Centre and states. The public sector healthcare system is three-tire, the primary health care, hospital healthcare and tertiary healthcare. The administrative set-up is somewhat as follows.

(a) Primary Health Sub-centre

(b) Primary Health Centers

(c) Community Health Centers

(d) District Hospitals

Ie) Tertiary care Hospitals and referred Centers

India has 1,37,000 sub centers, 28000 dispensaries, 23000 PHCs, 3000 CHCs and about 12000 secondary and tertiary hospitals. The whole administrative set-up may appear large, but most of the healthcare facilities are bleak and understaffing is more pronounced in rural health. About 15 percent of Indian population does not have access to healthcare due to reason of unavailability or due to economic reasons. Public healthcare systems are becoming extinct due to mushrooming growth of private hospitals. Insurance system may not suit Indian conditions since 94 percent of the labor force is working in the unorganized sector without having any sort of protection and large section of rural population would not be able to afford it and the government (Central and State) may not find the required budget.

Data from the National Family Health Survey-III (2005-06) clearly highlight the caste differentials in relation to health status. The survey reveals low levels of contraceptive use among the Scheduled Castes and the Scheduled Tribes compared to forward castes. Reduced access to maternal and child healthcare is evident with reduced levels of antenatal care, institutional deliveries and complete vaccination coverage among the lower castes. Stunting, wasting, underweight and anaemia in children and anaemia in adults are higher among the lower castes. Similarly, neonatal, postnatal, infant, child and under-five statistics clearly show a higher mortality among the SCs and the STs. Problems in accessing healthcare were higher among the lower castes.

The National Family Health Survey-II (1998-99) also documented a similar picture of lower accessibility and poorer health statistics among the lower castes.

The poor, a majority from the lower castes, migrate to different parts of the country in search of work. Their migrant status means they lose many benefits generally offered to the poorer sections as their below poverty line ration cards are not valid across state borders. The migrants find it difficult to register with the National Tuberculosis Programme at their place of work, resulting in out-of-pocket expenditure for treatment, discontinuation of medication when symptoms improve, relapse of the disease, medication resistance and premature death. Illness and its treatment usually wipe out all savings and are a common reason for indebtedness. Migrants are often considered vectors of communicable diseases and are not engaged by the public health system as they drive down indicators of health. The complete absence of schooling for their children implies a continuation of the cycle of poverty. Their inability to register with local electoral bodies means they fall off the radar of politicians and political parties.

The major barrier to mainstreaming healthcare and to scaling up effective interventions is caste inequality based on socio-cultural issues. The systematic discrimination of lower castes based on culture, tradition and religion needs to be tackled if interventions have to work. Tradition and culture maintain their stranglehold on inequality. Poverty and social exclusion have a multiplicative effect on the social determinants of health with those at higher risk for diseases also having a higher probability of being excluded from health care services.

It is widely recognized that the determinants of health are social and economic rather than purely medical. The poor health of people from the lower castes, their social exclusion and the steep social gradient are due to the unequal distribution of power, income, goods and services. Caste is inextricably linked to and is a proxy for socio-economic status in India. The restricted access of those from the lower castes to clean water, sanitation, nutrition, housing, education, healthcare and employment is due to a toxic combination of poor social policies and programmes, unfair economic arrangement and bad politics. The structural determinants of daily life contribute to the social determinants of health and fuel the inequities in health between caste groups. Viewing health in general as an individual or medical issue, reducing population health to a biomedical perspective and suggesting individual medical interventions reflect a poor understanding of issues. Social interventions should form the core of all health and prevention programmes, as individual medical interventions have little impact on population indices, which require population interventions.

Healthcare resources in India though not adequate, are ample. There has been a definite growth in the overall healthcare resources and health related manpower in the last decade. The number of hospitals grew from 11,174 in 1991 (57 percent private) to 19,128 (78 percent private) in 2005(Government of India 2006). In the beginning of the Eleventh Plan, the country had 1.25 million doctors and 0.8 million nurses, that translates into one doctor for every 1800 people. If other systems including Indigenous System of Medicine (ISM) and homeopathic medicine are considered, there is one doctor per 800 people. It not only satisfies but also betters the required estimate of one doctor for 1500 population (Government of India 2002). Approximately 15,000 new graduate doctors and 5,000 postgraduate doctors are trained every year.

To a casual observer this looks like a good proportion, however on further study, unequal distribution of resources becomes apparent. The ratio of hospital beds to population in rural areas is fifteen times lower than that for urban areas. The ratio of doctors to population in rural areas is almost six times lower than that in the urban population (Government of India 2006). Per capita expenditure on public health is seven times lower in rural areas, compared to government health spending for urban areas. Though the spending on healthcare is 5.2 percent of gross domestic product (GDP), the state expenditure is only 0.9 percent of the total spending. People using their own resources spend rest of it. Thus, only 17 percent of all health expenditure in the country is borne by the state, and 82 percent comes as 'out of pocket payments' by the people. This makes the Indian public health system grossly inadequate and under-funded. Only five other countries in the world are worse off than India with regard to public health spending like Burundi, Myanmar, Pakistan, Sudan, and Cambodia (WHO 2003). As a result of this dismal and unequal spending on public health, the infrastructure of health system is becoming ineffective. The most peripheral and most vital unit of India's public health infrastructure is a primary health centre (PHC). The major chunks of these units are suffering short of critical inputs and essential supplies. In a recent survey it was noticed that only 38 percent of all PHCs have all the essential manpower and only 31 percent have all the essential supplies (defined as 60 percent of critical inputs), with only 3 percent of PHCs having 80 percent of all critical inputs.

The reduction on public health spending and the growing inequalities in health and healthcare are taking its toll on the marginalized and socially disadvantaged population. The Infant Mortality Rate in the poorest 20 percent of the population is 2.5 times higher than that in the richest 20 percent of the population. In other words, an infant born in a poor family is two and half times more likely to die in infancy, than an infant in a better off family. A child in the 'Low standard of living' economic group is almost four times more likely to die in childhood than a child in the 'High standard of living' group. A child born in the tribal belt is one and half times more likely to die before the fifth birthday than children of other groups. Female child is 1.5 times more likely to die before reaching her fifth birthday as compared to a male child (NFHS III). The female to male ratios for children are rapidly declining, from 945 girls per 1000 boys in 1991, to just 927 girls per 1000 boys in 2001(Government of India 2001). Children below 3 years of age in scheduled tribes and scheduled castes are twice as likely to be malnourished than children in other groups. A person from the poorest quintile of the population, despite more health problems, is six times less likely to access hospitalization than a person from the richest quintile. This means that the poor are unable to afford and access hospitalization in a very large proportion of illness episodes, even when it is required. The delivery of a mother, from the poorest quintile of the population is over six times less likely to be attended by a medically trained person than the delivery of a well off mother, from the richest quintile of the population. A tribal mother is over 12 times less likely to be delivered by a medically trained person (NFHS III). A tribal woman is one and a half times more likely to suffer the consequences of chronic malnutrition as compared to women from other social categories. These figures speak for themselves and bring to the fore unequal distribution of resources and the effect of it on public health parameters. This unequal distribution of resources is further complimented by inability of universal access to healthcare due to various access difficulties. The recent reform measures introduced in the country as part of the Liberalization policies made the situation worse.

Since independence, the Indian government sought to establish healthcare system along the lines of recommendations of the Bhore Committee in 1946. One of the central guiding principles of the Committee was that no individual should be denied adequate medical care because of inability to pay for it (Banerji 1985). But since the inception of globalization and liberalization and acceptance of policy reforms by the government the health priorities began to be identified on the basis of cost benefit considerations. The rapid dismantling of the public health system on the one hand and the expansion of the private sector only for profit on the other is increasingly placing a higher burden on sections of populations due to increase in household health expenditures (Chandrasekher and Ghosh 2006). This ultimately landed in inequity and inequality in the accessibility affordability of healthcare facilities and system by the people of the country. It is apprehend that soon healthcare may go out of the reach of ordinary people. The country is facing acute health problems due to rising burden of chronic and degenerative illness on the one side and communicable infections on the other. The disease burden for India for all age groups by major causes of death reveals that 36 percent of deaths are due to communicable diseases, prenatal, maternal conditions and nutritional deficiencies, 11 percent due to injuries, 8 percent due to other chronic illness, 2 percent by diabetes, 7 percent by chronic respiratory diseases, 7 percent again by cancer and 29 percent by cardiovascular diseases. (Government of India 2006). The external pressures succumbed by the Government forced to cut short the allocation for preventive and promotive healthcare. This ultimately worsened the burden of curative healthcare budget of the people, especially the marginalised and vulnerable sections of Indian masses.

The new challenges that wait for us are very bizarre. India records the largest number of oral cancer patients and diabetes in the world. With 5.1 million HIV /AIDS cases it is second largest in the world after South Africa. With 16.5 percent of the global population, India contributes to a fifth of world share of diseases. Estimates suggest that by 2020 the number of HIV/ AIDS cases would increase three-fold and cardiovascular and diabetics incidence will double (WHO 1996).

Table 3.2: Disease Burden Estimates for 1990 and Projection of Estimates for 2020

Diseases	*Estimates for 1990 (in percent)*	*Projection for 2020 (in percent)*
Injuries	15	19
Non-Communicable	29	57
Maternal, child and Communicable	56	24

Source: WHO 1996

Medical Intervention and Impact on Population

In India mortality rate began to decline long before the benefits of the modern medicine were available to the population. In the pre-independence period the CDR of 47.2 per 1000 population in 1921 came down to 31.2 per 100 in 1941 registering a decrease of 16 points in 20 years without the general population experiencing the benefit of medical technology in any substantial way (Table 3.3) .

Table 3.3: CBR/CDR/ Expectations of Life at Birth and IMR in India 1921-2005

Year	*CDR*	*Changes in at birth CDR*	*Expectancy of life*		*IMR*
			Male	*Female*	
1921	47.2	–	19.42	20.91	174
1931	36.3	-10.9	26.91	26.56	174
1941	31.2	-5.1	32.09	31.37	161
1951	27.4	-3.8	32.45	31.66	146
1961	22.8	-4.6	41.89	40.55	146
1971	19.0	-3.8	46.40	44.70	429
1981	15.0	-4.0	54.10	54.70	110
1991	11.4	-3.6	58.10	58.60	80
2001	8.9	-2.5	62.30	65.27	68
2005*	7.6	-1.3	63.87	66.91	53

*Provisional: Census of India 2005 SRS 2006a

Source: Central Bureau of Health Intelligence 2006b; Government of India 2006

At the time of independence the major cause of death in British India were communicable diseases with fever accounting for more than half of the deaths. (Bhore Committee Report 1946) The fall in CDR continued for the next 10 years (1941-51) again with no appreciable availability of medical technology to the masses. It was only in the 1950s that is five years after independence; the first primary health center in the country was set up. Much of the fall in death rates was a consequence of a decrease in death due to fever. The public healthcare system in India is trailing and is in the midst of several challenges. India records the largest number of oral cancer patients and diabetes in the world with 5.1 million cases, it is the second largest in the world after South Africa. The Report of the National Commission on Macro Economics and Health (NCMH 2005), Equitable Development and Healthy Future states that "the probability of the poor falling sick is 2.3 times more than the rich and is an 18 year difference in life expectancy at birth between 72 years in Kerala and 58 years in Madhya Pradesh. This clearly reveals the regional inequality that exists in the deprivation of healthcare in India. When we compare the case of India with other developing and developed countries it can be seen that in all the three indicators of CDR, IMR and life expectancy India's position is far bleak and it is worse than Bangladesh and Sri Lanka (Table 3.4).

Table 3.4: CDR/IMR/Life Expectancy of Selected Countries

Country	*CDR*	*IMR (2005)*	*Life expectancy (2007)*
China	7	2.3	72.9
Australia	7.4	5	80.6
Sri Lanka	5.8	12	74.38
USA	8.2	7	78.0
Bangladesh	8.0	54	62.8
Switzerland	8.5	4	80.6
Pakistan	8.7	80	63.8
Norway	9.5	3	79.7
Nepal	9.2	56	62.0
UK	10.2	5	78.7
India	7.6	56	68.6
Germany	10.6	4	79.0

Source: Sathyimala and Kurian 2008.

Inequality in Healthcare Access

Universal access to healthcare is a norm in most of the developed countries and some developing countries (Cuba, Thailand and others). In India though pre-existing inequality in the healthcare provision is further enhanced by difficulties in accessing it, these access difficulties can be either due to

1. Geographical distance
2. Socio-economic distance
3. Gender distance

The issue of geographic distance is important in a large country like India with limited means of transportation and communication. Those who live in remote areas with poor transportation facilities remain away from the health systems. Incentives for doctors and nurses to move to rural areas are generally insufficient and ineffective. Equipping and re-supply of remote healthcare facilities is difficult and inadequacies due to poor supply deter people from using the existing facilities. Data from the 52nd round of NSSO show that 33 percent of people from rural areas and 10.4 percent from urban areas do not receive any medical attention at death. Of those who are reported to have received medical help, at least one-fourth have accessed by non-qualified practitioners and practitioners of other systems of medicine. Analyzing this data, Gupta and Sankar (2007) conclude that a rural death has almost 11 percent less probability of getting medical attention than an urban death and a person belonging to lower social class has 6 percent lower probability of attention before death.

Rural urban disparities in the availability of medical care and the lack of adequate resources determine access to medical care and between this two it is the lack of resources that emerges as the critical factor. Studies constituted at different levels reveal that (Sathymala 2006) despite all attempts to minimize direct costs to the patients in an NGO, Hospital in Bilaspur, less than 15 percent of the very poor use the facilities because they are unable to afford the total expenditure involved. Though in the past the Government attempted to provide free healthcare, since the 1990s as part of the global commitment to disinvestments a reversal is taking place with proliferation of private medical sector entry of private insurance in healthcare and introduction of payment in the government sector.[3] For the poor all that the Government will be obliged to provide "free" is a "minimum clinical package" along the lines suggested by World Bank. (1993)

Maternal mortality is clearly much higher in rural areas (UN 2001) as trained medical or paramedical staff attends fewer births and transport in case of pregnancy complications is difficult. Geographical difficulties in accessing healthcare facilities thus is an important factor, along with gender discrimination, that contributes to higher maternal mortality in women who live in remote areas especially the tribal women in India.

A different aspect of healthcare access problem is noticed in case of 'urban poor'. Data from urban slums show that infants and under-five mortality rates for the poorest 40 percent of the urban population are as high as the rural areas. Urban residents are extremely vulnerable to macroeconomic shocks that undermine their earning capacity and lead to substitution towards less nutritious, cheaper foods. People in urban slums are particularly affected due to lack of good housing, proper sanitation, and proper education. Urban slums are also home to a wide array of infectious diseases (Gangadharan 2005, 2008) that easily spread in highly concentrated populations where water and sanitation services are non-existent. Poor housing conditions, exposure to excessive heat or cold, diseases, air, soil and water pollution along with industrial and commercial occupational risks, exacerbate the already high environmental health risks for the urban poor. Lack of safety nets and social support systems, such as health insurance, as well as lack of property rights and tenure, further contribute to the health vulnerability of the urban poor. Though healthcare facilities are overwhelmingly concentrated in urban areas, the 'socio-economic distance' prevents access for the urban poor.

Another important access difficulty is due to gender related distance. It is said that health of society is reflected from the health of its female population. That is completely disregarded in many of the south Asian countries including India. Gender discrimination makes women more vulnerable to various diseases and associated morbidity and mortality. From socio-cultural and economic perspectives women in India find themselves in subordinate positions to men. The chance of income earning is very low among women in India and it is reflected in the poor work participation rates. The work participation rates of women and the chance of earning income is only half of men in India and in urban areas it is just 11.6 percent (Nirmala

2008). This coupled with lack of support mechanisms contributes to a poor quality of life.

Table 3.5: Access of Medical Care among Important States in India

Rank as per IMR	*State*	*IMR*	*Population served per allopathic govt. doctor*	*Population served for govt. hospital bed*	*per capita expenditure*			*Public expenditure as % of total*
					Public	*Private*	*Total*	
I	Madhya Pradesh	76	Na	3409	132	733	864	15.2
II	Odisha	75	76,56	2874	134	449	582	23.0
III	Bihar	61	-	28959	92	687	779	11.8
IV	Haryana	60	13284	3185	163	1408	1570	10.4
V	Gujarat	54	19332	1544	147	670	816	18.0
VI	Jharkhand	50	23005	20133	146	Na	Na	Na
VII	Himachal Pradesh	49	Na	845	493	812	1305	37.8
VIII	Tamil Nadu	37	7651	849	202	644	846	23.9
IX	Kerala	14	10308	1172	240	1618	1858	12.9
	India	58	na	2257	207	790	997	20.8

Source: CBHI(2006b) GOI, 2006 (108,114,128)

Table 3.5 presents some indicators of access to health services including population served per allopathic doctor, population served per government hospital bed and per capita health expenditure. The population served per allopathic government doctor and per government hospital bed, the two indicators reflecting medical care accessible to the poor are taken, Tamil Nadu is at the top (7651 and 849 respectively) and is far better than Kerala (10308 and 1172 respectively) even though it records an IMR double that of Kerala .The surprising finding is that Odisha with its high IMR has better population to allopathic government doctor ratio than Kerala, Haryana, Gujarat and Jharkhand (Table 3.5). It could be argued that expenditure on health may be better indicator for access to healthcare as the poor are now accessing the private sector. It shows that (Table 3.5) the total per capita expenditure on health (private and private combined) bears no relation to IMR ranking. Kerala, Haryana and Himachal Pradesh have the highest percept expenditure on health, yet this does not reflect in their IMR ranking. Madhya Pradesh has a total per capita expenditure of Rs 864, which is higher than in Tamil Nadu's Rs 846, yet these two states are at the two end of the spectrum of IMR.

Table 3.6: Medical Care Available at the Time of Pregnancy and Post Delivery

Rank as per IMR	*State*	*IMR*	*Birth assisted by medical personal (%)*	*Instant birth (%)*	*Mothers who had at least 3 ANC during pregnancy (%)*	*Mothers consuming IFA for 90 days or more when pregnant last (%)*	*Mothers receiving post-antenatal care from medical personal within 2 days of delivery (%)*
I	Madhya Pradesh	76	37.1	29.7	40.2	11.8	27.9
II	Odisha	75	46.4	38.7	60.9	32.8	38.3
III	Bihar	61	30.9	22	16.9	9.7	15.3
IV	Haryana	60	54.2	39.4	58.8	28.3	40.6
V	Gujarat	54	64.7	54.6	64.9	35.7	54.0
VI	Jharkhand	50	28.7	19.2	36.1	14.6	17.0
VII	Himachal Pradesh	49	50.2	45.3	62.6	38.6	40.8
VIII	Tamil Nadu	37	93.2	90.4	96.5	43.2	89.6
IX	Kerala	14	99.7	99.5	93.9	77.3	8707
	India	58	48.2	40.7	50.7	22.3	36.4

Sources: CBHI (2006b, 88, 89)

The number of states spending from public exchequer towards health sector which is lower than the all India average is very high in India (Table 3.5) and it reveals that Odisha , Madhya Pradesh ,Gujarat Tamil Nadu, Himachal Pradesh etc are far better than Kerala and these states has vital role in controlling the domination of private health care providers.

Table 3.7: Rural-urban Disparity in Health Indicators, 2005-06

Sl.No.	*Indicators*	*Rural*	*Urban*
1	TFR	3.0	2.1
2	Births delivered in hospitals (%)	31.1	69.4
3	Births assisted by health professionals (%)	39.1	75.2
4	Mothers who had at least 3 antenatal care visits for their last delivery (%)	42.8	73.8
5	Women whose body mass index is below normal (%)	38.8	19.8
6	Ever married women who are anemic (%)	58.2	51.5
7	Children 12-23 months fully immunized (BCG, measles and 3 doses each of polio and DPT (%)	38.6	57.5
8	Children 12-23 months who have received 3 doses of DPT vaccine (%)	50.4	69.1
9	Children 12-23 months who have received 3 doses of polio vaccine (%)	76.5	83.1
10	Children with diarrhea in the last 2 weeks taken to a health facility (%)	55.6	65.3
11	Children with acute respiratory infection or fever in the last 2 weeks taken to a health facility (%)	59.9	78.1
12	Children aged 6-35 months who are anaemic (%)	81.2	72.7
13	Underweight children below 3 years age (%)	49.0	36.4
14	Infant death(per 1000 live births)	62	51
15	Under five mortality	103.5	63.1
16	CDR	10.4	7.4

Source: Compiled from National Family Health Survey Report

Table 3.6 presents data on access to medical care at the time of pregnancy and during the period following delivery across nine states. It can be seen that institutional deliveries and help of medical personal during delivery is very low in most of the northern states compared to Kerala and Tamil Nadu. Similarly in the consumption of IFA tablets and taking of pre natal and postnatal care, wide range inequalities are existed among the states in India. The rural urban gap in health indicators is shown in the Table 3.7 and differencc in health status index among states in India is shown in Table 3.8

Table 3.8: Health Indicators of Major States in India

Sl.no	*States*	*CBR*	*CDR*	*TFR*	*IMR*	*MMR*	*Life expectancy*	*Estimated health index*
1	Andhra Pradesh	19.1	7.3	2.3	57	204	63.5	0.648
2	Assam	25.0	8.7	3.1	68	484	57.9	0.582
3	Bihar	30.4	8.1	4.3	61	436	60.8	0.670
4	Gujarat	23.7	7.1	2.9	54	137	63.4	0.643
5	Haryana	24.4	6.7	3.2	60	159	65.2	0.700
6	Karnataka	20.6	7.1	2.4	50	247	64.5	0.657
7	Kerala	15.0	6.4	1.8	14	136	73.5	0.805
8	Madhya Pradesh	29.4	9.0	4.0	76	411	56.9	0.560
9	Maharashtra	19.0	6.7	2.5	36	161	66.2	0.722
10	Odisha	22.3	9.5	2.7	75	377	58.5	0.582
11	Punjab	18.1	6.7	2.4	44	214	68.5	0.765
12	Rajasthan	28.6	7.0	4.1	68	484	61.1	0.625
13	Tamil Nadu	16.5	7.4	2.0	37	144	65.2	0.723
14	Uttar Pradesh	30.4	8.7	4.7	73	553	59.1	0.647
15	West Bengal	18.8	6.4	2.4	38	238	63.9	0.712

Source: Registrar General SRS Bulletin, various issues.

Financing of Health Expenditure

The total expenditure on health services in the country is estimated to be around 5 percent of the GDP (Table 3.13), whereas public expenditure on health services, however constitutes just 0.9 percent of GDP .In the health budget, out of the 5 percent of GDP, the government accounts for 21 percent, households 70 percent and the remaining 9 percent by others including local government, public sector units, private firms and external funds (Table 3.13) Similarly, the per capita public health expenditure is reduced at Rs 230 and in the family welfare segment Government spends only Rs 17 per woman in the age of 15-49 years. This implies that more than 70 percent of the health expenditure is borne by the private sector and that too by the households in the absence of any significant contribution by health insurance.

With the initiation of economic reforms, there has been a decline on public expenditure in social services in general and the health sector in particular. Health services are mainly the responsibility of the states. States' finances have been under great stress and as a result there has been a steady decline in funding of health sector. Reduction of public expenditure on health services has serious adverse equity implications. NSS surveys indicate that one of the principal reasons for poverty and destitution is the burden of out of pocket expenditure on health care. Another aspect of private sector dominated healthcare system is that preventive and promotive health services get neglected. Thus holistic approach to healthcare is a victim of private domination in the health sector. Another important concern of public healthcare system in India is the striking regional differences in health attainments and health expenditure across the country. The NCMH in its report submitted in 2005 has estimated the additional funds requirements in different states for providing basic health services and associated supportive services like water supply, sanitation and nutritional supplements (NCMH 2005). They clearly indicate that the requirements of backward states with relatively poor health indicators are vastly higher than the states that have achieved higher level of health performance.

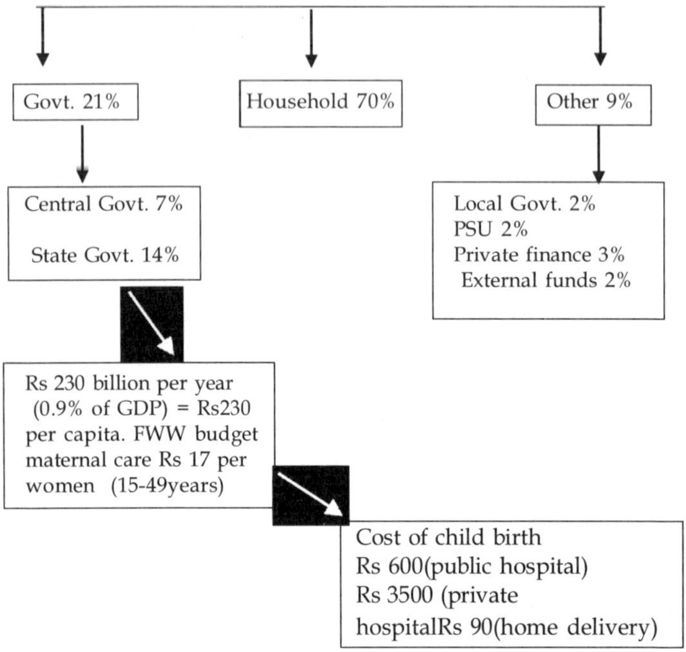

Fig.3.1: India Macroeconomics Health and RCH –Financing of Health Expenditure Total expenditure on health in India 2003-04 Rs 1100 billion (5 percent of GDP)

Though all the states spend 14 percent of the total government health expenditure but its extent varies from state to state which in turn is reflected in the health status of the people. A comparative analysis of various states reflects encouraging outcome for some of the middle-income states. In contrast, some of the BIMARU states have to go a long way to meet the achievement level of better performing states. The estimated health index was the highest in Kerala while it was lowest in Madhya Pradesh. This might be due to differences in health expenditure among various states as evident from Table 3.9.

Table 3.9: State-wise Health Expenditure (2005-2006)

State	*Real per capita health expenditure*	*Rank*	*Share of health expenditure to total expen-diture*	*Share of health expenditure in gross state domestic product*
Andhra Pradesh	109.75	5	4.04	0.87
Bihar	61.23	14	4.27	1.53
Gujarat	87.36	11	3.22	0.67
Haryana	92.06	9	2.94	0.55
Karnataka	125.34	4	4.22	0.88
Kerala	145.89	1	5.01	1.03
Madhya Pradesh	69.74	13	3.85	0.92
Maharashtra	115.03	8	3.5'1	0.60
Odisha	74.60	10	3.82	1.08
Punjab	154.51	2	3.70	0.87
Rajasthan	106.69	7	4.67	1.10
Tamil Nadu	119.83	3	4.51	0.86
Uttar Pradesh	52.83	12	3.81	0.89
West Bengal	107.50	6	4.83	0.89

Data from the National Family Health Survey (NFHS 2005-06) clearly reveals that caste differentials are related to health status. The survey documents low levels of contraceptive use among scheduled caste and scheduled tribes compared to forward castes. Reduced access to maternal and child healthcare is evident with reduced levels of antenatal care, institutional deliveries and complete vaccination coverage among the lower castes. Stunting, wasting, underweight and anemia in children and anemia among adults are higher among lower castes. Similarly neonatal, postnatal, infant, child and under-five statistics clearly show a higher mortality among the SC and STs. Problems in accessing healthcare were higher among the lower castes. The National Family Health Survey (NFHS II, 1998-99) documented a similar picture of lower accessibility and poor health statistics among the lower castes. Caste is a major indicator of health outcomes and mandated the need for interventions that changes social structures. The available data on nutrition and child health

(Table 3.10, 3.11, and 3.12) reveal precarious situation of marginalized groups in health status in the case of nutritional development and neonatal prenatal and child mortality rules both in the urban and rural, the condition of SCs and STs are pathetic compared to other better off social groups in the country.

Table 3.10: Nutritional Status of Children among Different Social Groups According to 3 Anthropometric Norms (percentage below -2sd)

Social group	*Weight for age*	*Height for age*	*Weight for height*
SC	47.9	53.9	21
ST	54.5	53.9	27.6
OBC	43.2	48.8	20.2
Others	33.7	40.7	16.3

Source: NFHS III 2005-0

Table 3.11: Differentials in Health Status among Social Group

Indicator	*IMR/1000*	*<5 Mortality*	*% Children underweight*
India	70	94.9	47
SC	83	119.3	53.5
ST	84.2	126.6	55.9
Other Disadvantaged	76	103.1	47.3
Other	61.8	82.6	41

Sources: NFHS III and NCMH 2005

Table 3.12: Infant and Child Mortality Rates in India among Different Social Group on Region-wise

Social groups	*NNMR*	*PNMR*	*IMR*	*CMR*	*Under-five mortality*
			Urban		
SC	40.1	20.2	60.4	25.2	84
ST	35.6	22.1	57.6	234	7
OBC	35.3	15.8	51.2	16.3	66.6
Others	29.3	13.7	43.5	14.1	57
			Rural		
SC	56.2	31.9	88.1	430	127.3
ST	55.1	31.8	86.9	48.8	131.4
OBC	54.7	27.6	82.9	32.7	112.2
Others	45.1	24.2	69.3	25.6	93.1

Source: NFHS III, 2005-06

It is widely recognized that the determinants of health are social and economic rather than purely medical .The poor health of people from the lower castes, their social exclusion and the steep social gradient are due to the unequal distribution of power, income, goods and services. Caste is inextricably linked to and is a proxy for socio-economic status in India. The restricted access of these from the lower castes to clean water, sanitation nutrition, housing, education, healthcare and employment is due to toxic combination of poor social policies and programmes, unfair economic arrangements and bad politics. The structural determinants of daily life contributed to the social determinants of health and fuel the inequities in health between caste group viewing health in general as an individual or medical issue reducing population health to a bio-medical perspective and suggesting, individual, medical interventions reflect a poor understanding of issues. Social interventions should form the core of all health and prevention programmes as individual medical interventions have little impact on population indices which require population interventions.

The Way Forward

The WHO and its commission on social determinants of health recommends three principles for action: improving the conditions of daily life, tackling the iniquitous distribution of power, money and resources and raising public awareness of issues measuring the problems and evaluating actions. Providing supplementary nutrition and psychosocial stimulation improves physical and mental growth in under privileged and stunted children.

The provision of primary and secondary education and accessible healthcare regardless of ability to pay is cardinal to success. Managing urban development with the provision of affordable housing, clean water and sanitation in addition to addressing rural land tenure and livelihoods is mandatory. The provision of fair and continuous employment and a universal social protection and public distribution system are necessary.

In the current context, given the socio-economic status, specific technology, resources and mechanism do exist to reduce ill health. If in the West, death due to tuberculosis for instance fell before the advent of specific medical technology, in today's situation with the availability of patent drugs and superior epidemiological understanding, the country should have been able to eliminate deaths and reduce incidence at a much-accelerated rate than the West. But it has not been able to do is a comment on the limit to modern medicine. Health planning then has to be a cognizance of both technology and specific socio economic control through which it medicate for an effective policymaking.

There are gender bias, economic bias, and status bias and bias of availability of funds within the healthcare delivery in India. There are differences in the accessibility of resources. Merely by professing equitable accessibility one cannot ensure equitable sharing of resources. To remove the socio-economic bias, rural healthcare system will have to be strengthened. In many instances doctors are not willing to work in the rural areas whatever may be the incentives given to them. This aberration can only be corrected by improving connectivity, security and job opportunities in the rural segment. Similarly, to remove gender bias and care of the girl child will have to be the motto.

Both the Central and state governments should take initiative to improve availability and accessibility of healthcare to the poor. This can also take initiative to provide social health insurance with affordability, equity and quality. Efforts must also be made to ensure quality of the public healthcare by providing suppliers, equipments and acumen on the one side and improving accountability of the public health services. It is also genuine to think of public private partnership in as much areas as possible for prevention, promotion and creative healthcare and also for sustaining support services as blood bank ambulance and communications.

Funds for healthcare will have to be made available to the urban and rural sector on equitable basis. Even the resources of the society will have to be spent in an equitable manner between the rich and poor to get out of the '10-90' syndrome. There is wide gap in the policies at the macro level and implementation at the micro level in India. The capacity created at the macro level fails to obtain directional capability at the micro level. So capability must be applied with community involvement at the grass root level with clean understanding of weakness and potential human failures and remain dynamic.

It can be concluded that with millions dying prematurely due to non-availability or unaffordability or both, of medical attention, it is only reasonable that the focus of development should be on matters related to providing universal access to health and its determinants such as water, sanitation, nutrition, primary education, communication and employment.

1. The pneumococcus is a bacterium that causes serious infections like meningitis, pneumonia and sepsis. In developing countries, even half of those children who receive medical treatment will die. Every second surviving child will have some kind of disability).

References

Banerji, Debabar. (1985). *"Health and Family Planning services in India"*, New Delhi: Lok Prakash.

Bellamy. (2004). *The State of World's Children 2005: Childhood under Threat.*

Ben, Sholmo. , Y. I. R. White, M. Marmot (1996). "Does the Variation of Socio-Economic Characteristics of an area Affect Mortality?" *BMJ*, 312, 1013-4.

Braveman, P. (2006). "Health Disparities and Health Equity: Concepts and Measurements", *Annual Review of Public Health*, 27, 67-194.

Cassel.J. (1976). "The Contribution of the Social Environment to Host Resistance: the Fourth Wade Hampton Frost Lecture." *American Journal Epidemiology*, 104, 107

Chandrasekhar,C.P. and Jayanti Ghosh. (2006). "Health Expenditure in India" ,Business Lane 10 September ,http://www.thehindubussinessline.com./2006/09/19stories/200609190145++100-htm

Deogaonkar, Milind. (2004). *European Journal of Sociology.*

Gangadharan, K. (2005). *Utilization of Health Services in Urban Kerala A Socio Economic Study*, New Delhi: Serials Publications.

Gangadharan, K. (2008). *Living Environment and Health in Urban Slum*, New Delhi: Manglam Publications.

Government of India. (2001). *Census of India 2001*, Provisional Population totals, Registrar General and Census Commissioner

Government of India. (2002). Ten*th Five-Year Plan 2002-2007*, Vol. II.

Government of India. (2006). *Health Information of India*, Director General of Health

Government of India. (2006_b). *National Family Health Profile.* http:/cbhigghs.nic.in/wrileverddata/mainlinmfile/file975.pdf.

Govt of India. (2006). Estimates of Mortality Indicators http://www.searo.who.in thinkfiles2007, mortality-stations India pdf.p.bi.

Govt. of India. (2005). *Report of the National Commission on Macro Economics and Health*, New Delhi: Govt. of India: Ministry of Health and Family Welfare.

Gupta, Indrani. and Deepa Sarkar. (2007). Medical Attention at Death Evidence from India http:/iegindia.org/dis_ind_45.idf.

http://www.global issues.org/issue 587/health- issues

International Institute of Population Studies. (1999). *National Family Health Survey-II.* Mumbai: International Institute of Population Studies.

International Institute of Population Studies. (2006). *National Family Health Survey III,* Mumbai: International Institute of Population Science.

Kaplan, G. E. Pamuk, J.W. Lynch R.D. Cohen. (1996). "Inequality in Income and Mortality in The United States: Analysis of Mortality and Potential Pathways," *BMJ,* 312,996-1103.

Kennedy, B. P. I. Kawachi, D. Prothrow-Stith. (1996). "Income Distribution and Mortality: Cross Sectional Ecological Study of Robin Hood Index in the United States", *BMJ,* 312, 1004-

Nirmala, J. (2008)."Women and Empowerment in Demography, Economic Inequality," in V. B. Jugale, *Women and Other Essays,* New Delhi: Serial Publications.

Rao, Sujatha K. S.Selvaraju, Somilnagpal and S.Sakithivel. (2005). "Financing of Health in India," in *Financing and Delivery of Healthcare Services in India,* Background Papers, New Delhi: NCMH, Govt. of India.

Report of UNICEF New York: United Nations.

Sathyamala. C. and N.J Kurian. (2008). *Health Sector Issues and Challenges in India Social Development Report 2008,* New Delhi: Council for Social Development.

Satyamala. (2006). "Health Security for the Poor a View From the Grass Root," in Suja Prasad and C. Satyamala (Eds), Security Health for all: Dimensions and Challenges, New Delhi: iho.

Services, Central Bureau of Health Intelligence, Ministry of Health and Family Welfare.

United Nations. (2001). *World Population Monitoring: Population, Environment and Development* (ESA/P/WP.164), (Draft), New York: Population Division, Department of Economic and Social Affairs.

WHO. (2004). *Maternal Mortality in 2000,* Estimates Developed by WHO, UNICEF and UNFPA, Report of the WHO Geneva, Switzerland.

Wilkinson, R G. (1992). "Income Distribution and Life Expectancy". *BMJ,* 304,165-

World Bank. (1993). *World Development Report: Investigating in Health,* New Delhi: Oxford University Press.

World Health Organization. (1996). *Creating Healthy Cities in the 21st Century,* Background Paper, UN Conference on Human Settlements: Habitat II, Istanbul 3-14 June.

World Health Organization. (1996). *The World Health Report.*

World Health Organization. (2003). *The World Health Report.*

Public Expenditure on Health: Global Scenario with Particular Referene to India

Harvinder Kaur & Gursimran Kaur

Health has always been a valued possession, as shown by the numerous ancient religious injunctions to preserve health through a variety of means. It is still considered the most valuable thing in life. The Millennium Poll, a huge worldwide survey prepared for the Millennium Report of the Secretary-General of the United Nations, revealed that health consistently ranked number one in the things men and women desired in life (The Report of Working Group-I of the *Commission on Macroeconomics and Health 2002).*

No doubt, most of the expenditure on health is borne by individuals themselves in most of the countries, but in recent years there has been a significant shift in the attention being paid to health of the citizens within development policies of a nation. Once seen as 'non-productive' sector, it is now viewed as the driver of economic growth (Mills *et. al.* 2008). The role of World Health Organization (WHO) is significant in creating consciousness amongst the governments of different nations to strengthen health system of the citizens. Governments, through ministries of health and other related ministries and agencies, play an important role in health development, through strengthening health systems and generation of human, financial and other resources. This allows health systems to achieve their goals of improving health, reducing health inequalities, securing equity in healthcare financing and responding to population needs (Regional Committee for the Eastern Mediterranean 2006). However, the issue of health is assigned either to central/federal government or to state/provincial governments and territories or to both in a federal nation.

The present paper analyses global scenario regarding the issue of expenditure on health and the role of the government. India's position amongst member countries of WHO has been explored. The role of Government of India has also been compared with that of other selected federal nations like Argentina, Brazil, Canada, Germany, Mexico and United States with respect to public expenditure on health.

Section I

Health Expenditure: Global Scenario and India's Position

Global health expenditure is less than 10 percent of GDP. However, it has been improving as it has increased from 9.2 percent in 1997 to 9.7 percent in 2007. The role of the state in providing health care services is increasing at the world level and general government expenditure on health as percent of total expenditure on health has reached to the level of 60 percent during 2007 from less than 58 percent during 2000. Out of total government expenditure at the global level, 15.4 percent has been made on health. Amongst World Health Organization region, total expenditure on health as percent of GDP was the highest (13.6 percent) in region of the Americas, followed by European region (8.8 percent) and it was the second lowest in African region (6.2 percent) and the lowest in Eastern Mediterranean region (4.1 percent) in 2007 (*World Health Statistics* 2010).

The total expenditure on health as percent of GDP during 1997 was the highest (13 percent) in USA. During 2007, no doubt it increased to 15 percent in USA but it was the country Kiribati (19.1 percent) which took the lead and as a result deaths per 1000 live births have declined in this country (www.unicef.org).

It was the lowest in Madagascar (1.8 percent) in 1997 but was the lowest in Myanmar (1.9 percent), a country suffering from a high burden of communicable diseases (Guin and Gupta 2010) in 2007. While categorizing total expenditure on health as percent of GDP into four ranges, it has been found that 82 countries were spending less than 5 percent and 102 countries were spending between 5 to 9.9 percent during 1997. But only 6 countries' total expenditure on health was in the range of 10 to 14.9 percent during 1997. While the scenario has improved in the next decade, the number of countries increased in the medium and high range and four countries had entered in the highest range of greater than 15 percent of total expenditure on health as percent of GDP in 2007. Most of the countries spent in the range of 5 to 9.9 percent of total expenditure on health as percent of GDP during 2007. The rank of India on the basis of total expenditure on health as percent of GDP was very low i.e., 109 (amongst 190 countries) during 1997 but instead of improvement, the position had further lowered to 160 (amongst 191 countries) during 2007.

Table 4.1: Total Expenditure on Health as percent of GDP of Member States of WHO

Range of Expenditure	*Number of Countries*	
	1997	*2007*
< 5 (Low)	82	63
5 to 9.9 (Medium)	102	107
10 to 14.9 (High)	6	17
15 or > 15 (Very High)	Nil	4
Total countries	190	191
Rank of India	109 (5.3 %)	160 (4.1%)

Note: Exclude Democratic Republic of Korea and Somalia.
Source: Calculated from the data available in *World Health Report, 2003* and *World Health Statistics, 2010.*

It is also important to analyse the position of different countries with regard to per capita expenditure being incurred on health. The countries have been categorized into four groups of up to 10 US $, 11 to 100 US $, 101 to 1000 US $ and more than 1000 US$ of per capita expenditure on health. The larger number of countries' per capita total expenditure was of the lower range of 11 to 100 US $ in 1997 but It was the higher range of 101 to 1000 US $ in 2007 (Table 4.2). The number of countries where per capita total expenditure on health at average exchange rate was in the highest range of more than 1000 US $ was 26 in 1997 which increased to 40 by 2007. Improvement with respect to per capita total expenditure on health has been noticed in the same category as well as many countries have entered in the higher categories.

Table 4.2: Per Capita Total Expenditure on Health at Average Exchange Rate (US $)

Range of Expenditure	*Number of Countries*		*Improvement in the same category*
	1997	2007	
Up to 10 US$ (Low)	12	4	Democratic Republic of the Congo, Ethiopia
11 to 100 US$	81	60	Angola, Bangladesh, Benin, Bolivia, Cameroon, Central African Republic, (Medium) Comoros, Congo, Djibouti, Ghana, Guinea, Guinea-Bissau, Haiti, India, Indonesia, Kenya, Kyrgyzstan, Lao People's Democratic Republic, Lesotho, Madagascar, Mauritania, Mongolia, Mozambique, Nepal, Nicaragua, Nigeria, Rwanda, Senegal, Solomon Islands, Sri Lanka, Sudan, Syrian Arab Republic, Timor-Leste, Uganda, United Republic of Tanzania, Uzbekistan, Vanuatu, Viet Nam, Yemen, Zimbabwe.
101 to 1000 US $ (High)	70	87	Antigua and Barbuda, Bahrain, Barbados, Belize, Botswana, Brazil, Brunei Darussalam, Cambodia, Chile, Colombia, Cook Islands,

			Costa Rica, Cuba, Dominican Republic, El Salvador, Estonia, Fiji, Gabon, Germany, Grenada, Iran, Jamaica, Jordan, Kuwait, Latvia, Libyan Arab Jamahiriya, Lithuania, Malaysia, Marshall Islands, Mauritius, Mexico, Micronesia, Namibia, Oman, Palau, Panama, Peru, Poland, Russian Federation, Saint Kitts and Nevis, Saint Lucia, Saint Vincent and the Grenadines, Saudi Arabia, Seychelles, South Africa, Suriname, The former Yugoslav Republic of Macedonia, Trinidad and Tobago, Tunisia, Turkey, Venezuela.
> 1000 US $ (Very High)	26	40	Andorra, Australia, Austria, Belgium, Denmark, Finland, France, Greece, Ireland, Israel, Italy, Japan, Luxemburg, Monaco, Netherlands, New Zealand, Norway, San Marino, Spain, Sweden, Switzerland, United Kingdom, United States of America.
Total countries	189	191	
Rank of India	148	157	
	(23US $)	(40 US $)	

Note: Excludes Democratic Republic of Korea and Somalia.

Source: Calculated from the data available in *World Health Report, 2003* and *World Health Statistics, 2010.*

So far as India is concerned, the per capita total expenditure on health is very low, however it has improved from 23 to 40 US $. India's rank has worsened from 148 in 1997 to 157 in 2007. Thus, India is a poor performer with respect to per capita total expenditure on health as 156 countries are better placed than India.

Public Expenditure

Economic development of a nation is directly related to the better health of its people. Therefore, improvement in the health of the people is on the agenda of the governments of almost all the nations of the world. Governments all the world over allocate a part of the total expenditure on health which ranges from 11 to 99 percent. Government expenditure on health as percent of total expenditure was the highest in Kiribati in 1997 (99.1 percent) which declined to 84.0 percent in 2007. It was the country Tuvalu where this share turned the highest (99.8 percent), but the country where it was the lowest was Guinea (11.0 percent) experiencing comparatively a very low life expectancy at birth (54), a high neonatal mortality rate per 1000 live births (39), high infant mortality rate (93) and also very high adult mortality rate (331) in 2007. While splitting the countries on the basis of the share of public expenditure on total health expenditure into four categories of less than 25 percent, 25 to 49.9 percent, 50 to 74.9 percent and more than 75 percent (Table 4.3), it has been noticed that a large number of countries (more than 80) fall into the third category of high range. Almost governments of similar number of countries (49 and 47) are spending 25 to 49.9 percent and greater than 75 percent of the total expenditure on health. A very little variation in this respect has been observed during the decade from 1997 to 2007. So far as the role of the government in India in providing health care services is concerned, it does not hold a sound position as public expenditure as percent of total expenditure on health was very less (nearly 16 percent) in 1997. However, this has improved and reached to 26 percent in 2007. The rank of India is very poor in this respect too despite the fact that it has improved from 187 in 1997 to 178 in 2007.

Table 4.3: Government Expenditure on Health as Percent of Total Expenditure

Range of Expenditure	Number of Countries	
	1997	2007
<25 (Low)	9	10
25 to 49.9 (Medium)	46	49
50 to 74.9 (High)	89	85
75 or > 75 (Very High)	46	47
Total countries	190	191
Rank of India	187 (15.7 %)	178 (26.2 %)

Note: Exclude Democratic Republic of Korea and Somalia.
Source: Calculated from the data available in *World Health Report, 2003* and *World Health Statistics, 2010.*

It also seems important to analyze the importance being given to the issue of health of citizens amongst all other functions of the governments of different nations. The share of public expenditure on health as percent of total public expenditure is different in almost all the countries. As percent of total government expenditure, the expenditure on health was the highest i.e., 32.5 percent in Andorra during 1997 which declined to 21.3 percent in 2007. It was the lowest in Nigeria (2.1 percent) in 1997. In 2007, it was the highest in Slovakia (29.9 percent) and the lowest in the country Myanmar (0.9 percent) in 2007. In the country where government spends a meagre share of its finances like in Myanmar in 2010, a large number of children (92,000) died due to curable diseases such as diarrhea, pneumonia and malaria (news.xinhuanet.com).

While categorizing the share of expenditure on health as percent of total government expenditure into three ranges, it has been noticed that 85 countries were spending less than 10 percent on health and 99 countries were spending between 10 to 19.9 percent and only 6 countries were in the high range of greater than 20 percent during 1997 (Table 4.4). In 2007, the largest number of countries was spending 10 to 19.9 percent public expenditure on health as 11 new countries entered in this range. The issue of health of the citizens is not the top priority of the Government of India as the share of health in total public expenditure is very low. It has remained less than 4 percent and its rank is also very-very poor which is 187 since 1997.

Table 4.4: General Government Expenditure on Health as Percent of Total Government Expenditure

Range of Expenditure	*Number of Countries*	
	1997	*2007*
<10 (Low)	85	76
10 to 19.9 (Medium)	99	110
20 or > 20 (High)	6	5
Total countries	190	191
Rank of India	187 (3.2 %)	187 (3.7 %)

Note: Exclude Democratic Republic of Korea and Somalia.

Source: Calculated from the data available in *World Health Report, 2003* and *World Health Statistics, 2010.*

Social security expenditure on health includes outlays for purchase of health goods and services by schemes that are mandatory and controlled by government. Such social security schemes that apply only to a selected group of the population, such as public sector employees only, are also included. Table 4.5 exhibits social security expenditure on health as percent of general government expenditure on health. It was the highest in Slovakia (96.7 percent) followed by Bosnia and Herzegovina (95.4 percent) in 2007. A large part of the resources to finance social security programmes have been provided by international donors in these countries (Bartlett and Xhumari 2007). While categorizing this expenditure into four ranges, it was found that no social security expenditure on health was incurred by 99 countries during 1997. While 31 countries were incurring less than 25 percent on social security expenditure in 1997 followed by 26 countries which were spending between 25 to 49.9 percent, 20 countries were spending in the high range of 50 to 74.9 percent and 11 countries were spending more than 75 percent. In 2007 the position improved and the governments of twenty-two countries began spending money and 4 more countries entered in the high and very high range of expenditure on health for the purpose of social security by 2007. So far as India is concerned, it has been found that a very low share (17.2 percent) of public expenditure on health is spent for the purpose of social security expenditure on health.

Table 4.5: Social Security Expenditure on Health as percent of General Government Expenditure

Range of Expenditure	*Number of Countries*	
	1997	*2007*
Nil	99	77
<25 (Low)	31	51
25 to 49.9 (Medium)	26	24
50 to 74.9 (High)	11	15
75 or > 75 (Very High)	20	24
Total countries	187	191
Rank of India	n/a 69	(17.2 %)

Note: Exclude Democratic Republic of Korea and Somalia.

Source: Calculated from the data available in *World Health Report, 2003* and *World Health Statistics, 2010.*

While comparing the position of different countries on the basis of per capita government expenditure on health, it has been noticed that large number of countries (71) were included in the range of $ 11 to $ 100 in 1997, whereas in 2007 a number of countries were spending in the range of 101 to 1000 US $ (Table 4.6). In quite a large number of countries per capita government expenditure on health was up to $ 10 in 1997, but the number of countries in this lowest range had declined in 2007. The number increased in the high range categories indicating that governments have started giving more emphasis on health of the citizens. The per capita government expenditure on health is very low in India. It was only $ 11 in 2007. India's position among the 191 countries of the world is low, but it has improved its position during 177 to 167 from 1997 to 2007.

Table 4.6: Per Capita Government Expenditure on Health at Average Exchange Rate (US $)

Range of Expenditure	*Number of Countries* 1997	2007	*Improvement in the same category*
Up to 10 US $ (Low)	41	19	Bangladesh, Democratic Republic of the Congo, Ethiopia, Nepal, Niger, Pakistan, Sierra Leone, Tajikistan, Togo, Uganda.
11 to 100 US $ (Medium)	71	63	Angola, Armenia, Bhutan, Cape Verde, Chad, Congo, Djibouti, Dominican Republic, Egypt, Guatemala, Honduras, Kenya, Kyrgyzstan, Lesotho, Mauritania, Mongolia, Morocco, Nicaragua, Paraguay, Peru, Philippines, Republic of Moldova, Senegal, Solomon Islands, Sri Lanka, Swaziland, Syrian Arab Republic, Timor-Leste, Turkmenistan, Vanuatu, Zambia, Zimbabwe.
101 to 1000 US $ (High)	56	78	Antigua and Barbuda, Argentine, Bahamas, Bahrain, Barbados, Bosnia and Herzegovina, Botswana, Brazil, Brunei Darussalam, Bulgaria, Chile, Colombia, Cook Islands, Costa Rica, Croatia, Cuba, Cyprus, Czech Republic, Dominica, Estonia, Grenada, Hungary, Jamaica, Jordan, Kazakhstan, Kiribati, Kuwait, Lebanon, Libyan Arab Jamahiriya, Lithuania, Marshall Islands, Mexico, Micronesia, Namibia, Nauru, Oman, Palau, Panama, Poland, Republic of Korea, Russian Federation, Saint Kitts and Nevis, Saint Lucia, Saint

			Vincent and the Grenadines, Saudi Arabia, Seychelles, Singapore, Slovakia, South Africa, Suriname, Tunisia, United Arab Emirates, United Kingdom, Venezuela.
> 1000 US $ (Very High)	21	31	Australia, Austria, Belgium, Canada, Denmark, Finland, France, Germany, Iceland, Ireland, Italy, Japan, Luxemburg, Netherlands, New Zealand, Norway, Sweden, Switzerland, United States of America.
Total countries	189	191	
Rank of India	177 (4 US $)	167 (11 US $)	

Note: Excludes Democratic Republic of Korea and Somalia.

Source: Calculated from the data available in *World Health Report, 2003* and *World Health Statistics, 2010.*

Private Expenditure

In a large number of countries (around 90), 25 to 50 percent of total expenditure on health was private expenditure and in quite a large number of countries (around 50), half to three-fourth was the share of private expenditure in total expenditure on health. The share of private expenditure was the highest in Guinea (89.0 percent) and the lowest in Tuvalu (0.2 percent) in 2007. Nearly three-fourth of the total expenditure on health is private expenditure in India.

"Out-of-pocket expenditure is any direct outlay by households, including gratuities and in-kind payments, to health practitioners and suppliers of pharmaceuticals, therapeutic appliances, and other goods and services whose primary intent is to contribute to the restoration of enhancement of the health status of individuals or population groups. It is a part of private health expenditure." (stats.oecd.org). Out-of-pocket expenditure as percent of private expenditure on health is categorized into low, medium, high and very high range. As percent of private expenditure on health, more than three-fourth expenditure was made as out-of-pocket expenditure in a large number of countries (138 countries in 1997 and 129 countries in 2007) (Table 4.7). While 50 to 74.9 percent out-of-pocket expenditure as percent of private expenditure on health was made by people of 41 countries, in 18 countries it was 25 to 49.9 percent in 2007. In India, while during 1997 the entire private expenditure on health was out-of-pocket expenditure, it was around 90 percent in 2007.

Table 4.7: Out-of-pocket Expenditure as percent of Private Expenditure on Health

Range of Expenditure	*Number of Countries*	
	1997	*2007*
<25 (Low)	3	3
25 to 49.9 (Medium)	16	18
50 to 74.9 (High)	31	41
75 or > 75 (Very High)	138	129
Total countries	188	191
Rank of India	69 (100 %)	73 (89.9 %)

Note: Exclude Democratic Republic of Korea and Somalia.

Source: Calculated from the data available in *World Health Report, 2003* and *World Health Statistics, 2010.*

Section II

Public Expenditure on Health in Selected Federal Nations including India

In order to compare the importance being given to the issue of health of people in India with other selected nations, the position regarding public expenditure on health in comparison to private expenditure on health as percent of GDP and per capita expenditure on health has been discussed.

In the Indian federal set-up, amongst the three layers of the government, the Constitution of India placed 'Health' in the State List. There is no health related item in the Union List. In the Concurrent List, there are six items relating to health (Madan and Shukla 2010-11). However, the Central government in India is making expenditure under the centrally-sponsored programmes for the control of communicable diseases like National AIDS Control Programme and National S.T.D. Control Programme and for control of non-communicable diseases like National Cancer Control Programme and National Mental Health Programme. Beside it, some expenditure for health is made by the central government under the central sector schemes. Under these schemes, the highest amount is being spent on strengthening of institutions for medical education, and training and research. National Leprosy Eradication Programme, National Rural Health Mission, National Vector Borne Disease Control Programme, National Iodine Deficiency Disorder Control Programme and National Programme for Control of Blindness are other programmes of the central government of India. Similarly, in Argentina, by constitutional mandate the provinces are the technical administrative units responsible for the health care and protection of the population *(Profile of the Health Services System of Argentina,* 2002). While the Constitution of Canada assigns to the provinces and territories exclusive jurisdiction over health care, the federal government has also played a role - affected primarily through transfers that cover part of the expenses incurred by provinces and territories (www.gov.nl.ca). In Germany, health care is governed at the national level by the federal assembly, the federal council and the federal ministry for health and social security. The federal government is responsible for setting the health policy for delivery of medical services (Tulchinsky and Varavikova 2009).

Total expenditure on health is the sum of public and private health expenditure. It covers the provision of health services (preventive and curative), family planning activities, nutrition activities and emergency and designated for health but does not include provision of water and sanitation (www. tradinge conomics.com). Total expenditure on health as percent of GDP varies in these countries. It is about 5 percent (lowest) in India and less than 6 percent in Mexico, 8 percent in Brazil, nearly 10 percent in Argentina, Canada and Germany and is the highest (more than 15 percent) in United States. Public expenditure on health as percent of GDP is improving in all the selected countries (Fig. 4.1). It is the highest (more than 8 percent) in Germany. It is in the high range of 7 to 8 percent of GDP in Canada, United States and one higher of GDP is 4 times Germany but it is very low (nearly 1 percent) in Indian federation. Public expenditure on health as percent of GDP in Argentina is higher as compared to India. Private expenditure on health as percent of GDP is in the range of 2 to 5 percent in all the selected countries except United States where it is more than 8 percent. It has improved in Argentina, Brazil, Canada and Germany but declined in India, Mexico and United States during 2003 to 2007. Private expenditure on health as percent of GDP is about 4 percent in India, Canada, Germany and Mexico. While it is nearly 5 percent in Argentina and Brazil, it is more than 8 percent in United States. But as percent of GDP, public expenditure as compared to private expenditure on health is lower in India, Brazil, Mexico and United States. While in Argentina, Canada and Germany, it is the public expenditure which is higher than private expenditure as percent of GDP.

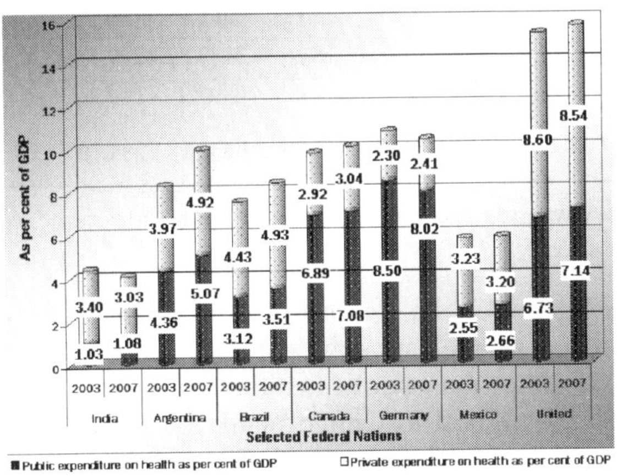

Source: www.tradingeconomics.com.

Fig. 4.1: Public and Private Expenditure on Health as Percent of GDP

The ultimate aim of expenditure on health is to increase life expectancy at birth and to reduce death rates. Germany and Canada are the mature federal nations and public expenditure on health as percent of total expenditure on health is as high as 70 percent in these countries. Public expenditure on health as percent of total government expenditure is 45 to 50 percent in Mexico, United States and Argentina (Table 4.8) while it is less than one-fourth in India. Therefore, in comparison to other countries, India is a poor performer on the health indicators.

Table 4.8: Public Expenditure and Per capita Expenditure on Health and Major Health Indicator in Selected Federal Nations Including India

	Public Expenditure on Health as percent of				Per Capita Expenditure on Health (US $)		Life Expectancy at Birth	
	Total Expenditure Health		Total Government Expenditure					
	2003	2007	2003	2007	2003	2007	2003	2007
India	23.18	26.18	3.55	3.75	23.91	40.29	63.62	68.59
Argentina	52.34	50.76	14.79	13.92	284.13	662.62	75.48	76.32
Brazil	41.29	41.59	4.41	5.37	229.48	605.66	71.13	72.24
Canada	70.21	69.98	16.73	18.13	2688.13	4409.12	79.83	80.34
Germany	78.72	76.88	17.54	18.16	3183.82	4209.18	78.42	78.95
Mexico	44.17	45.40	15.54	15.50	396.96	564.13	72.3	75.63
United States	43.91	45.54	18.56	19.45	5852.1	7284.70	77.14	78

Source: www tradingeconomics.com and www.indexmundi.com.

A growing per capita expenditure in all the nations reveals that people as well as governments are becoming more conscious about the issue of health. Per capita expenditure on health is the highest in United States and the lowest in India amongst the selected countries. India and Argentina are more comparable as in these countries it is the responsibility of the states/provinces to take care of health of citizens. Per capita expenditure on health in India is 16 times lower than Argentina.

Life expectancy is the highest in Canada and the second highest in Germany and it is the public expenditure out of total expenditure on health which is the highest (Germany) and the second highest (Canada) (more than 70 percent) in both of these countries. It may thus be concluded that whenever the government shoulders a greater responsibility of health of its citizens, life expectancy of the people improves.

Conclusion

The role of the government in providing better healthcare services to the people has been assuming significance at the global level. Global health expenditure is nearly 10 percent of GDP. The proportion of the government expenditure and private expenditure on health as percent of total expenditure on health at the world level is in the ratio of 60:40 which indicates the increasing role of the state in providing healthcare services. Total expenditure on health as percent of GDP has also been improving in the countries of the world. A large number of countries (107) are spending 5 to 9.9 percent of GDP on health. Every government is incurring less or more share of public expenditure on health. A large number of countries (more than 80) are spending half to three-fourth of total public expenditure on health. Quite a large number of countries (77) are not incurring social security expenditure on health. However, an improvement has been observed with this regard as many new countries have started incurring expenditure and many countries have entered in the higher range of social security expenditure on health.

More than three-fourth share is of out-of-pocket expenditure in private expenditure on health in large number of countries. Per capita total expenditure on health in large number of countries (87) is in the high range, followed by the number of countries (60) which are spending in the medium range. The increase in the number of countries in the high and very high range of per capita expenditure on health indicates that the issue of better health has gained momentum. Per capita government expenditure on health is in the high range in 78 countries and is in the medium range in 63 countries.

India's position is very poor amongst 191 member nations of WHO with respect to total expenditure on health as percent of GDP (160), per capita total expenditure on health at average exchange rate (157), general government expenditure on health as percent of total expenditure on health (178), general government expenditure on health as percent of total government expenditure (187), social security expenditure on health as percent of general government expenditure on health (69), per capita government expenditure on health at average exchange rate (167), and out-of-pocket expenditure as percent of private expenditure on health (73). Therefore, India should try its best to improve its position in this regard.

When we compare India with other selected countries it is found that India is shouldering least responsibility regarding the health of its people. The countries such as Canada and Germany where the share of public expenditure on health is the highest, life expectancy is also the highest. Thus, in India there is a need to increase the share of public finances for health sector.

References

Bartlett, Will. and Merita Xhumari. (2007). "Social Security Policy and Pension Reforms in the Western Balkans", *European Journal of Social Security*, Vol. 9, No. 4, December.

Guin, Pradeep. and Indrani Gupta. (2010). "Communicable diseases in the South-East Asia Region of the World Health Organization: towards a more effective response", *Bulletin of the World Health Organization*, 11 January.

The Commission on Macroeconomics and Health. *Health, Economic Growth, and Poverty Reduction (2002).* The Report of the Working Group I.

Mills, Anne, Sara Bennett and Lucy Gilson. (2008). "Health, Economic Development and Household Poverty: The Role of the Health Sector", in Anne Mills and Sara Bennett and Lucy Gilson (ed.), *Health, Economic Development and Household Poverty: From understanding to action*, Routledge International Studies in Health Economics, Oxon.

Pan American Health Organization. (2002). *Profile of the Health Services System of Argentina*, Program on Organization and Management of Health Systems and Services, Division of Health Systems and Services Development,

Regional Committee for the Eastern Mediterranean. (2006). *The Role of Government in Health Development* , Fifty-third Session, Technical Discussion I, July 2006.

Tulchinsky, Theodore H. and Elena Varavikova. (2009). *New Public Health*, London : Elsevier Academic Press.

World Health Organization. (WHO). *World Health Report, 2003*, Geneva.

World Health Organization (WHO), *World Health Statistics, 2010*, Geneva.

Webography

- news.xinhuanet.com
- stats.oecd.org
- www.gov.nl.ca
- www.indexmundi.com
- www.tradingeconomics.com
- www.unicef.org

Health Financing Reforms in India: Lessons from Other Countries

S. Sandhya

Introduction

There are two basic theoretical frameworks on which different health systems can be analysed—libertarian and egalitarian (Culyer *et al* 1981). The former values consumer sovereignty and market forces while the latter is committed to the pursuit of community health - equal health as a right to everyone, and inability to pay should not deny access to this fundamental human right. The egalitarian approach favours equality of opportunity (physical proximity and lowering of financial barriers), i.e., equal access and opportunity to the poor in the use of health care. The United States of America follows the libertarian approach, with its private insurance-based system and buys health care using public fund insurance for deserving poor and the elderly (Peabody *et al* 1996). Australia and other OECD countries follow egalitarian approach with social insurance system and the governments of these countries take into account externalities, such as preventing communicable diseases, protection of environment, etc., and provide merit goods. The health outcomes are better in these countries than in the United States[1], which follows libertarian approach. The government's role as an agent to reduce risk and improve welfare has both an economic value to society in terms of maintaining household productivity and humanitarian value of helping the disadvantaged. Even the argument for interventions in health care, so as to reduce poverty, is largely economic. Economic theory suggests that governments may or should intervene in health care system to redress the failure of the market mechanism.

The basic needs approach to development focuses on welfare aspects and explicitly considers inequality in society. For the eradication of mass poverty and attaining equity[2] in society, economic growth alone is not adequate. A comprehensive range of economic and social policies is needed. Equity is associated with social justice and fair distribution of resources. Under basic needs approach, social services are extended to different social groups based on needs. Health, along with education and other human services, forms the social sector. In this approach, the most vulnerable groups are attended first.

In India, initially the state concentrated on the development of infrastructure for healthcare system. Due to fewer number of rural health facilities and low coverage, and an insignificant presence of private sector in the delivery of modern healthcare, the Bhore Committee (1946) recommended that the state be the main provider of healthcare. While this line was followed in the post-independence period, by the Eighties, investments by the state in the hospital sector started decreasing. Over a period of time, problems of inadequate resources and poor management of available resources in the public sector resulted in inefficiency[3] giving scope for much criticism. India had very large private medical sector, especially for non-hospital care. While the colonial state developed the hospital sector at a slow pace, individual private practice expanded without any state intervention. Investment in private hospital sector was very small until the mid-1970s, after which it expanded (number of hospitals increased from 4,465 in 1976 to 11,174 in 1991). There are two reasons for this – the first reason is that the state is unable to provide healthcare to the growing population and its health needs, and started providing subsidies and soft loans, duty and tax exemptions, etc, to the private sector and also the private sector is interested in capital intensive services (hospitals). The second reason is that the introduction of modern healthcare in the form of Primary Health Centres paved the way for the private sector by creating a market for modern healthcare in the peripheral regions. Parallel to public sector in the Nineties, the private sector penetrated the market with corporate hospitals and super specialty care characterised by ultramodern and sophisticated technologies, resulting in an increase in the cost of healthcare (Gopalan 1994, Sen *et al* 2002). Against this background, the present paper focuses on the following in the Indian context based on the experiences of a few developed and developing countries: a) The role of state in the provision of health services; b) Priority setting for the major health problems in India; c) Magnitude and issues in health provision by private sector; d) Health policies and health expenditure; e) Different sources of health financing and health outcomes; and f) Reforms in healthcare in different countries with respect to user fees and lessons for India.

Role of Government in the Health Sector

The crucial assumptions[4] of perfect competitive market are not applicable in healthcare because of its unique characteristics[5] and there is a market failure in healthcare. The justification for the state to intervene in healthcare market is: a) to ensure equity; b) the presence of externalities and public goods; c) to promote both technical and allocative efficiency; and d) to contain the ever increasing cost of medical care. Further, the absence of socially optimum supply of hospitals, and dependency of health care on drugs (inappropriateness of agency relationship) and the related regulatory problems also justify for the state to intervene in the healthcare market. No country in the world has a completely free market for the healthcare because of fundamental market failures in this area and also health service is inherently uncertain (Arrow 1963). It is widely agreed that a healthcare system left to market forces alone will not be socially optimal in terms of quantity, quality or cost (Hsiao 1995) and would not lead to an effective and efficient healthcare system (Rosenthal and Newbrander 1997). Healthcare markets suffer from significant deviations from the pure competitive market model provided in economics and these deviations can result in significant losses to social welfare.[6] Also, there is a market failure in health insurance.[7] Thus, the economic basis for public production and subsidy emphasises public action to compensate market failure to provide an efficient allocation of resources (Arrow 1963, Griffin 1989, Akin and de Ferranti 1984, 1987). Theoretically it is not possible to achieve equity in the market because of three reasons. First, the market for healthcare does not concern itself with any particular modality for income distribution. Poor and those generally vulnerable to ill health do not have the ability to purchase healthcare. Secondly, in the free market, individuals are assumed to be self-interested and their desire is to maximize their own utility, which is against achieving social equity in terms of needs not backed by purchasing power. Further, there is an option demand for the hospitals - they should be available as a standby in case of emergencies such as accidents, outbreak of epidemics, etc. Option demand cannot be expressed effectively in the private market. The hospitals have no way of charging the people who have an option demand. Also, those who have an option demand will conceal their true preferences in the hope that others who have such demands will contribute to the support of the hospitals. As a result, in the absence of public financing, there will not be a socially optimum supply of hospitals (Sgontz 1979). Thirdly, giving cash subsidies to people lead to problems such as identifying the targets, and even if done there is no guarantee that people spend the money for healthcare. In the best interest of society, the state would like its sick people to take treatment, especially for contagious and communicable diseases. Thus, there is a case for government intervention in healthcare market. The role of government is to correct market failures and ensure equity to poor and vulnerable people. Another reason for the state to intervene is the role of pharmaceuticals in healthcare. Because of inappropriateness of the agency relationship between the consumer (patient) and the provider (doctor) in health care, neither the buyer (patient) nor the drug seller (pharmacist) has a control on the sale of drugs, only the doctor has. In developing countries, pharmaceutical drugs now account for 30 to 50 percent of total healthcare expenditure, compared with less than 15 percent in established market economies (Velasquez *et al* 1998). India spends 20 percent of its public health expenditure on drugs. More expensive and less essential drugs dominate the drug production in India (Government of India 1975). The supplier-induced demand and the link between profits and the sale of drugs through the health services or individual practitioners would result in over prescriptions and loss of resources to the society. Hence, the society or the state is in a better position to make informed choices about the overall levels of health expenditures and its allocation than the individual citizens. Apart from the above reasons, the Constitution of India, under Article 21, guarantees the right to life as a Fundamental Right: "No person shall be deprived of his life or personal liberty except under procedure established by law". Directive Principles of State Policy (Articles 41, 42 and 47) speak of the duty of the state to make provision in health matters. In a number of judgments the Supreme Court has reminded the state and the medical profession of their duties in protecting the lives of citizens.

Priority Setting in Healthcare System of India

Despite overall achievements in India in other fronts after Independence, millions of people lack access to basic food, shelter, and safe drinking water. Diseases arising out of acute malnutrition persist, and more than a third of population remains illiterate (Kumar and Mukherjee *et al* 1993). In spite of a nationwide supplementary nutrition programme (ICDS) for pregnant women and lactating mothers and children aged 1-4 years, the data of National Family Health Survey-2 (1998-99) show that 36.8 percent of women are with body mass index of 18.5 kg/m2 or less, indicating chronic energy deficiency. Anaemia in women varies from 41.9 percent in high income groups to 60.2 percent in low income groups. Among the children below three years, 47 percent are underweighted, and 18 percent are severely underweighted (NFHS – 2). Though the percentage of population below the poverty line has declined from 36 percent in 1993-94 to 26 percent in 1999-2000 (*Economic Survey* 2000-01), the overall picture indicates that social infrastructure in India has remained relatively neglected. This is true in health sector also. The combined factors of population and unsatisfactory health status makes India account for a fifth of the global burden of diseases with a 17 percent share of the world's population. Of the global burden, India accounts for 23 percent of child diseases, 20 percent of maternal deaths, 30 percent of TB cases, 68 percent of leprosy cases, and 14 percent of persons infected with HIV (Misra *et al* 2003). Similar trends are seen in poverty reduction, sanitation, and access to safe drinking water and literacy – all-important determinants of health status suggesting a holistic approach to health sector. These are reflected in the health indicators of the people as given below. Major issues affecting health scene in India are: high infant mortality (68 per 1,000 live births in 2000, accounting for one-fifth of total deaths), and high maternal mortality (407 per one lakh deliveries in 1998, which was far higher than the target of 200 set for 2000 by the *National Health Policy, 1983*). The reason for high maternal mortality rate may be due to the fact that 46 percent of the deliveries are attended by untrained professionals (Sample Registration System 1998). Two major diseases, which cause morbidity and mortality among children are – diarrhea and acute respiratory infections (ARI). The Survey by the Registrar General, National Institute of Communicable Diseases and National Family Health Survey, etc. have reported several episodes of diarrhoea particularly among children in the age of 6-23 months. Incidence of ARI has been found to be high among low birth weight and malnourished babies. National level studies based on a large sample [Gumber 1997, 42nd and 52nd Rounds of National Sample Survey (NSS)] have shown that India is facing a double burden of communicable and chronic diseases. The above statistics suggest the need to strengthen primary healthcare services along with qualitative improvement in health related sectors such as water, sanitation, nutrition, etc. and not to privatise them. Despite this expenditure on water supply, sanitation and nutrition is not up to the mark. In one of the states in India, viz., Andhra Pradesh, health-related sectors like water supply, sanitation, and nutrition received only about 3 percent of total public expenditure (Narayana 2003). This is against the recommendation of 15 percent allocation by Bhore Committee or 10 percent by Mudaliar

Committee as also that of the World Health Organisation. The allocation could not reach even 6 percent level recommended by the Health for All report of the Indian Council of Medical Research. With the onset of demographic transition[8], the percentage of aged (60 +) had increased from 5.7 in 1961 to 6.7 in 1991 in India. According to NSS, nearly half the population aged 60 and above was suffering from a chronic disease in 1986-87; and about three-fourths of elderly were economically dependent. Gumber (1997), in the combined analysis of morbidity data from NSS (42nd round) and NCAER Surveys (1991 and 1992), found that annual hospitalisation rates were high among elderly people and non-hospitalisation rates were concentrated in younger and older age groups. Similar findings were noticed in the 52nd round of NSS data. Improved survival among the aged implies an increasing demand for health services (Verbrugge 1984, 1989). The cost of management per medical case for those above 70 years is estimated to be four to five times higher than that for less than 5 years age group (Ogawa *et al* 1986).

Epidemiological Transition: It refers to long-term changes in the health conditions of a society. It involves four fundamental shifts[9]. During the process of economic transition of any country, chronic diseases and stress related diseases are on the rise due to urbanisation and industrialisation. In 1990, when the burden of diseases was analysed, in the established market economies, 9.7 percent of the burden was due to communicable diseases, 78.4 percent was due to non-communicable diseases and 11.9 percent was due to other diseases. The corresponding percentages were 71.3, 19.4 and 9.3 in Sub-Saharan Africa, and 50.5, 40.4 and 9.1 in India (Murray, Lopez and Jamison 1994). Similar distribution was noted for India as a whole in 1998 (WHO 1999) and for India and five states (World Bank 1997 and 2001). Among the communicable diseases, TB and malaria pose special threat. Data from NSS 52nd round on morbidity also indicate that TB was one of the major chronic diseases. This situation called for emphasis on secondary and tertiary level care and not privatisation. The major causes of death in developing countries in 1985 were infection (36 percent), circulatory problems (19 percent) and others (21 percent). The corresponding percentages in industrial countries were 9, 50 and 15 (Bulatao and Stephens 1990). The mortality data by causes in India (WHO 1999, Health Information of India-2000 & 2001, 2003)) show that the percentage of communicable diseases was 42, non-communicable diseases were 48 and injuries were 10. Among women deaths in India, 65 percent was due to infections and only 2.5 percent was due to childbirth (Gupta 1996). Keeping all these in view the policy should emphasise on public health problems and not reproductive problems.

Utilisation of Health Services: Data from 42nd round of NSS (1989) on utilization of health services indicate that the government services were the dominant services for treatment of all except those from higher income groups in both rural and urban areas. For acute illnesses private practitioners provided the majority of treatments at all economic levels. The survey also indicates that public hospitals provided an important source for in-patient care of the poor. Non-poor patients also significantly used these facilities. The richest 20 percent enjoyed three times the share of public subsidy for health compared with the poorest quintile (NCAER 1991). It also shows that for diseases that required longer treatment, such as tuberculosis, and skin diseases, and for complicated diseases, public hospitals were chosen for treatment. The reason could be that the treatment for chronic diseases was "non-productive" and not lucrative and so the private sector did not show interest in providing these services. On the contrary, the private sector was interested in treating greater proportion of shorter stay (acute) cases than the longer stay cases. The 52nd round NSS data show that 20 percent of the people used government sources and 80 percent used private sources for the outpatient care. Similar findings were observed by NFHS-2 survey also. The reason for this could be that the existing public health infrastructure was far from satisfactory as is well documented in the Draft National Health Policy 2001 "For the outdoor medical facilities in existence, funding is generally insufficient; the presence of medical and para-medical is much less than required by the prescribed norms; the availability of consumables is frequently negligible; the equipment in many public hospitals is often obsolescent and unusable and buildings are in a dilapidated state" indicating the poor quality of services in public sector. There is a negative correlation between the income and the utilisation of public sources. Among the hospitalised treatments about 56 percent were from non-governmental (52nd NSS survey). A study by the author (1993) on health seeking behaviour of 600 rural mothers (300 IRDP beneficiary households and 300 - non-beneficiaries – both the samples were from poor households) from 9 villages in Hayathnagar Mandal of Rangareddy district indicates that two-thirds of mothers and children took treatment from private sector for illnesses (most of them are common illnesses treated as outpatients). The same study pointed out the main reasons for not utilising the public sector facilities. These were unsuitable timings of the facilities, non-availability of health personnel, non-availability of drugs, and long waiting time. Other utilization studies show that one-third of in-patients and three-fourths of outpatients utilized private health care facilities (Duggal and Amin 1989, Yesudian 1990, Visaria and Gumber 1994). Gumber's (1997) analysis across states found that the reliance by people on public sector was more in less developed states as compared to more developed states. The reason in the former could be non-availability of private sector service providers. It was further found that among the nine major states, the lower socio-economic groups and the scheduled caste population used public facility more often than the higher socio-economic groups.

Poverty, Health and Health Expenditures at the Household: There is a broad view of the prevalence of a vicious circle of poverty, malnutrition and ill health. The major health problems in the developing countries arise from poverty and poor environmental conditions. Better nutrition, sanitation, immunisation and preventive health education could prevent almost 80 percent of this conditions[10]. The major determinant of morbidity and mortality in the country was malnutrition. Poor households spent 80 percent of total income on food. Even then they met only 80 percent of the suggested dietary requirements (Lipton 1988). It is observed in many studies that the mortality and morbidity were clustered among children, women in reproductive ages and the elderly, particularly among those belonging to the poor households. Among these, again the risk of morbidity was higher among the young, casual labourers and self-employed households with limited resource base. They suffered considerable hardship due to frequent and prolonged illnesses and chronic diseases. Table 5.1 indicates that poorer households spent a greater share of their income on healthcare than the rich households. Sierra Leone study (Fabricant *et al* 1999) concludes that part of the high relative expenditure on health by the poorest groups was due to their greater medical needs. Members of the poor households were nearly 20 percent more likely to be ill (inclusive of all illnesses) than their wealthy neighbours. In about 29 percent of all cases, formal medical treatment was deferred for financial reasons, more so among the lowest income quintile (34.8 percent). In most of the developing countries, it was noticed that poor households spent greater share of income on general health care as well as maternal health care than the rich households (Whitehead *et al* 2001).

Table 5.1: Percentage of Health Expenditure by Households According to Their Income in Different Countries

Country	*Lowest income quartile*	*Upper income quartile*
Nepal 1993	10.0	6.0
Vietnam 1996	19.3	3.9
Bangladesh 1997	10.2	2.3
Thailand 1997	21.0	2.0
Gambia 1994	6.0	3.4
Egypt 1995	14.4	8.7
Azerbaijan, Cuba 1996	25.0	17.5
Sierra Leone 1999	25.6	3.7
NCAER 1992-3 $	7 - 8	2 - 3
Madhya Pradesh 1993	10.0	2.0
Rangareddy, Andhra Pradesh, 1993		
Out of total income	2.2	na
Out of non-food expenditure	10.0	na

Source: As quoted in Fabricant, *et al* 1999. $ - Shariff, Abusaleh. 1995.

The frequent illnesses among poor in many countries result in: a) loss of wages leading to more financial burden for treatment as in Vietnam (Segall *et al* 2000) and China (Yu *et al* 1997) (see also Pryer 1989); b) struck in debt trap as in Vietnam (Tipping 2000); c) selling off other assets and foregoing other necessities for treatment, sometimes resulting in impoverishment as in Cambodia, Uganda, Thailand and Kenya (Corbet 1989; Chamber 1989) (see, for further details, Visaria 1990; Hsiao 1994); and d) untreated morbidity as in India (Iyer and Sen 2000).

Magnitude and Issues in Private Sector in India

Despite the relatively greater spread of public facilities, a higher proportion of health services are provided by the private sector than by government facilities in India (Chatterjee 1988). India probably has the largest private health sector in the world (Duggal and Nandraj 1991). Most of the manpower in health is in private sector (Jasani and Ananthram 1993). According to information available about hospitals and hospital beds by ownership, about 57 percent of the 11,174 hospitals were in the private sector in 1991, and 32 percent of the total hospital beds (664,135) were in private sector, while the government and the local government agencies owned the rest of 32 percent of the beds (CEHAT Database 1995). The spatial distribution of health services indicates a clear urban bias. The national average of urban hospitals and beds was fifteen times the norm recommended in 1987 (Chatterjee 1993). The main issues in private sector in India are quality and increasing cost of health. (Gopalan 1994; Sen *et al* 2002). Bhat (1997) has concluded that a level of awareness about the Consumer Protection Act and other regulations among private practitioners would result in increase in health care costs to consumers. Cost of treatment between public and private sector narrowed between 42nd and 52nd NSS rounds. The reason was that in the public sector, patients were asked to buy drugs, injections, diagnostics, etc. The private sector expenditure is dominated (67 percent) by curative care at primary level, with only a third spent on secondary and tertiary in-patient care (World Bank 1995).

Quality of Care: Private sector consists of various kinds of practitioners. While a large percentage of people use private services, it is likely that a large part of it is from under-qualified practitioners. In many national studies, including the 42nd NSS round, the distinction between various kinds of practitioners was not made. Vishwanathan and Rhode (1990) report that 38 percent of those described by village mothers as 'doctors' had some type of medical qualification or registration and that only 3 percent were MBBS. Rhode and Vishwanathan (1995), in another study, noted similar findings. Berman (1996), in his analysis of healthcare expenditure in India remarked that "private sector has contributed for health improvement in India, not by its quality but by its size and frequency of treatment". Yesudian (1990) has noted that the private healthcare practice significantly affected both the cost and quality of available healthcare services. Private physicians and hospitals rendered superfluous services and high cost services (Uplekar 1989; Duggal and Amin 1989). They also had greater incentives, freedom, and ability to provide higher quality services than public providers with respect to the nontechnical aspects of quality (Berman and Rannan 1993). Yesudian (1994) has observed that medical malpractice and medical negligence seemed to be rampant in the private sector. The number of cases filed in Consumer Redressal Commissions (district, state and national levels) demonstrates the evidence of growing concerns about the quality of private practice.

Overuse of Drugs and Irrational Practices: Many studies have noted that private sector overuses drugs and encourages irrational practices. In Jalgaon district of Maharashtra, it was found that 72.5 percent of the patients for diarrhoea, 66.7 percent for cough and cold, 87.5 percent for malaria, 61.1 percent for measles and 76.5 percent for heart diseases received injections (Duggal and Amin 1989). The prescriptions of doctors were highly influenced by the pharmaceutical industry. Several studies have shown that 80 percent of the investigations prescribed by doctors were not really required. Half of the scans done on patients with coronary heart disease were unnecessary. If 99 percent of the CT scans reported normal, what was the need for them? (Data News Features 2002). In the coastal districts of

Andhra Pradesh, caesareans and hysterectomies were on the rise, with unqualified practitioners referring patients to nursing homes for a commission. This 'cut' practice operated in most urban-centred private hospitals (Nandraj 1994). Recent studies of private hospitals in Kolkata and Mumbai (Nandraj *et al* 2000b) confirm the inadequate facilities therein, as well as the frequency of medically unnecessary procedures. The private sector might use more capital-intensive techniques than was required. The fact that CGHS had banned four leading corporate hospitals in Hyderabad in 2004 from its list indicates the severity of the problem. Bhat (1996) found that regulation of private sector in India was largely ineffective due to totally inadequate capacity for enforcement. State governments, which were legally responsible for licensing and registration lacked up-to-date figures on both qualified and unqualified practitioners. Registration systems were terribly out-of-date, both in terms of registering new practitioners as well as removing from local lists those who were deceased or who were relocated. A study by Andhra Pradesh Vaidya Vidhana Parishad in Andhra Pradesh (1993) found that the number of beds in private hospitals to be almost double of those officially registered with government authorities (DGHS 1991).

Health Policies and Health Expenditure

Reasons for Mortality Decline: The mortality rates started declining much before the medical interventions and techniques prior to 19th Century in Europe. Other sectors (non-health) such as education, water, sanitation, housing, etc., played an important role in improving the health of the people during that period. Broader changes in standards of living and environmental sanitation played an important role (Griffiths 1926). Similar observations were noted for England and Wales for their mortality reduction (McKeown and Record 1962). In these European countries, the incidence of cholera, typhoid, plague, tuberculosis, and measles declined before there were any effective methods of treatment. The improvements in health care were partly due to greater food production and better means of distribution, which resulted in higher levels of nutrition. Late in the Nineteenth Century further improvements resulted in the wider availability of clean and plentiful water supplies and the construction of efficient systems of sewage disposal (United Nations 1973). Attention has also been drawn to improvement in personal hygiene (Razzell 1974). Differences in health standards cannot be explained by differences in the extent of provision of more expensive services like doctors or hospitals (Maxwell 1975). The experience shows that inter-sectoral approach played a significant role in the health transition of Western countries. In contrast to the experience of the West, there has been general agreement that the reduction of mortality in contemporary developing countries has been largely a medical achievement (Arriaga and Davis 1969). But, in some countries, the probable supplementary significance of nutritional and economic changes had also been stressed (Gray 1974). In Sri Lanka, the health improvement could be achieved due to a combination of improvements in health sector and non-health sector - rapid growth of agricultural sector, universal free education and rural housing (Marga Institute 1984). The multi-sectoral approach adopted by China for improving health conditions as well as the emphasis within the health sector on prevention, community mobilisation and finance and on bare-foot doctors was found responsible for health improvement from 1950 to 1982 and drew attention of other countries (World Bank 1984). The "shared growth" model in Taiwan and South Korea aimed at capacity expansion of the people despite low investment of government in primary health care for the poor, and the "welfare state" model in Chile and Costa Rica aimed at publicly funded social services including primary health care during post-1960s gave similar reductions in the risk of early deaths (McGuire 2001). In India, Krishnan's (1975) analysis of data for different states for the period 1951-61 show that the decline in mortality was not due to public health programmes alone, and economic development and social changes particularly literacy had a larger effect. He found that the indirect effects of literacy in reducing mortality seemed to be almost as large as the direct effect of the doctor-population ratio. Demographic Health Survey Reports for Bangladesh (1993-94), Indonesia (1994), Pakistan (1990-91) and Philippines (1993) show that women who attended school and those from higher social classes were more likely to use medical services, and had supervised deliveries than less educated, poorer women. Similarly, under-five mortality rates were much lower for children of educated (secondary and higher level) women in the above countries (Asian Development Bank).

Health Policies: The main aim of the National Health Policy of India 1983, was 'Health for All by the Year 2000 A.D'. The National Health Policy of 2001 emphasised achieving "an acceptable standard of good health amongst the general population of the country". Both were specified to achieve the goal "through universal provision of comprehensive primary health care services". The 2001 policy stipulated ensuring more equitable access to health services across the social and geographical expanse of the country. It realised the most cost-effective method of achieving equity was to increase the outlay in primary health sector (from the current level of less than 20 to 55 percent). The policy should emphasise on an integrated approach of water and sanitation for controlling diseases such as Malaria, Cholera, etc. But, in reality, the Health Policy of India 2001 clearly de-linked health from development and promoted healthcare on the basis of available technologies, not necessarily on the disease profiles of the people (Qadeer 2002). There was no mention of other sectors such as food security, nutrition, drinking water supply, sanitation etc. in the policy document, in spite of the empirical evidence that the extremely insecure and severely insecure states in terms of food had low health indicators (Swaminathan 2001).

Health Expenditure: In India, health is a state subject. However, the central government also spends directly on some vertical programmes and family planning programme. The total outlay in the First Five Year Plan (1951-56) was Rs.1,900 crore, out of which, 3.3 percent was spent on health and 0.1 percent on family welfare and the corresponding percentages in the Ninth Five Year Plan were 2.31 and 1.76 respectively. It shows that there has been a reduction of outlay on health and increasing outlay on family planning. If the government's intervention emphasises a) correcting failures in health insurance market, it should subsidise hospital care, b) improving health outcomes, it should subsidise prevention and treatment of infectious diseases through primary care, and c) improving equity, it should subsidise rural health. Let us examine where government's health expenditure in India is going. The expenditure on health as a percentage of GDP was 6.7 percent in India. The share of private health sector in India was 4.7 percent of the GDP and that of public sector was 1.3 percent (World Bank, 1993). Of the public expenditure, 71 percent had been allocated to hospital care (Griffin 1992). In most public systems, resource constraints fell most heavily on non-hospital activities, so was the case in India. Tulsidhar (1993) has estimated that 62 percent of the Health Ministry's spending by the Centre and the states went to medical sector during 1986-89. Reddy and Selvaraju (1994) in the longitudinal analysis of the governments' expenditure between 1974-91, found that in the combined expenditure of central, state and union territory governments, the major share (65 percent) was under 'medical' head, mostly curative, which supported clinical services in hospitals, and about 25 percent was spent on preventive care. Thus, it indicates that government intervention in India was to correct the failure of health insurance market. Public health interventions were more efficient than medical care spending (Jamison and Mosley 1991), but the government's expenditure was mostly towards medical, not a cost effective method of spending. People are not satisfied with the public services in many primary care settings because of absence of drugs, trained staff and limited hours of service. As a result, the demand is: a) shifted to more intensive public delivery settings; b) is shifted to the private sector; and c) remains unsatisfied (Mulou *et al* 1992). A study in India by Prakash (1998) shows that about 40 percent of the patients attending a general medicine out-patient department in one of Mumbai's largest public teaching hospitals needed only primary health care indicating that public hospitals that constituted secondary and tertiary level care were both overburdened and underutilised. Apart from the above, the polarisation of health between different states and different groups of people in society is striking in India

(Kumar and Mukherjee 1993). Health spending in India is higher in richer states and in those states having lower infant mortality rates. Central government allocations are negatively related to state infant mortality rate. The Central government's spending is not targeted to the poorest areas and those with the worst health indicators. The share of urban India in total public health expenditure was nearly 2.5 times larger than its share in the population. The sharp decline occurred in the expenditure on malaria, tuberculosis and leprosy programmes, which mostly struck the poor (Gupta 1995), further aggravating the public health. Lal *et al* (1994) applied CBA to Malaria Control Programme and found that every rupee invested in malaria control had produced a direct return of Rs.22.10. They estimated the labour days saved as 1,329.0 million man-days per year indicating the huge social benefit of controlling malaria indicating that the social benefits of controlling malaria were much higher.

Sources of Health Care Financing, Health Outcomes and Equity

There are a number of methods for financing health care services: (1) personal payment (out-of-pocket), (2) voluntary insurance, (3) social insurance, (4) general revenues, (5) charity, (6) industry, and (7) external financing. Around the world, the first four sources mainly finance health services and the contribution of the last three are negligible. Of the first four sources, the former two are private and the latter two are public.

Personal Payment (Out-of-pocket, Fee-for-Service Payment): This method provides services through independent practitioners or a group of practitioners—clinics or hospital emergency rooms (e.g., in India, they are called as super specialty clinics or nursing homes or hospitals). Here, the provider's responsibility is directly to the patient. The strengths of this method are that everyone can seek care if they can pay for it, consumers have the freedom of choice of providers and there are incentives to improve the quality by the providers. Though there is out-of-pocket payment in public sector also, but its share is limited to the extent of 10 to 15 percent of the total (Mahal *et al* 2001). But this method leads to inequity in spatial distribution of services as in India (Chatterjee 1993; Sebastian 2003). Roemer's study has found that 60 percent of the doctors in Malaysia were engaged in private practice in the country's major cities (Roemer as cited in Sorkin 1976). Musgrove (1986) has examined Peruvian data for 1984 and has shown that the inequality of medical attention, expensive resources, especially doctors, were heavily concentrated in the capital city, Lima. Even in countries where the general revenues support health services for a majority of the population – as in most Asian and African countries – persons in the middle and upper classes still finance much of their health care through direct payment. In India, private spending contributed 87 percent according to WHR (2000), and 82 percent according to World Bank (2001). Out of this private spending, the bulk was from out-of-pocket, estimated at 75.2 percent by Peter Berman (1996) (These figures have been reproduced from Ellis *et al* 2000), and 84.6 percent by WHR (2000). Latest estimates from National Accounts Statistics indicate that private expenditure on healthcare in India was over Rs.1,000 billion and 90 percent of this was out-of-pocket[11] (Duggal 2001). Most payments in private payment were on fee for- service basis—an inflationary and cost-escalating method that induced over supply of care (Jimenez 1987). In China, the fee-for-service payment diverted the public health workers to activities for which fee could easily be charged rather than those with the highest priority for public health (World Bank 1997). The alarming increase in caesarean deliveries in Chennai (about 40 percent against the normal figure of 5 percent) has been attributed to the above method (Muraleedharan 2000).

Voluntary/Private Insurance: Health systems that rely primarily on private insurance arrangements have the following problems: a) cannot cover the vulnerable sections of the society; b) encourages cream skimming, which can result in limited access to health care for certain categories of patients; and c) less successful in cost containment than are those that rely on public financing (Newhouse 1993). Though the cost sharing is meant to tackle "moral hazard", the US data from Rand Health Insurance Experiment (Brook *et al* 1983) show that cost sharing by non-elderly patients reduced the number of medical care visits and this resulted in less favourable clinical outcomes among patients with less income, those with hypertension and those with poor vision. The American system characterised by privately financed care and insurance denied 15 percent of its population adequate access to care. Similar conclusion was drawn in a review article: "The United States' so-called medical care model is not benefiting the majority of the working class and lower middle class (60 percent of the US population); it benefits only the top 20 percent as well as the large employers and financial interests that control the system" (Navarro 1999). Evans (1990) points out that the costs of insurance and administration in 1987 were about 0.6 percent of GNP in the United States and only 0.1 percent in Canada. Woolhandlet and Himmelstein (1991) point out that administrative cost was 4 to 6 percent of total health spending in the United Kingdom compared to 22 percent in the United States indicating the wastages in American health care system. Penetration of commercial insurance into health care all over Latin America weakened the long established government national health services. Thus, there is a need to finance health care through general revenues.

In India, private health insurance is quite insignificant (covers only 1.7 million people accounting for 0.16 percent of population) and also most of it is for tertiary care. The reimbursement to providers in India is mostly by fee-for-service method and contributes in escalating the cost of medical care[12]. The capitation fee method[13] is quite negligible and found only in Employees Social Insurance Scheme (ESIS) and in some public sector companies. In the public sector, health care is delivered by salaried staff, but inadequate supplies and corruption (private practice and bribes) in it add to the fee-for-service method. The private practice *per se* is not bad but it operates under unrestrained market mechanism, reminding the government's role to regulate it more stringently.

Social Insurance: Risk pooling is the main aim of all insurances. But what is good about social insurance is ensuring an adequate coverage based on ability to pay and not according to pay. Thus, it ensures equity, finance and access. A social insurance or security system involves the imposition of special taxes on workers and employers exclusively for the benefit of workers and their families. The quality of services provided in social insurance hospitals is better than those at government hospitals. But, the problems with social insurance are high administrative costs, risk of moral hazard, and high-cost care depending on payment mechanism to the providers. Evidence suggests (Misra *et al* 2003) that over the past five years the General Insurance Company's claims in India have been growing at more than 30 percent per year - which substantially exceeded the growth of public health care spending or individual spending. It seems plausible that this growth in part was due to the moral hazard response to insurance and other reason could be cost escalation which needed to be probed by further analysis. It is estimated that Central Government Health Scheme, Employees State Insurance Scheme and Mediclaim together covered only a small fraction (less than 9 percent) of the Indian workforce—mostly from the organised sector (Ellis *et al* 2000). In developed countries, where social insurance is a major source of financing, although many employees will be partially covered by their employers and unions (as in Germany, France, Austria and Japan), the unemployed, and retired, the poor rural populations, employers' dependents are not covered who need the provision of health leading to inequity (Chernichovsky 1995).

General Revenues: In every country of the world, general tax revenues are used for financing certain components of medical care. It can meet the objective of equity in finance, based on progressive tax structure. In many countries, financing from this source is predominant. In Canada, Sweden, United Kingdom, Germany, Costa Rica, the major single source of financing is tax revenues or social insurance or a combination of both. Most of the above countries have public expenditures averaging above 80 percent of the total health expenditures. Experiences from these countries show that equity in access and healthcare outcomes are positively correlated, and together, they are directly related to the share of public finance in total health expenditure. China, Malaysia, South Korea and Sri Lanka, with 30 to 60 percent of total health expenditures coming from public finance, have shown better outcomes (infant mortality) and equity (WHO 1995) than India with a 20 percent share of public finance (World Bank 1993).

Reforms in Health Care

One of the main aims of reform is about improving management, and achieving better healthcare. Management can be improved through improved efficiency. This is believed to be achievable through increased competition, cost reduction and government regulations of its delivery by others as opposed to direct delivery by the government. One reason for controlling health spending is that there is strong evidence that more healthcare spending does not necessarily buy better health (Newhouse 1993). In response to worsening economic conditions and reduced public finance for health services, most developing countries, since the 1980s, have undertaken health reforms. In many industrialised countries, the major motivation is cost containment or giving society the value for the huge sums of money it spends on healthcare. There are four unpleasant lessons to be learnt at the institutional level if cost containment is to succeed: (1) the government must be given a strong regulatory hand; (2) there must be some amount of universal health care coverage; (3) freedom of choice must be limited; and (4) technology assessment must be superintended by a willingness to apply strict standards of efficacy based on some substantive view of human well-being - and by a willingness to use these standards to reduce or eliminate the use of effective technologies when affordable, not just those that are ineffective or marginally effective (Callahan 1990). In developed countries, some of the above are applicable, whereas in India only the second one is applicable. For Latin America, reform is a response to the devastating effects that the economic crisis of the 1980s had on public and private spending. For the newly-industrialised countries of Asia, where rapid economic growth has created both the need and possibility of extending access to healthcare, reform is seen as a solution for achieving equity and cost containment (Hsiao 1990). India introduced economic liberalisation in 1991. Along with other reasons, health care reform was inspired by the 1987 document of the World Bank entitled "Financing Health Services in Developing Countries: An Agenda for Reform". Further, in India, public health expenditure had declined from 1.3 percent of GDP in 1990 to 0.9 percent in 1999. While central budgetary allocation remained stagnant at 1.3 percent, the states' allocation (which accounted for over 70 percent of the total health care expenditure of the country (Gupta 1996) fell from 7.0 percent to 5.5 percent during the above period. To overcome these problems, India moved towards reforming the health sector. The World Bank, in its *World Development Report 1993* spells out the need for reform in health sector in terms of the need to deal with misallocation, inequity, inefficiency and exploding costs. The document provides two specific types of strategies that have been introduced by governments - 1) reform of financing strategies, and 2) reform of public sector organisations. The financing strategies are introduction of user fees and provision of insurance or risk coverage. Through user fees the idea is to shift some of the burden of financing healthcare from the public sector to the private sector beneficiaries (households). But what user fees did was not shifting the burden of financing but shifting the burden of providing essential services to the poor. Simply they priced them out of medical market. Organisational reforms shifted some decision making from central planning agencies to those in closer touch with local conditions and client needs. The following sections deal with the review of available literature on user fees only.

User Charges - Experiences from Other Countries: Introduction of user fees[14] is demand side control measure in regulating unnecessary services. Typically, in economic evaluation, the willingness-to-pay approach is used to justify the introduction of user fee for government health services. The important argument against the willingness-to-pay is that the poor are the hardest hit by user fees. In the absence of market prices, as is typically true in health sector, questions in surveys are increasingly being asked to elicit information about hypothetical willingness-to-pay. Briscoe and de Ferranti (1988) indicate the potential for this approach in the valuation of water projects, but its applicability in health needs to be assessed.

Because of consumer ignorance of effectiveness of intervention, inability of people to estimate risks (Weinstein 1989); willingness-to-pay assessments would probably have limited application to health. Also, it is increasingly clear that paying for health services is not the same as ability to pay. Many poor people cannot afford to pay but still do so, at the cost of other essential expenditure for items such as basic nutrition (Ministry of Health and Family Welfare 2001). The role and effect of user fee for publicly provided health services in developing countries were evolved during the mid-1980s. The early supporters (Akin *et al* 1987) of user fee believed that the fees could be designed to improve efficiency (through appropriate price signals[15]), reduce overuse, attain financial sustainability (through significant resource mobilisation), leading to better quality, and equity (through targeted prices and exemptions). It may also serve as a revenue generating mechanism for the government not for improving the resource availability of the health sector as practised in Ethiopia. Several theoretical arguments have been used to justify the feasibility of these goals. Zero prices hinder a health system from efficiently directing users to places where unit costs for particular services are lowest. Also user fees are recommended when health expenditure is high or rising quickly to moderate demand and containing costs (Shaw and Griffin 1995). It is believed that user fee will divert some patients from private sector to government sector, as there will be improvement in the quality of services (hypothetical) in the latter. But sometimes, greater privatisation leads to a shift of patients who can pay from public to private sector, leading to further decline in the quality of care in the public sector. Opponents of user fees believe that user fees shift healthcare costs from the better-off to the sick, thus one has to make a trade-off between raising revenue and maintaining access to care based on need rather than ability to pay.

User fee works well if several factors are present: fees can be retained in health facility; the community and managers can decide how fee revenue is spent; patients are charged by-pass-fees when they go straight to secondary providers. Also, providers are made accountable for funds, exemption mechanisms are in place and patients are assisted with ways of financing healthcare when they are not able to pay at the point of service use. The World Bank strategy has been powerfully reinforced by the practice of making user fees a condition of loans and aid from international donors, for example, in Kenya and Uganda. In Sub-Saharan Africa, chronic scarcity of resources in the face of old and new challenges such as AIDS forced them to adopt reforms. Even though the external assistance is not substantial in India, it shapes the priorities of health policy to a greater extent.[16] As an instrument for controlling costs by managing demand, user fees had limited success. From several industrialised countries there is evidence that increasing fees did reduce the use of health services, though not necessarily service costs (Fahs 1992, Nolan 1993 and OECD 1994). The experience of some of the countries, which implemented user fees in terms of cost recovery and its impact on quality of services, utilisation and equity (maintaining exemptions), has been given below from which one can draw lessons for India.

Cost Recovery and Equity: In many countries of Africa, user charges were introduced after the launch of Bamako Initiative (BI) in 1987 with a view to mobilise revenue (Shaw and Griffin 1995). Top down user fee model was introduced through Structural Adjustment Programme; but BI followed a reverse approach, viz., at the primary health centre level. A survey of 37 sub-Saharan African countries shows that 33 had cost recovery programmes or planned to introduce one (Nolan and Turbat 1993). Some studies from Africa show that revenue from user fees has traditionally covered only 6 - 8 percent of recurrent expenditure aggregated at the national level even without taking the accounts of the administrative cost of fee collection process (Mwabu 1990). At the health facility level, revenue from user charges as a percentage of total income is way beyond – 6 to 8 percent, and positively affects the quality of healthcare being provided. To this limited extent, user fee has achieved its objective. But many empirical studies show that user fees did not add much to the revenue. Cost recovery ratio (fee revenues as percentage of recurrent government expenditures) in 16 African countries from the early to mid-1980s ranged from less than one percent to about 12 percent, averaging about 5 percent (Vogel 1991). When the administrative costs of collecting fees from this are taken out, it becomes much less than 5 percent (Creese 1991). In Zimbabwe, user charges were introduced in 1992. But the cost recovery level was very poor amounting to only 3.5 percent. This might be because of low prices, a weak billing and collection system. Another reason is that generally the revenue was not retained by the health sector. This could have demoralised the health personnel to collect the fees. Fee revenues were not used to improve the quality but only to sustain the service reflecting the decline in the utilisation of healthcare by 50 percent, mainly the poor people in rural areas and other vulnerable sections of the society (Mills *et al* 2001). User charges were high in China and cost recovery was also high in China (around 36 percent) (Creese 1997). There is evidence to show that the higher the share of user charges in the total mix of financing for health, the greater the relative share of the financing burdens falling on poor people (Van Doorslaer *et al* 1993).

Exemptions: In the Sine Saloum Rural Health Project in Senegal, exemptions were allowed at the discretion of the health worker (Stinson 1982). In an attempt to reach the individual poor with healthcare, the government of Thailand exempted poor people from payment of fees. But the geographical distribution of the free medical care budget was not in accordance with the geographical distribution of the poor and as such defeating the objective of the system (Mills 1991). Litvack and Bodart (1993) point out that lack of effective exemption mechanism even in a well-organised system of user fees collection resulted in reduced access to poor. In Ghana, PNDC Law 207 (1988) regulation specifies that the outpatient consultancy fees increase from rural health centre to district to regional and to teaching hospital. There are total exemptions for TB and leprosy and only cost of drugs are charged for other communicable diseases such as meningitis, tetanus, hepatitis B, etc. An evaluation study in 25 institutions (Ghana Statistical Service, 1995) in Volta region of Ghana noted that the exemptions for poor were not working due to lack of proper definition of poor people, insufficient copies of policy documents for consultations and failure of the reimbursement of the total amount spent. Among the total 1,894 exemptions, 52 percent were for health staff and only 16 percent were for paupers. Analysis by Creese and Kutzin (1995) concludes that user fees can be costly to implement and income-based exemptions in particular have widely proved difficult to manage. An evaluation study in one of the regions of Ghana viz., Brong Ahapo (Coleman 1997), concludes that government institutions were no longer complying with the Hospital Fees Regulation of 1985. Fees charged were way above the standard levels. Exemptions and waivers were totally disregarded. It also found that the reasons for this were (1) lack of knowledge by service providers about the fees structures; (2) revenue generation had become the key objective of user charges, leading to inequitable and undesirable considerations of user fees, thus ignoring other objectives of cost containment; (3) lack of awareness among public about waivers; and (4) no penalties to the health facilities for not complying with the law. It also found that wherever exemptions were granted, the institutions did not have the records of the amount of money not collected from the patients. It is, therefore, difficult to believe that exemptions were actually granted. Another study by Nyonator and Kutzin (1999) in Volta region of Ghana also came out with similar conclusions. Official exemptions were largely nonfunctional, difficult to maintain, might be because of free-rider problem. Frequently, the poor were unable to benefit from exemptions, while non-poor persons (e.g., civil servants) could do (Gilson *et al* 1997). Tanzania Human Resources Development (HRDS) of 1994 used by Social Sector Review of the World Bank (1996) reports "people were alienated by poor services, especially shortage of drugs caused partly by mismanagement and scarcity of funds". Health workers used to supplement their wages through drug sales. Without reforms in management, patients would continue to get poor services. The Gender Networking Project in Tanzania (1997) states "pregnant women and rural poor are unable to access crucial medical services", although these groups were supposedly exempted to pay user fees. Fees were imposed for AIDS, mental illness and other diseases. There is evidence to show that the increases in maternal mortality (C

Hongoro, S K Chandiwana, unpublished report) and in the incidence of communicable diseases such as diphtheria and tuberculosis have been attributed to user fees (International Child Development Centre 1993).

User Fees and Utilisation of Services: As an instrument for controlling costs by managing demand, the user fees had limited success. From several industrialized countries there is evidence that increasing user fees did reduce the use of health services, though not necessarily service costs (Fahs 1992, Nolan 1993 and OECD 1994). Changes in the utilisation of services by the poor depend on their perception about increase in the quality of services relative to the increase in user fees. When there was improvement in the quality of services, utilisation had increased. Sierra Leone in 1989 was one of the poorest countries in Africa characterised by a decade of declining producer prices, high inflation and internal corruption. People responded positively to Bamako Initiative drug supplies and the presence of better-trained paramedical staff, resulting in increased utilisation of PHC services. The beneficial effects of user fee on equity were challenged (Gilson 1988 and Creese 1991). A cross-sectional analysis of household survey data from two developing countries shows that utilisation by poorer persons was reduced to a greater extent than that by the rest of the population (Gertler and Van der Gaag 1990). Recognisable improvement in the quality is also essential for the political acceptability of fee increases, as revealed by Kenya's experience (Collins *et al* 1996). There was evidence from Cameroon (Livack and Bodart 1993) that despite fee increase, utilisation by poor increased because of increase in the quality of services. The studies conducted in Ghana (1989), Peru (1987), Swaziland (1990) and Zaire region (1989) reveals that user fees decreased the service utility and mostly poorer population. In Swaziland most affected were poor, those who needed multiple visits. People felt that ailments were not serious to justify the costs. It was found that attendance for sexually transmitted diseases dropped cited in Bir 2000). But many empirical studies concluded that there were difficulties in initiating and sustaining quality improvements. A study in Burkina Faso (Sauerborn *et al* 1994) analyses the elasticity of demand by age and income sub-groups and concludes that increase in price resulted in decrease in access to those at higher risk of ill health and death, the young and the poor, who were pushed out of the system. Gertler and Hammer 1997 review many studies which used cross-sectional household surveys to estimate the price elasticity of demand for outpatient services. A few early studies using questionable data found completely inelastic demand - prices had no effect on utilisation. Most studies have found that higher prices were associated with lower utilisation, but that overall own price elasticities were low well below unity. Further, they reveal that price sensitivity differed by economic and demographic group. The poor appeared to be more price sensitive than the rich and children's utilisation seemed to be more price sensitive than adults. Gertler and Molyneaux (1996) estimate the price elasticity for outpatient services in Indonesia using longitudinal panel data in which public sector user fees varied experimentally. It was found that with increase in price there was a significantly lower utilisation in both rural and urban areas, more so in urban areas, where there were more private-provider alternatives. Two longitudinal studies from Kenya (Collins *et al* 1996) and Ghana (Waddington and Enyimayew 1990) find that the 1985 increase in user fees resulted in sharp and significant reduction in the utilisation of curative and ambulatory care immediately, but rose again to near previous levels. The time required for recovering and the residual decrease in utilisation depended mainly on the rate of increase in fees, on the degree of quality improvement that was introduced, and the availability of alternative sources of care. A review of user fees and other determinants on utilisation of health services (formal and informal health sectors) in Africa (Hutton 2002), indicates that if there were no other changes, the introduction of user fees reduced utilisation, particularly from poorer households. On the whole, the African example shows that user fees were not for accumulation of capital and it did not increase the efficiency of healthcare in several African countries. In China, user fees for some public health services, such as immunisation, resulted in limiting the demand for them, particularly among the poor (World Bank 1997). At the level of health facility, user fees increased the non-salary component (Parker and Knippenberg 1991; McPake *et al* 1992; Bennett and Banda 1994). Where such inputs were severely underfunded (Kutzin 1995; Creese and Kutzin 1997), even a small amount of funding for non-salary inputs might have greater impact on productivity than implied by cost recovery 'averages'. Untreated morbidity is dangerous because it involves huge social costs due to externality in health sector. TB is a leading cause of mortality in China. The introduction of user charges has led to untreated TB (World Bank 1993).

Indian Context: In India, the *Working Group Report on Health Financing and Management for the Eighth Five Year Plan* (1990-95) recommended that the government might give a large subsidy to healthcare services. User fees should be introduced but the payment should be graded – poor people must get the health services totally free of cost. The graded user charges should be linked with equity and efficiency. In the Ninth Five-Year Plan (1997-2002), the Government of India clearly put forward user charge as a strategic decision. The main assumption for the success of the user fees model is that a majority of the users are part of the publicly funded system. But it is far from this in the case of India. In India, the government policies on cost recovery vary from state to state, although it is safe to say that only a small percentage of costs are recovered through fees. A study from Maharashtra (Satia and Deodhar 1993) has found that exemptions from charges in public hospitals and dispensaries were clearly set down by regulation for those with income of less than Rs.180 per month in urban and Rs.150 in rural areas. Civil servants and their families, medical and nursing staff and medical students were exempted from paying. No fees were to be charged for immunization and most maternal and child health services. Despite the completeness of the scheme, hospitals collected less than one percent of costs in 1984-85. The reason was – the system depended on self-declaration of income, and almost everyone declared that they earned less than Rs 180. For 15 major states in India the average cost recovery was about 3.8 percent. It was highest in Punjab at 7.7 percent and lowest in Rajasthan at 2.8 percent (World Bank 1997). The cost recovery in Andhra Pradesh, on an average was 2.7 percent (Andhra Pradesh: *Agenda for Economic Reforms 1997*). A review of user fees in Gujarat, Madhya Pradesh, Rajasthan, and West Bengal (Bhat 2000) shows that it contributed below 2 percent to hospital budgets. The impact of user fees on utilisation, especially by the poor, is not known clearly in India. But the experience from other countries shows that user fee can be highly regressive (Reddy and Vaudomoortele 1996). A study by Deolalikar and Vashishtha in 1992 reveals that price elasticity of demand for primary healthcare services was virtually zero, implying that an increase in user cost would not adversely affect the demand for such services. However, one has to be careful in drawing such conclusions because the elasticity of demand has many components such as treatment cost, and time cost and opportunity cost of time. Kerala introduced user charges in government hospitals including five medical colleges. The government of Kerala was unable to increase the user charges by even a minimum of 10 to 20 percent of the rate, which existed in 1994. The fee hike was widely opposed by the public, various political parties and social organisations. The protests over hike in hospital charges in Kozhikode and other places show that sections of the people who are availing medical services almost free are not going to tolerate the changes. As a result the government has rolled back the hospital fee hike recently. If such is the plight of Kerala state, one can imagine the fate of other states. User charges were introduced in all government hospitals at the district level in Karnataka from March 1988. Green card holders and people with an income limit of Rs. 11,850 per year (accepted norm under Jawahar Rozgar Yojana) were exempted. In 1995, the government constituted District-level Health Committees, which were made responsible for collecting user charges. The user charges are used for improving the quality of healthcare such as buying drugs, repair and maintenance of equipment, ambulance, supply of water and sanitation. Evaluation studies are needed to examine the achievement of objectives of user fees. A major study on user charges in Chamoli district in Uttaranchal, Indore in Madhya Pradesh, Jamnagar in Gujarat, Ramanthapuram in Tamil Nadu, Guwahati in Assam was conducted by Sharma

(2001). The study was based on community-based responses from 4,000 households interviewed on their willingness and economic capacity to pay user charges for healthcare provided in government facilities. Except in Ramanthapuram district, a majority of the respondents were willing to pay irrespective of their socio-demographic background. But, the respondents expected quality, accessibility, and availability of doctors and the health staff. Further, 96 percent of them also felt that poor should be exempted from paying user charges. In Rajasthan, a Medical Relief Society was formed in 1995 in all government hospitals with more than 100 beds. The sources of funds for this society were from seed money by the State Government. The societies were given powers to transfer operational control of diagnostic machines and authorised to levy user charges and retain income from auction of other support services. They were authorised to accept grants and donations and loans. User charges were collected in the order of Rs.2 for out-patients, Rs.5 for in-patients, and Rs.10 for in-patients referred by private practitioners, Rs.2 for visitors and Rs.100 - Rs.600 for bed charges for Private Cabins/Cubical/Cottage Wards. Charges were exempted for families living below the poverty line, widows, freedom fighters, destitute, citizens over 70 years and retired government servants. The average cost recovery was 10 to15 percent of the hospital budget in Rajasthan. Funds were used for the maintenance of buildings, repairs of equipment, purchase of new equipment, improving sanitation and cleanliness and for free medicines for below poverty level families. There was improvement in the quality and utilisation of services. 73 percent of the users had positive perception, 22 percent of the users were indifferent and 74 percent of the doctors expressed increase in hospitalisation. It indicates that wherever user fees were used for improving the quality of the care, there was positive impact on the utilisation of the care.

Conclusions

No country in the world has completely free market in health care because of fundamental market failures in this area. Also, due to market failure in health insurance, the role of pharmaceuticals and social welfare loss, healthcare needs government intervention in its financing and provision. The experience shows that inter-sectoral approach played a significant role in the health transition of Western countries as it happened before the medical revolution. The experience from developing countries, especially Sri Lanka and China, shows that health outcomes are better when health policy is viewed as an integration of health and non-health sectors (holistic approach), rather than health sector alone. India followed basic needs approach in the development of infrastructure for health services. In India, health policy is not integrated to overall development of the country, thus resulting in poorer health outcomes. Inter-sectoral approach to health is important for India because it is characterised with high malnutrition which can be reduced with better food supply, high incidence of communicable diseases which can be avoided with better water and sanitation facilities and high infant mortality which can be reduced with overall socio-economic development. The major health related problems in India are high malnutrition, poverty, illiteracy and poor water quality and poor sanitation. The health status problems in India are high infant and maternal mortality which are the result of a wide range of disease morbidity. India has the double burden of both communicable and chronic diseases. The population in older age is increasing, leading to high demand on public health services. The country spends nearly 6 percent of GDP on health, of which 4.7 is from private sources and only 1.3 from public sources amounting to only 20 percent of health expenditure and hence, has shown poor health outcomes and inequity. Countries with a larger share of public health expenditure have shown better outcomes and equity than India (World Bank 1995). It notes that out of this public expenditure in India, 65 percent was spent on medical sector – an inefficient way of spending resulting in poor health outcomes. To achieve better outcomes and equity, the government must intervene in subsidising prevention and treatment of communicable diseases and subsidising rural health and not to subsidise medical (mostly hospital) sector. Utilisation of health services from NSS 52nd round reveal that for in-patients, among the lowest 20 percent fractile group (based on monthly per capita expenditure), about 60 percent used public sector facilities and the corresponding percentage was about 35 for the top 20 percent fractile group. It also shows that 20 percent of the people used government sources and 80 percent used private sources for the out-patient care. Similar findings were observed by NFHS-2 survey also. The reason for this may be that the existing public health infrastructure is far from satisfactory and is of poor quality as is well documented in *Draft National Health Policy 2001*. This has been emphasised by many utilisation studies. With increase in the cost of health services due to various reasons, the poor are going to private sector by selling their meagre assets, or borrowing money from moneylenders or sometimes unable to take treatment due to financial burden, which is dangerous because of externalities. There is evidence (Sen *et al* 2002) for the worsening of class-based inequalities in terms of access to health services for both men and women and more so, for women and also between scheduled castes and scheduled tribes and non-scheduled castes and non-scheduled tribes. Given the general economic problems and inequities in terms of healthcare access between poor and non-poor, rural and urban, men and women, the Government of India initiated economic reforms in 1991. Reforms were introduced in health sector also in mid-1990s. Consequently, the share of social sector in the overall outlay of the budget of the country has reduced including health, resulting in fall in operational expenditure of health sector leading to inefficient public services. Simultaneously, private sector is spearheading its expansion with high service costs. There are no regulations on the quality of health services in the private sector. In such a scenario, the main question is whether the government should shed away its responsibility in terms of finance as well as provision of health services. The World Bank has advised the governments to follow two measures in health care financing – introduction of user fees and provision of insurance. Also, user fees are recommended when health expenditure is high or rising quickly to moderate demand and containing costs. The main assumption behind user fees to be successful is that majority of the users are part of the publicly funded system. In healthcare in

India, this is far from the case. The experience of African countries reveals that the cost recovery is not high and the administrative cost of collecting revenue is huge. The exemptions of fees for poor people are difficult to maintain, as there are free-riders. The studies show that there is an increase in infant mortality rates of African countries after the reforms. Also, the maternal mortality and the incidence of communicable diseases and TB are on the rise when a user fee is implemented. User fees lead to further inequity in terms of access to care and result in untreated morbidity. Thus, the user fee did not achieve the objectives for which it was being introduced. In India, given the political economy and inequity in terms of access and urban bias in the provision of health services, user fees show mixed results. The review of a few studies that are available has shown that cost recovery was low in different states. When it was so low one had to decide whether it was worthwhile to collect the fees because the time and energy spent by the personnel in collecting could be saved for some other fruitful work (opportunity cost of time). The introduction of user fees was successful in Rajasthan where it was retained in the institution and was used to improve the quality of services in terms of providing drugs, maintaining and repairing the equipment. Not many studies have focused on the change of utilisation of services due to user charges and whether the decline is due to unnecessary need or unable to pay has to be addressed in future studies. India should also think of containing costs through supply side measures such as fixed budgets, which was successful in Canada, and establish tight control over the acquisition of advanced technologies as done in the US where the hospital has to demonstrate that demand exists, before getting the body scanners. The State should play an active role in strictly implementing regulatory mechanisms for private sector to control the cost of health care and ensure the quality of care rather than evading its Constitutional obligations.

Notes

1 Although private enterprises may have greater incentive to operate more efficiently than their public counterparts, the private systems for healthcare generate monopolies (even at the level of individual provider), which may prevent economies of scale and impose high information and transaction costs on the consumers, the insurers, and even care providers. Ultimately, in private and market-based system, these costs can yield less value or output on a market wide basis than in public based systems. In addition, the free market system may generate more care for cost, but not more health, partly because technical medical advances in particular specialties do not necessarily prolong overall health and quality of life.

2. Sen (1977) defines equity as equal access to equal need.

3. The reason for this can be explained as a large percentage of the outlay of health sector is accounted for by salaries and non-salary components such as medicines, equipment and fuel which are inadequately funded (Duggal 1995). The health indicators are better if the non-salary component in the total health expenditure accounts for 50 percent or more as in China, Korea and Sri Lanka (Griffin 1992).Whenever there is a mixed public/ private system, the private sector provides services which derive more benefits and quick profits such as curative care, surgeries, etc., leaving the unprofitable activities such as immunisation, public health activities to the public sector, thus labeling the latter as more inefficient. But one should not compare the services of private sector with that of public sector, because in the latter, the goals are not clear like that of former. It may not be important for a government department to make profit, provided it performs functions that are essential for the community or for another department. In the case of health care, support is needed by the government because health is essential for overall development.

4. a) There should be numerous producers; b) consumers are fully informed and knowledgeable about the product; c) prevailing distribution of income is fair; d) consumer is sovereign; and e) no externalities.

5. a) Risk and uncertainty of (i) occurrence of illness, (ii) relationship between health improvement after treatment, and (iii) financial costs for treatment. b) Health is a merit want, c) Existence of externalities. d) Licensure and asymmetry of information. e) Certain health activities have public good characteristics [the social benefits are greater than the individual's (private) benefits].

6. Social welfare loss – The insured people need not pay for medical care at the time of treatment, hence, the quantity of healthcare demanded will be more, thus leading to social welfare loss.
7. Adverse selection, moral hazards of provider and consumer and economies of scale are the reasons for market failure in health insurance.
8. Accompanied with increase in industrialisation, urbanisation and rural to urban migration, there is a shift from joint family set up to nuclear family set up, making the aged population more vulnerable in the absence of social security system.
9. (a) The passage from a predominance of common infections, malnutrition, and reproductive events as leading causes of death to preponderance of non-communicable diseases, injuries, and new infections. (b) A shift in importance from child to adult mortality, especially among the elderly. (c) A relative predominance of morbidity over mortality in defining the overall health picture of the population. (d) A change in the social meaning of disease, which ceases to be an acute event that is resolved when the patient either is cured or dies, and instead becomes a chronic and often stigmatized condition.
10. This has brought the importance as well as crisis of public health in India.
11. Most of the out-of-pocket expenses are borne by households engaged in low-income informal economic activities.
12. In USA, it encourages providers to increase the number of individual procedures billed for, with significant cost increases resulting from more quantity and intensity of care (Gabel and Redisch 1979).
13. Providers are paid a fixed amount per person covered for a defined set of services over a defined period of time.
14. User charge is the money paid directly by the patient to the health care provider at the time of delivery of services such as fees for service, price for drugs and immunisation, or for injections, diagnostic facility. It is different like other forms of health care financing such as pre-payment schemes and insurance.
15. Price signals from user charges, it is argued, can help restore efficiency in the referral system.
16. External assistance in India is channeled through centrally sponsored programmes for communicable diseases such as AIDS, malaria, tuberculosis and blindness. The funding is in the form of assistance for equipment, drugs, supplies and training. External funding changes the total approach of the programme. For example, the revised National Tuberculosis Programme supported by the World Bank is

called DOTS (Directly Observed Treatment Short course) which is totally away from the earlier National TB programmes, which has been integrated into the general health services as a 'non-vertical' programme. AIDS is also not a leading cause of mortality in India, but lot of funds is pumped into this programme. At present, 65.63 percent of the external funding is spent for family welfare in the form of construction of infrastructure buildings, mainly sub-centres, whereas the real problems, as observed by many studies (Sandhya 1993) and even acknowledged by Draft National Population Policy 2001, at the sub-centre level are unsuitable timings of health workers, lack of drugs, non-availability of health workers for all days.

References

Akin, J., N. Birdsall, and D. de Ferranti. (1987). *Financing Health Services in Developing Countries: An Agenda for Reform.* Washington D C: World Bank.

Arriaga, E.E. and K. Davis. (1969). "The Pattern of Mortality Change in Latin America", *Demography*, 6(3): 223-42.

Arrow, K. J. (1963). "Uncertainty and the Welfare Economics of Medical Care", *American Economic Review*, 53 (5): 941-67.

Asian Development Bank.(1999). *Health Sector Reform in Asia and the Pacific – Options for Developing Countries.* Manila: Asian Development Bank.

Bennet, Sara., Ellias Ngalande-Banda and Ole Teglgaard.(1994). *Public and Private Roles in Health: A Review and Analysis of Experience in sub-Saharan Africa.* Current Concerns SHS Working Paper number 6, Geneva: WHO.

Berman, P. (1996). "Health Care Expenditure in India", in Monica Dasgupta, *et al* (eds.), *Health, Poverty and Development in India.* New Delhi: Oxford University Press.

Berman, P., and R. Rannan-Eliya. (1993). *Factors Affecting the Development of Private Health Care Provision in Developing Countries.* Health Financing and Sustainability Project. Major Applied Research Paper No. 2. Bethesda, MD: Abt Associates.

Bhat, R. (2000). "Issues in Health: Public-Private Partnerships", *Economic and Political Weekly*, XXXV (52 and 53): 4706-16.

Bhat, R. (1996). "Regulation of the Private Health Sector in India", *International Journal of Health Planning and Management*, 11:253-274.

Bhat, R. (1997). "Regulation of the Private Health Sector in India." In W. Newbrander (ed.), *Private Health Sector Growth in Asia: Issues and Implications.* Chester, U.K: Wiley & Sons, Ltd.

Bhore Committee. (1946). *Report of the Health Survey and Development Committee.* (Vol. 1 to 3). New Delhi: Government of India.

Bir, T. (2000). "User charge: A Policy Option for Health Service Development in Developing Countries like India", *Health and Population – Perspectives and Issues,* 23 (2): 71- 84.

Briscoe, J. and D. De Ferranti. (1988). *Water for Rural Communities: Helping People Help Themselves.* Washington, D.C: World Bank.

Brook, R.H. *et al.* (1983). "Does Free Care Improve Adult Health? Result from Randomised Controlled Trial", *The New England Journal of Medicine,* 309 (23): 1426-1434.

Bulatao, Rodolfo. A. and Stephens, Patience. (1990). "Estimates and Projections of Mortality by Cause: A Global Overview, 1970-2015", in D T Jamison, W H Mosley, (eds.), *Evolving Health Priorities in Developing Countries,* Washington, DC: World Bank, Population, Health, and Nutrition Division.

Callahan, Daniel. (1990). *What Kind of Life? The Limits of Medical Progress.* New York: Simon and Schuster.

Chamber, R. (1989). "Health, Agriculture and Rural Poverty: Why Seasons Matter", *Journal of Developmental Studies,* 18.

Chatterjee, Meera. (1988). *Access to Health.* New Delhi: Manohar Publications.

Chatterjee, Meera. (1993). *Health for Too Many: India's Experiments with Truth.* In Rohde, J., Meera Chatterjee and David C Morley (eds.) *Reaching Health for All.* New Delhi: Oxford University Press.

Chernichovsky, Dov.(1995). "Health System Reforms in Industrialised Democracies: An Emerging Paradigm", *The Milbank Quarterly,* 73(3): 339-73.

Coleman, Nii Ayite. (1997). *The Uneven Implementation of User Fees Policy in Ghana.* (Research Paper) Takemi Program in International Health, Boston: Harvard School of Public Health.

Collins, H. David, Jonathan D. Quick, Stephen N. Musau, and Daniel L. Kraushaar. (1996). *Health Financing Reform in Kenya: The Fall and Rise of Cost Sharing, 1989-94).* Stubbs Monograph Series No. 1. Boston: Management Sciences for Health and U.S. Agency for International Development.

Corbett, J. (1989). "Poverty and Sickness, High Cost of Ill Health", *IDS Bulletin,* 20 (2): 58-62.

Creese, A. (1991). "User Charges for Health Care: A Review of Recent Experiment", *Health Policy and Planning,* 6(4): 309-19.

Creese, A. (1997). "User Fees", *British Medical Journal,* 315:202-203 (July 26).

Creese, A. and J. Kutzin (1995). 'Lessons from Cost Recovery in Health', SHS/NHP, Forum on Health Sector Reform. (Discussion Paper No 2) Geneva: World Health Organisation.

Culyer, A.J., A. Mayhard, and A. Williams. (1981). "Alternative Systems of Health Care Promotion: An Essay on Motes and Beams", in M. Olsen (ed.). *A New Application to the Economics of Health Care* Washington D.C: American Enterprise Institute.

Data News Features. (2002). *Andhra Pradesh 50 Years*. Hyderabad : Data News Features.

De Ferranti, D. (1984). "Strategies for Paying for Health Services in Developing Countries", *World Health Statistics Quarterly*, 37 (4): 428-42.

Deolalikar, Anil B. and Prem. Vashishtha. (1992). *The Utilisation of Government and Private Health Services in India.* Washington D.C.: The Futures Group Project, AIHA.

Directorate General of Health Services (DGHS). (1991). *Health Information India.* New Delhi: Ministry of Health and Family Welfare.

Duggal, Ravi. (2001). "Our National Health Policy – A Critique". *Health Action*, 14(11): 20-24.

Duggal, Ravi. and S. Amin (1989). *Cost of Health Care: A Household Survey in an Indian District.* Bombay: The Foundation for Research in Community Health.

Duggal, Ravi. and S. Nandraj. (1991). "Regulating the Private Health Sector", *Medico Friend Circle Bulletin*,173-174, July/August.

Ellis, P. Randall, Alam Moneer, and Indrani Gupta. (2000). "Health Insurance in India: Prognosis and Prospectus". *Economic and Political Weekly*, XXXV (4): 207-217.

Evans, R. G. (1990). "Tension, Compression and Shear: Directions, Stresses, and Outcomes of Health Care Cost Control," *Journal of Health Policy and Law*, 15 (1): 101-29.

Fabricant, J. Stephen, Clifford, W Kamara and Anne Mills. (1999). "Why the Poor Pay More: Household Curative Expenditures in Rural Sierra Leone," *International Journal of Health Planning Management.* 14(4): 339-40.

Fahs, M.S. (1992). "Physician Response to the United Mine Workers' Cost-sharing Programme: The Other Side of the Coin", *Health Services Research*, 27 (1):25-45.

Gertler, P. J. (1996). "The lessons of User fee experience in Africa", *Health Policy and Planning*, 12(4):273-85.

Gertler, P. J. and J. S. Hammer. (1997), *Strategies for Pricing Publicly Provided Health Services.* Policy Research Working Papers. Washington DC: World Bank.

Gertler, P. J. and J. van der Gaag. (1990). *The Willingness to Pay for Medical Care: Evidence from Two Developing Countries*, Baltimore, Maryland: John Hopkins University Press.

Gertler, P. J. and J. W. Molyneaux. (1994). "How Economic Development and Family Planning Programmes Combined to Reduce Indonesian Fertility", *Demography*, 31(1): 33-63.

Ghana Statistical Services. (1995). *The Pattern of Poverty in Ghana: 1988-1992*, Accra: Ghana Statistical Service.

Gilson, L. (1988). "Government Health Care Charges: Is Equity Being Abandoned?" Evaluation and Planning Centre Discussion Paper No. 15. London.: School of Hygiene and Tropical Medicine. University of London.

Gilson, L. (1997). "Review Paper: The Lessons of User Fee Experience in Africa", *Health Policy and Planning*, 12 (4): 273-85.

Gopalan, C. (1994). "Challenges to Public Health Systems", *Economic and Political Weekly*, 29 (20): 1204-09.

Government of India. (1975). *Report of the Committee on Drugs and Pharmaceuticals* (Hathi Committee), New Delhi: Government of India.

Government of India. (2001). *Economic Survey, 2000-01 Economic Division*. New Delhi: Ministry of Finance, Government of India.

Gray, R. H. (1974). "The Decline of Mortality in Ceylon and the Demographic Effects of Malaria Control", *Population Studies*, 28 (2): 205-29.

Griffin, C. Charles. (1989). "Strengthening Health Services in Developing Countries through the Private Sector", Discussion Paper No.4, Washington, D. C: International Finance Corporation.

Griffin, C. Charles. (1992). *Health Care in Asia: A Comparative Study of Cost and Financing*, World Bank Regional and Sector Studies. Washington D C: The World Bank.

Griffiths, G. T. (1926). *Population Problems of the Age of Malthus*. Cambridge: Cambridge University Press.

Gumber, Anil. (1997). "Burden of Diseases and Cost of Ill Health in Indian Setting: Priorities for Health Interventions during the Ninth Plan", *Margin*, 29 (2): 133-72.

Gupta, Amit Sen. (1996). "Economic Reforms, Health and Pharmaceuticals: Conferring Legitimacy to the Market", *Economic and Political Weekly*, XXXI (48): 3135-45.

Gupta, S. P. (1995). "Economic Reforms and Its Impact on Poor", *Economic and Political Weekly*, 30(22): 1295-1320.

Hsiao, W. C. (1994). *Co-operative Health Care for the Rural Chinese Population*, Boston: Harvard School of Public Health.

Hsiao, W. C. (1990). "Lessons for Developing Countries from the Experiences of Affluent Countries about a Comprehensive Health Financing Strategy", A Paper Presented at the International Seminar on Comprehensive Financing Strategy in Selected Asian Nations, Bali, Indonesia.

Hsiao, W. C. (1995). "Abnormal Economics in the Health Sector", In P. Berman (ed.), *Health System Reform in Developing Countries: Making Health Development Sustainable.* Cambridge, MA: Harvard University Press.

Hutton, Guy. (2002). "Is the Jury Still Out on the Impact of User Fees in Africa? A Review of the Evidence from Selected Countries on User Fees and Determinants of Health Service Utilisation", *East African Medical Journal* [Online], 81(4). Pp. S45-S60.

International Child Development Centre. (1993). "Central and Eastern Europe in Transition: Public Policy and Social Conditions", Regional *Monitoring Report No 1.* Florence:UNICEF.

International Institute of Population Sciences. (2000). *National Family and Health Survey (NFHS) 1998-99.* Mumbai: International Institute of Population Sciences and ORG Macro.

Iyer, A., Gita Sen. (2000). "Health Sector Changes and Health Equity in the 1990s in India", In S. Raghuram (ed.) *Health and Equity, Technical Report Series* 1.8. Bangalore: HIVOS.

Jamison, D.T. and W.H. Mosley. (1991). "Disease Control Priorities in Developing Countries: Health Policy Responses to Epidemiological Change," *American Journal of Public Health,* 81(1): 15-22.

Jimenez, Emmanuel. (1987). *Pricing Policy in the Social Sectors: Cost Recovery for Education and Health in Developing Countries.* Washington D C: The World Bank.

Krishnan, P. (1975). "Mortality Decline in India 1951-61", *Social Science and Medicine,* 90: 475-479.

Krishnan, T. N. (1995). "Access to Health and Burden of Treatment in India: An Inter-State Comparison", A Paper Presented at the International Workshop on Health Insurance in India, Bangalore, September, 20-22.

Kumar, A. K. Shiva. V.N. Mukherjee. (1993). "Health as Development – Implications for Research, Policy and Action", Economic *and Political Weekly,* 28(16): 769-74.

Kutzin, J. (1995). 'Lessons from Cost-Recovery in Health', *Discussion Paper, WHO/SHS/ NHP/95.5* Geneva: World Health Organisation.

Lal, Shiva. *et al.* (1998). "Economic Impact of Malaria Control in India," *Abstract of Scientific Papers.* 42nd All India Annual Conference of Indian Public Health Association. Chennai : 26-28 June.

Lipton, M. (1988). "Attacking Under-nutrition and Poverty: Some Issues of Adaptability and Sustainability", Pew/Cornell Lecture Series on Food and Nutrition Policy, Cornell University.

Litvack, J. and C. Bodart. (1993). "User Fees and Improved Quality of Health Care Equals Improved Access: Results of a Field Experiment in Cameroon", *Social Science and Medicine,* 37(3):369-83.

Mahal, A., S. Abdo, David Yazbeck, H. Peters. and G. V. N. Ramana. (2001). *The Poor and Health Service Use in India.* Electronic document: www.Worldbank.org/poverty/health/library/incidence2.htm. (Accessed on September 12, 2005)

Marga Institute. (1984). *Inter-Sectoral Action for Health,* Colombo.

Maxwell, R. (1975). *Health Care: The Growth Dilemma.* London: Mc Kinsey.

McGuire, James W. (2001). "Social Policy and Mortality Decline in East Asia and Latin America", *World Development,* 29 (10): 1673- 97.

McKeown, T., and R.G. Record. (1962). "Reasons for the Decline of Mortality in England and Wales during the 19th Century", *Population Studies* 16 (2): 94-122.

McPake, A., K. Hansom and A. Mills. (1992). *Experience to Date of Implementing the Bomako Initiative: A Review and Five Country Case Studies.* London: London School of Hygiene and Tropical Medicine.

Mills, A. (1991). "Exempting the Poor: The Experience of Thailand", *Social Science Medical Journal,* 33(11):1241-52.

Mills, A., S. Bennett and S. Russell. (2001). *The Challenge of Health Sector Reform: What Must Governments Do?* Basingstoke: Palgrave.

Ministry of Health and Family Welfare. (2001). *Draft National Health Policy,* New Delhi: Ministry of Health and Family Welfare, Government of India.

Misra, Rajiv., Rachel Chatterjee, Sujatha Rao. (2003). *India's Health Report,* New Delhi: Oxford University Press.

Mulou, N., J Thomason and K Edwards. (1992). 'The Rise of Private Practice: A Growing Disquiet with Public Services?' *Papua New Guinea Medical Journal,* 35(3): 7-14.

Muraleedharan, V. R. (2000). *Private-Public Partnership in Health Care Sector in India: A Review of Policy Options and Challenges.* Background Paper for the World Bank Study on the Indian Health System. Chennai: Indian Institute of Technology.

Murray, Christopher., J. L. Lopez, Alan. D. and Jamison, T. Dean. (1994). *The Global Burden of Diseases in 1990: Summary Results, Sensitivity Analysis and Future Diseases.* Geneva: World Health Organisation.

Musgrove, P. (1986). "Measurement of Equity in Health", *World Health Statistics Quarterly*, 39 (4): 325-35.

Mwabu, Germano. (1990). "Financing Health Services in Africa. An Assessment of Alternative Approaches", *Population, Health, and Nutrition. Working Paper 457*, Washington D C: World Bank.

Nandraj, S. (2000). 'The Private Health Sector: Concerns, Challenges and Options,' (Mimeo), Mumbai: Centre for Enquiry into Health and Allied Themes.

Nandraj, S. (1994). "Beyond the Law and the Lord: Quality of Private Health Care", *Economic and Political Weekly*, XXIX (27): 1680-85.

Narayana, K.V. (2003). "Size and Nature of Health Care System", in C. H. Hanumantha Rao and Mahendra Dev, S. (eds.). *Andhra Pradesh: Development, Economic Reforms and Challenges Ahead*. Hyderabad: Centre for Economic and Social Change.

National Council of Applied Economic Research. (1991). *Household Survey of Medical Care*. New Delhi: NCAER.

National Council of Applied Economic Research. (1992). *Rural Household Health Care Needs and Availability*, New Delhi: NCAER.

National Sample Survey Organisation (NSSO). (1992). NSS 42nd Round (July 1986 to June 1987), Morbidity and Utilisation of Medical Services. *Sarveskhana*, 15 (4): 50- 75.

National Sample Survey Organisation (NSSO). (1998). *NSS 52nd Round (1995-96), Morbidity and Treatment of Ailments*. NewDelhi: Department of Statistics, Government of India.

Navarro, Vicente. (1993). *Free for All? Lessons from the RAND Health Insurance Experiment*. Cambridge: M A: Harvard University Press.

Navarro, Vicente. (1999). "Health and Equity in the World in the Era of "Globalisation", *International Journal of Health Services*, 29(2): 215-226.

Nolan, B. (1993). "Economic Incentives, Health Status, and Health Services Utilisation", *Journal of Health Economics*. 12: 151-69.

Nolan, B. and Vincent Turbat. (1995). *Cost Recovery in Public Health Services in Sub-Saharan Africa,* Washington D C: The World Bank.

Nyonator, Frank. and Kutzin, Joseph. (1999). Health for Some? The Effects of User Fees in the Volta Region of Ghana. *Health Policy and Planning*,14 (4): 329-341.

Ogawa, Naohiro., *et al*. (1988). *Long-Term Prospects Based upon the Population Economic Medical Model: Phase II*, Tokyo: Nihon University, Population Research Institute.

Organisation for Economic Co-operation and Development (OECD). (1994). *The Reform of Health Care Systems: A Review of Seventeen OECD Countries*. (Health Policy Studies No 5.) Paris: OECD.

Parker, D. and Knippenberg, R. (1991). *Community Cost -Sharing and Participation: A Review of the Issues*, Bomako Initiative Technical Report Series Number 9, New York: UNICEF.

Peabody, J.W. Lawson, J. and Bickel, S. (1996). "The Health Care System in Australia: Is Down Under Right Side Up?" *Journal of American Medical Association*. 276 (24): 1944-50.

Planning Commission. (1998). *Approach Paper to the Ninth Five-Year Plan, 1997-98*. New Delhi: Planning Commission.

Prakash, Padma. (1998). "Lacunae in Medicare", *The Hindu*, Chennai, January 10.

Pryer, Jane. (1989). "When breadwinners Fall Ill: Preliminary findings from a Case Study in Bangladesh", *IDS Bulletin*, 20 (2): 49-57.

Qadeer, Imrana. (2002). "Draft National Health Policy 2001-I: Debt Payment and Devaluing Elements of Public Health", *Economic and Political Weekly*, XXXVII (1): 12-15.

Razzell, P. E. (1974). "An Interpretation of the Modern Rise of Population in Europe - A Critique", *Population Studies*, 28 (1): 5-17.

Reddy, C. and Vandomoortele, J. (1996). "User Financing of Basic Social Services: A Review of Theoretical Arguments and Empirical Evidence", *Staff Working Paper*, New York: UNICEF.

Reddy, K.N. and Selvaraju, V. (1994). *Health Care Expenditure by Government in India: 1974-75 to 1990-91*. New Delhi: Seven Hills Publications.

Rhode, JE and Vishwanathan, H. (1996). *The Rural Private Practitioner*. New Delhi: Oxford University Press.

Rosenthal, Gerald. and William Newbrander. (1997). "Public Policy and Private sector Provision of Health Services", in Newbrander, W. (ed.) *Public Health Sector Growth in Asia: Issues and Implications*. New York: John Wiley and Sons Limited.

Sandhya, S. (1993). "Health Seeking Behaviour and its Financial Implications," in Session Financing Health Care Services: Who is Responsible? XVI Conference of Indian Association for the Study of Population, Bhubaneswar.

Satia, J. K. and Deodhar, N. S. (1993). "Hospital Costs and Financing in Maharashtra", in Peter Berman and M. E. Khan (eds.) *Paying for India's Health Care*. New Delhi: Sage Publications.

Sauerborn, R., A. Nougtara and E. Latimer. (1994). "The Elasticity of Demand for Health Care in Burkina Faso: Differences across Age and Income Groups", *Health Policy and Planning*, 9(2): 185-192.

Sebastian, Ouseparmpil. (2001). "Providing Quality Health Care", *Health Action* 14(11): 25- 26.

Segall, M. Tipping, G. Lucas, H. *et al*. (2000). "Health Care Seeking by the Poor in Transitional Economies: The Case of Vietnam", *Research Report No. 43*. Sussex: Institute of Development Studies.

Sen, A. (1977). "Rational fools: A Critique of the Behaviour Foundations of Economic Theory", *Philosophy and Public Affairs*. 6(4): 317-44.

Sen, Gita, Aditi Iyer and Asha George. (2002). "Structural Reforms and Health Equity – A Comparison of NSS Surveys, 1986-87 and 1995-96", *Economic and Political Weekly*, XXXVI (14): 1342-52.

Sgontz, Larry. G.(1972). "The Economics of Financing Medical Care: A Review of Literature", *Inquiry* 9(4): 3- 19.

Sharma, B.B.L. (2001). *Health Financing in India: Some Issues*. New Delhi: National Institute of Health and Family Welfare.

Shaw, R. Paul., and Charles. C. Griffin. (1995). *Financing Health Care in Sub-Saharan Africa through User Fees and Insurance,* Washington D C: World Bank.

Sorkin, A. (1976). *Health Economics of Developing Countries.* Lexington, KT: LexingtonBooks.

Stewart, Art. (1988). "Cost-containment and privatisation: an international analysis", in Daniel Drache and Sullivan Terry (eds.), *Market Limits in Health Reform – Public Success, Private Failure,* London: Routledge.

Swaminathan, M. S. (2001). *Food Insecurity Atlas of Rural India,* Chennai: M S Swaminathan Research Foundation.

Tipping, G. (2000). *The Social Impact of User Fees for Health Care on Poor Households. Commissioned Report to the Ministry of Health,* Hanoi: Vietnam.

Tulsidhar, V. B. (1993). "Expenditure Compression and Health Sector Outlays", *Economic and Political Weekly,* 28 (45): 2473-2477.

United Nations. (1973). *Determinants and Consequences of Population Trends,* New York: United Nations.

Uplekar, M. (1989). *Implications of Prescribing Patterns of Private Doctors in the Treatment of Pulmonary Tuberculosis in Bombay, India,* Research Paper No. 40, Takemi Program in International Health. Cambridge: Harvard School of Public Health.

Van Doorslaer, E. Wagstaff, A. Rutten, F. (1993). *Equity in the Finance and Delivery of Health Care: An International Perspective,* Oxford: Oxford University Press.

Velasquez, G. Madrid, Y. Quick, J. (1998). *Health Reform and Drug Financing: Selected Topics in Health Economics and Drugs* DAP Series No 6. [WHO/DAP/98.3] Action Programme on Essential Drugs. Geneva: World Health Organisation.

Verbrugge Lois, M. (1989). "Recent, Present, and Future Health of American Adults", *Annual Review of Public Health,* Vol. 10. Palo Alto: California Annual Reviews.

Verbrugge Lois, M. (1984). "Longer Life but Worsening Health: Trends in Health and Mortality of Middle-aged and Older Persons," *Milbank Memorial Fund Quarterly,* 62 (3): 475-519.

Visaria, Pravin. (1990). 'Poverty, Development and Change in India: Some Reflections,' Working Paper No: 29, Ahmedabad: Gujarat Institute of Development Research.

Visaria, Pravin. and anil Gumber. (1994). *Utilisation of and Expenditure on Health Care in India, 1986-87.* Ahmedabad Gujarat Institute of Development Research.

Vishwanathan, H. and Rhode, J. E. (1990). *Diarrhoea in Rural India: A Nationwide Study of Mothers and Practitioners,* New Delhi: Vision Books.

Vogel, R. J. (1991). "Cost Recovery in the Health Care Sector in Sub-Saharan Africa", *International Journal of Health Planning and Management,* 6: 167-91.

Waddington, C. and K. Enyimayew. (1990). "A Price to Pay, Part 2: the Impact of User Charges in the Volta Region of Ghana", *International Journal of Health Planning and Management,* 5: 287-312.

Weinstein, N. D. (1989). "Optimistic Biases about Personal Risks", *Science,* 246:1232-3.

Whitehead, M., G.Dahlgren, and T. Evans, (2001). "Equity and Health Sector Reform: Can Low Income Countries Escape the Medical and Poverty Trap?" *Lancet,* 358 (9284): 833-6.

Woolhandlet, S. and D. Himmelstein. (1991). "The Deteriorating Administrative Efficiency of the United States Health Care System", *New England Journal of Medicine,* 324 (18):1253-8.

World Bank. (1984). *China: The Health Sector,* The World Bank Country Study, Washington D C: The World Bank.

World Bank. (1993). *World Development Report: Investing in Health,* New York: Oxford University Press.

World Bank. (1995). *India: Policies and Finance Strategies for Strengthening Primary Health Care Services.* Report No. 13042-IN, Population and Human Resource Division, South Asia Country Department II, Washington D C: World Bank.

World Bank. (1996). *China: Issues and Options in Health Financing,* Washington, DC: World Bank.

World Bank. (1997). *India: New Directions in Health Sector Development at the State Level: An Operational Perspective*, Population and Human Resource Division, South Asia Country Department II, February.

World Bank. (2001). *India: Raising the Sights – Better Health Systems for India's Poor*, Washington, DC; World Bank.

World Bank. 1975. *Health Sector Policy Paper.* Washington D C: World Bank.

World Health Organisation. (1995). *Western Pacific Region Data Bank on Socio-Economic and Health Indicators.* Geneva: World Health Organisation.

World Health Organisation. (1999). *World Health Report.* Geneva: World Health Organisation.

Yesudian, C.A.K. (1990). *Utilisation Patterns of Health Services and its Implications for Urban Health Polic,* Cambridge: Takemi Program in International Health, Harvard School of Public Health.

Yesudian, C.A.K. (1994). "The Nature of Private Sector Health Services in Bombay", *Health Policy and Planning*, 9 (1).

Yu H, Cao. S. and H. Lucas. (1997). "Equity in the Utilisation of Medical Services: A Survey in Poor Rural China", *IDS Bulletin*, 28: 16-23.

Trends and Determinants of Early Neonatal Mortality in India

Binod Bihari Jena & Prakash Chandra Sahoo

Introduction

High child mortality in many parts of the world has identified the need for reduction of under-five and infant mortality rate by two-thirds between 1990 and 2015 as two important targets of the Millennium Development Goal (MDG, 2000). Therefore, the two indicators of child mortality become common while measuring progress in child wellbeing in any country. In 2009, 8.1 million children across the world died before their fifth birthday. Most of these children lived in developing countries and died from a disease or a combination of diseases that could easily have been prevented or treated (UNICEF 2010). However, the rate of decline in under-five mortality is still grossly insufficient to reach the MDG goal by 2015, particularly in Sub-Saharan Africa and South Asia. It is alarming that among the 64 countries with high mortality rates only 9 are on track to meet MDG-4 (UNICEF 2010). Therefore, the reduction in infant and under-five mortality remains a primary concern for most developing countries. While strategies such as immunization, oral rehydration and control of acute respiratory infections have contributed to the decline of deaths among children above one month of age, but the reduction in neonatal deaths (deaths under four weeks of age) has not been significant.Consequently, there has been shifting of mortality to neonatal period which is a serious concern in developing countries and the MDG-4 requires major reductions in neonatal mortality rate (Lawn, 2005).

Globally for the year 2000 an estimated 4 million babies died during the neonatal period and three-quarter of these deaths occurred in the early neonatal period i.e., during first week of life (WHO 2005, cited in Lawn 2005). Almost all (99 percent) those neonatal deaths come from low and middle-income countries and the remaining from rich countries. The highest numbers of neonatal deaths occurred in South-Central Asian countries and highest rates are generally in sub-Saharan African countries (Lawn 2005). In 2000, 27 percent of the global neonatal deaths were from India (WHO 2005) and during the same year the world average early neonatal mortality rate was 23 per thousand of live births and its share in neonatal mortality was 75 percent. The early neonatal mortality rate in least developed regions (31) was nearly 8 times more that of the more developed regions (4) and for less developed regions it was 25 (WHO 2006). Hence, the reduction of early neonatal mortality is a major concern in less and least-developed regions.

In India the infant mortality rate continued to remain high as compared to all developed countries and many of the developing countries. It has declined from 139 in 1972 to 53 in 2008 indicating a reduction of 62 percent. This decline was mainly because of the substantial reduction of deaths during the post-neonatal and late neonatal period. During this period post-neonatal mortality and late neonatal mortality has declined to 74 percent and 78 percent respectively, whereas the early neonatal mortality has been declined only 23 percent. Currently more than two-third (66 percent) of infant deaths comprised of neonates most of who die within the first week of life. The share of early neonatal deaths has been increasing over the years and in the year 2008 it has reached to 77 percent of all neonatal deaths and 51 percent of infant deaths and 39 percent of under-five mortality (SRS 2009). According to 2010 MDG evaluation report it is not possible for India to achieve the Millennium Development Goal-4 for child survival as both under-five and infant mortality rate continued to remain high due to their slow rate of reduction.

The report particularly emphasizes the need for the reduction in early neonatal deaths since it constitutes more than 51 percent of total number of infant deaths in 2008 (WNTA 2010). Therefore, a faster rate of reduction in infant mortality rate can only be possible through a higher rate of reduction in early neonatal mortality rate and hence it is important to focus the crucial first seven days of life in order to reduce the under-five and infant mortality rate to the targeted level that will meet India's Millennium Development Goal-4 for child survival.

Earlier studies show that the reduction of early neonatal deaths remains challenging because it is predominantly caused by biological and genetic factors and it can be little influenced by public health measures (Achyut *et al* 1997). Other studies show that along with biological factors, socio-economic, cultural, environmental, demographic factors and factors related to pregnancy and delivery significantly impact on newborns survival during early neonatal period. Study conducted by Saksena and Srivastav (1980) using data from Dufferin Hospital Lucknow during the year 1976-77 found that among the biological factors the age of mother at birth, parity, period of gestation, birth weight and sex of the child and among the socio-economic factors, religion and occupation of father are significantly associated with perinatal mortality. The younger mothers give birth to a greater proportion of low-birth weight babies and therefore the reduction of infant and neonatal mortality has centered upon the reduction of birth weight (Saugstad 1981).

Among the causes of death in the early neonatal period, the major causes are low birth-weight, birth asphyxia, bacterial infection and congenital malformation (Chavan 1992).The caste and education of mother and her demographic factors, variable related to pregnancy and delivery have significant effect on the survival of infants in the first week of life (Achyut *et al.* 1997). There were two sets of factors - one relating to mother (like demographic, nutrition, genetic, etc.) and the second relating to health seeking behavior and availability of quality care services were found responsible for neonatal mortality (James and Subramanian 2004).

However, recent studies show that providing necessary information on birth preparedness, recognitions of danger sign, educating pregnant women and caretakers about antenatal care, safe delivery practices and home based neonatal care can reduce early neonatal mortality to a large extent. A study in rural Gadchiroli, Maharashtra shows that the primary cause of death were sepsis/pneumonias (52.5 percent), birth asphyxia (20 percent), prematurity (15 percent), hypothermia 2.5 percent and other unknown (10 percent) (Bang 2005). With the intervention on home based neonatal care (HBNC) neonatal mortality decreased from 62 to 25 in the intervention area which has contributed by the reduction of 24 points in early neonatal mortality rate and of 20 points the late neonatal mortality rate (Bang and Reddy 2005). A cluster randomized behavioral intervention study conducted in some villages of Uttar Pradesh shows that newborn care packages and behavioral education which encouraged improving birth preparedness, hygienic delivery, thermal care including skin to skin care, umbilical cord care and breastfeeding resulted reduction in neonatal deaths in the intervention group compared with the control group (Kumar *et al* 2008). The present study attempts to examine how socio-economic and environmental, demographic and biological, and programmatic and newborn care factors affect the survival of newborns during early neonatal period.

Objectives of the Study

I. To examine the levels and trends in early neonatal mortality rate.

II. To study the age patterns of mortality in early neonatal period.

III. To examine the factors affecting early neonatal mortality

Data Sources and Methodology

The data sets used in this study are National Family Health Survey (NFHS) and Sample Registration System (SRS). The Sample Registration System (SRS) in India is the largest demographic survey in the world covering about 1.4 million households and over 7.1 million populations. It has continued to be the main source of information on fertility and mortality indicators both at the state and national level. The system has a unique feature of dual recording, which involves collection of data through two different procedures viz., continuous enumeration and retrospective half-yearly surveys. The Sample Registration System provides direct estimates on early neonatal mortality for India and bigger states (population of 10 million and above) from 1995 onwards but for the period 1972-1994 it is estimated indirectly from perinatal mortality rate (PMR) and still birth rate (SBR).The SRS data are used to show the levels and trends of early neonatal mortality rate (ENMR) in India and its bigger states, while the NFHS data sets are used to examine the age patterns of death during early neonatal period, differential in early neonatal mortality rate among different sub-groups of population and the determinants of early neonatal mortality. The NFHSs are large scale demographic and health surveys in India conducted to provide national and state level estimates on fertility, family planning, infant and child mortality, reproductive, maternal and child health care, nutrition of women and children and socioeconomic conditions. For the study of age patterns of early neonatal deaths all the three rounds of NFHS data sets are used while for the analysis of determinants of early neonatal mortality only NFHS-3 data are used. The analysis is carried out by using SPSS-17 version and all births those have taken place during last five years before the survey are taken in account. In this study the following quantitative methods are used to calculate early neonatal mortality rate and its differentials and determinants.

i. Procedure for Estimation of Early Neonatal Mortality rate (ENMR)

$$\text{ENMR} = \frac{\text{Deaths of infants in 0-6 days after birth}}{\text{live Births}} \times 1000$$

$$\text{ENMR} = \frac{PMR - SBR}{1000 - SBR} \times 1000$$ (if deaths during 7 days are not available)

Where, PMR is Perinatal Mortality Rate and SBR is Still Birth Rate. Before estimating ENMR three points moving average of PNMR and SBR is taken to remove any random fluctuation.

ii. Bivariate Analysis (cross tabulation):

iii. Multivariate Analysis (Binary logistic regression and predicted probability of dying)

Results and Discussion

1. Levels and Rural-Urban Differentials in Early Neonatal Mortality Rate in India and its Bigger States

The latest published estimates of early neonatal mortality rate for the year 2008 in India and its bigger states are shown in Table 6.1. The all India average of early neonatal mortality rate was 27 per thousand of live births. Among the bigger states there were wide variations. Madhya Pradesh had the highest rate of early neonatal mortality (38), followed by Chhattisgarh (36), Odisha (34) and Uttar Pradesh (33). On the other hand, Kerala had the lowest mortality rate (5), followed by Tamil Nadu (15), Delhi (15), Maharashtra (19) and Karnataka (20). If we compare among north and south Indian states, it is evident that the rates were higher in all northern Indian states (Uttar Pradesh, Madhya Pradesh, Bihar, Chhattisgarh and Rajasthan) than all the south Indian states (Kerala, Tamil Nadu, Karnataka, Andhra Pradesh). There also exists large differential in early neonatal mortality rate between rural and urban areas in India as well as in all the states as shown in Table 6.2. The early neonatal mortality rate in rural areas was more than urban areas both in India and all the states except Delhi. In India the rate of early neonatal mortality in rural areas (31) was nearly two times that of urban areas (16) and among states it varies from one and half times to more than three times that of urban areas.

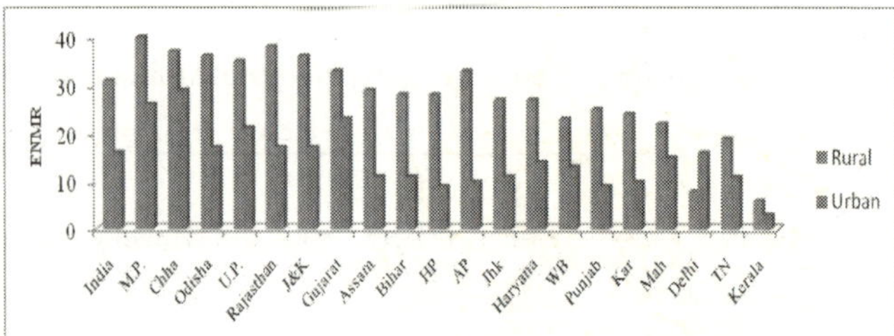

Fig. 6.1: Rural-urban Differentials in Early Neonatal Mortality Rate in India and Bigger States, SRS, 2008

Table 6.1: Levels of Early Neonatal Mortality Rate and Its Share in NMR, IMR and U5MR, India, 2008

India and Bigger States	*ENMR*	*NMR*	*IMR*	*U5MR*	*Share of ENMR NMR (%)*	*Share of ENMR IMR (%)*	*Share of ENMR to USMR (%)*
India	27	35	53	69	77	51	39
Madhya Pradesh	38	48	70	92	79	54	41
Chhattisgarh	36	39	57	71	92	63	51
Odisha	34	47	69	89	72	49	38
Jammu & Kashmir	33	39	49	55	85	67	60
Rajasthan	33	43	63	80	77	52	41
Uttar Pradesh	33	45	67	91	73	49	36
Gujarat	30	37	50	60	81	60	50
Assam	27	34	64	88	79	42	31
Bihar	27	32	56	75	84	48	36
Himachal Pradesh	27	33	44	50	82	61	54
Andhra Pradesh	26	34	52	58	76	50	45
Jharkhand	24	25	46	65	96	52	37
Haryana	24	34	54	65	71	44	37
West Bengal	21	26	35	42	81	60	50
Punjab	20	28	41	49	71	49	41
Karnataka	20	24	45	55	83	44	36
Maharashtra	19	24	33	41	79	58	46
Delhi	15	19	35	40	79	43	38
Tamil Nadu	15	21	31	36	71	48	42
Kerala	5	7	12	14	71	42	36

Source: Sample Registration System, Registrar General of India, 2009,
Note: ENMR: Early Neonatal Mortality Rate, NMR: Neonatal Mortality rate, IMR: Infant Mortality Rate,
U5MR: Under-five Mortality Rate. All the rates are per thousand of live births

The share of early neonatal mortality rate with the different components of child mortality is shown in Table 6.1. The percentage share of early neonatal mortality rate in neonatal mortality rate was 77 percent in the year 2008. Its share in infant mortality rate was 51 percent whereas in under-five mortality rate its share was 39 percent in the year 2008. Among bigger states its share in neonatal mortality varies from the lowest 71 percent each in Kerala, Tamil Nadu, Karnataka and Haryana to highest 96 percent in Jharkhand. Its share in infant mortality rate varies from 42 percent in Kerala and Assam to 67 percent in Jammu and Kashmir and its share in under-five mortality varies from the lowest 31 percent in the same state Assam to the highest 60 percent in the same state Jammu and Kashmir.

2. Trends in Early Neonatal Mortality Rate, Neonatal Mortality Rate and Share of Early Neonatal Mortality Rate to Neonatal Mortality Rate in India (1972-2008)

The trend analysis of early neonatal mortality helps to know the past, present and as well as to predict the future scenario of early neonatal mortality rate for remedial policy interventions. The trend values of early neonatal mortality rate, neonatal mortality rate and the percentage share of early neonatal mortality rate to neonatal mortality rate during the period 1972-2008 are shown in the Figure 6.2. During the period 1972-74, the early neonatal mortality rate was 35 and then increased to the highest value of 47 during 1978-80 and thereafter declines continuously and finally reaches to 27 in 2008. In case of neonatal mortality during the period 1972-74, the rate was 70 and then reached the highest level at 79 during the period 1975-79 and after that declined continuously. The trend of the share of early neonatal mortality rate to neonatal mortality rate shows that it was 50 percent during the period 1972-74, and then it went up to 77 percent in 2008 with some fluctuations. The trend line of neonatal mortality rate is steeper than the trend line of early neonatal mortality rate indicating a higher rate of decline in neonatal mortality than early neonatal mortality rate. At same time the general trend line of the share of early neonatal mortality rate to neonatal mortality rate is increasing over the years.

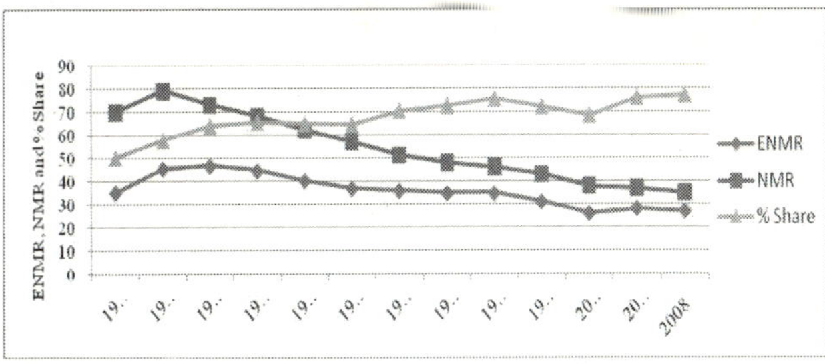

Fig. 6.2: Trends in Early Neonatal Mortality Rate, Neonatal Mortality Rate and Share of Early Neonatal Mortality Rate to Neonatal Mortality Rate, India, 1972-2008

Table 6.2: Rural-Urban Differentials in Early Neonatal Mortality Rate in India and Bigger States, 2008

India and Bigger States	*Early Neonatal Mortality Rate* Total	Rural	Urban
India	27	31	16
Madhya Pradesh	38	40	26
Chhattisgarh	36	37	29
Odisha	34	36	17
Uttar Pradesh	33	35	21
Rajasthan	33	38	17
Jammu & Kashmir	33	36	17
Gujarat	30	33	23
Assam	27	29	11
Bihar	27	28	11
Himachal Pradesh	27	28	9
Andhra Pradesh	26	33	10
Jharkhand	24	27	11
Haryana	24	27	14
West Bengal	21	23	13
Punjab	20	25	9
Karnataka	20	24	10
Maharashtra	19	22	15
Delhi	15	8	16
Tamil Nadu	15	19	11
Kerala	5	6	3

Source: Sample Registration System: Register General of India, 2009

3. Reduction in Early Neonatal Mortality Rate among Bigger States of India during the Period 1972-2008

Table 6.3 shows the levels of early neonatal mortality rate and its average annual reduction among bigger states during the period 1972-2008 in India. The average annual reduction of early neonatal mortality rate was in the range of 0.5 (Madhya Pradesh) to 2.1 percentage point (Kerala) among selected bigger states during the period 1972-2008. Ten bigger states had average annual reduction of more than 1 percent and remaining three states (Madhya Pradesh, Odisha and Rajasthan) had average annual reduction of less than one percent. The average annual reduction of early neonatal mortality rate in Bihar and West Bengal were 2.5 and 3.0 respectively during the period 1982-2008 while the all India average annual reduction was just 0.6 percent during the period 1972-2008.

Table 6.3: Percentage Reduction in Early Neonatal Mortality Rate among Bigger States of India during the Period 1972-2008

India and Bigger	*ENMR-1972*	*ENMR-2008*	*Percentage of States Average Annual Reduction (1972-2008)*
India	35	27	0.6
Andhra Pradesh	46	26	1.2
Tamil Nadu	32	15	1.5
Karnataka	37	20	1.3
Kerala	22	5	2.1
Maharashtra	41	19	1.5
Gujarat	57	30	1.3
Haryana	40	24	1.1
Punjab	41	20	1.4
Rajasthan	48	33	0.9*
Madhya Pradesh	47	38	0.5
Uttar Pradesh	58	33	1.2
Bihar	45	27	2.5#
West Bengal	41	21	3.0#
Odisha	46	34	0.7
Assam	55	27	1.4

Source: Sample Registration System, Registrar General of India, 1972-2008

Note: ENMR =Early Neonatal Mortality Rate

* Average annual reduction during 1973-2008

Average annual reduction during 1982-2008

4. Age Patterns of Mortality in Early Neonatal Period during the three Rounds of NFHS

Fig. 6.3 presents the percentage distribution of deaths according to age at death during the first week of life in the three rounds of National Family Health Survey (NFHS). From the Table, it is clear that deaths during these seven days are unevenly distributed with a maximum number of deaths occurring within first 24 hours (day zero) of newborns life. The age patterns of mortality are similar in all the three rounds of NFHS. In day zero during NFHS-1 and NFHS-2 the share was 36.4 percent and 35.6 percent respectively, but in NFHS-3 it has increased to 41.7 percent. From the data, it appears that the deaths are concentrated towards day zero of newborn. In all the three rounds, the highest percentage of deaths have occurred on day zero; followed by day one and day three. During the first three days altogether more than two-thirds of the total deaths have occurred. The number of deaths and the corresponding percentage share in each day during the early neonatal period in all the tree rounds of NFHS is shown in Table 6.4.

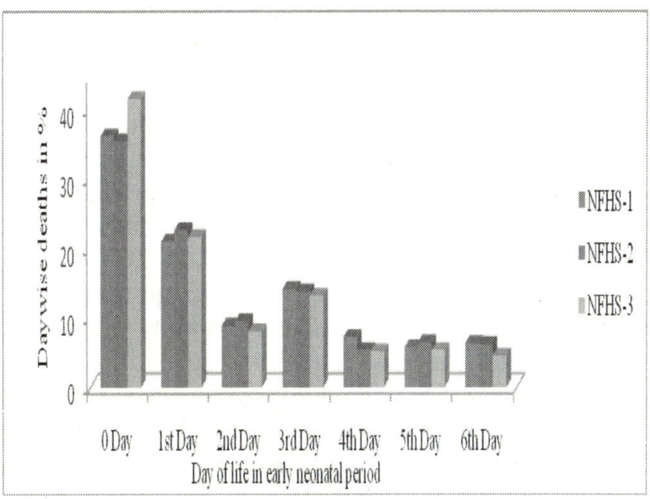

Fig. 6.3: Age Patterns of Morality in Early Neonatal period during the three Rounds of NFHS in India

Table 6.4: Age Patterns of Mortality in Early Neonatal Period during NFHS-1, 2 & 3

Age in Days	*(NFHS-1:1992-93)*		*(NFHS-2:1998-99)*		*(NFHS-3:2005-06)*	
	Deaths	*Percentage*	*Deaths*	*Percentage*	*Deaths*	*Percentage*
0 day	749	36.4	633	35.6	703	41.7
1st day	434	21.1	405	22.8	367	21.8
2nd day	184	8.9	170	9.6	137	8.1
3rd day	293	14.2	246	13.8	224	13.3
4th day	150	7.3	96	5.4	88	5.2
5th day	119	5.8	116	6.5	91	5.4
6th day	131	6.4	111	6.2	77	4.6
Total	2060	100	1777	100	1687	100

5. Result from Bivariate Analysis: Differentials in Early Neonatal Mortality Rate

Socio-economic and Environment Differentials in Early Neonatal Mortality Rate

It is essential to study the gross differentials in early neonatal mortality rate according to various socio-economic and environment, demographic and biological, and programmatic and newborn care factors. Table 6.5 reveals the variations in early neonatal mortality rate, according to mother's socio-economic condition and living environment. Among different caste groups, the rate of early neonatal mortality was highest for newborns born to mothers who belong to Scheduled Caste (33), followed by Schedules Tribes (31), OBC (30) and lowest for General Caste (28). Among religious groups, Hindus have the highest rate of early neonatal mortality (31), followed by others (26) and Muslims (24). With regard to mother's place of residence there exists huge difference between rural and urban areas. The rate was 32 in rural areas but 23 in urban areas. Only at higher level of mother's education, there is positive impact on newborns' survival during the early neonatal period. It was highest for mothers with no education (35) and having primary education (35) and lowest for mothers having only secondary or higher education (21). Like education, mass media exposure has also some impact on early neonatal mortality rate. Mothers who were exposed to mass media, the mortality rate was 27 and for those who were not exposed to mass media the early neonatal mortality rate was 33 per thousand of live births.

Early neonatal mortality rate also varies with the occupational status of mother. The rate of mortality was higher for those infants whose mothers were working in primary sector (36) and lower for women either working in service sector (27) or not working (27). The possible reasons for higher mortality rate among women working in primary sector are because of the negative impact of heavy work during pregnancy, more exposure to infections, and not utilizing antenatal care. Father's occupational status is also positively associated with the survival of infants in the early neonatal period. The mortality rate was 31 if father works in a primary sector and 26 for non-primary sector. Among wealth quintiles the highest disparity was seen between upper and lower quintile. The mortality rate was 35 in lowest wealth quintile, 29 in middle and 23 in upper wealth quintiles.

The impact of households' living environment on the rate of early neonatal mortality is assessed in terms of sources of drinking water, types of sanitation facilities and types of cooking fuel used in households. The early neonatal mortality rate was 33 for households with inadequate sanitation facilities and 21 for households with improved sanitation facilities. Household with improved sources of drinking water the early neonatal mortality rate was 29 and households without improved sources, the early neonatal mortality was 32. The early neonatal mortality was higher (32) for households where no smoke free cooking fuels were used compared with households using smoke free cooking fuels (19).

Table 6.5: Socio-economic and Environment Differentials in Early Neonatal Mortality Rate in India, NFHS-3 (2005-06)

Socio-economic Factor	*Number of Early Neo-natal Deaths*	*Number of Live Birth*	*Early Neo-natal Morta-lity Rate*	*Confidence Interval (95%)*
Caste of Mother				
Scheduled Castes	383	11739	32.6	29.4-35.8
Scheduled Tribes	165	5389	30.6	26.0-35.2
OBC	685	22962	29.8	27.6-32.0
Others	403	14560	27.7	25.0-30.3
Religion				
Hindu	1384	44152	31.3	29.7-33.0
Muslim	233	9641	24.2	21.1-27.3
Others	68	2593	26.2	20.2-32.5
Place of Residence				
Rural	1361	42135	32.3	30.6-34.0
Urban	325	14303	22.7	20.3-25.2
Mother's Education				
No Education	978	28237	34.6	32.5-36.8
Primary	275	7920	34.7	30.6-38.7
Secondary and above	433	20280	21.3	19.4-23.4
Mass Media Exposure				
No Exposure	887	26602	33.3	31.2-35.5
Exposure	799	29835	26.8	25.0-28.6
Mother's Occupation				
Not working	942	35384	26.6	24.9-28.3
Primary sector	676	18527	36.5	33.8-39.2
service sector	69	2515	27.4	21.0-33.7
Father's Occupation				
Primary sector	1280	41055	31.1	29.5-32.9
Service sector	385	14682	26.2	23.6-28.8
Wealth Index				
Lower quintile	947	27031	35.0	32.8-37.2
Middle quintile	321	11181	28.7	25.6-31.8
Upper quintile	418	18226	22.9	20.8-25.1
Sources of Drinking Water				
Improved	1289	44501	28.9	27.4-30.5
Not Improved	228	7070	32.2	28.1-36.4
Sanitation Facilities	250	11434	21.8	19.2-24.5
Improved				
Not Improved	1436	45004	31.9	30.3-33.5
Types of Fuel used				
Smoke Free	195	10239	19.0	16.4-21.7
Not Smoke Free	1322	41327	31.9	30.3-33.7

Demographic and Biological Differentials in Early Neonatal Mortality Rate

Table 6.6 shows early neonatal mortality rate according to demographic and biological characteristics of both the mother and the newborn infant. First, while analysing mother's characteristics, it was found that mother's age at any child's birth and mother's age at her first birth puts severe impact on the survival of babies in the early neonatal period. Mothers whose age were less than 20 years at the time of child's birth, the early neonatal mortality rate was highest at 43 followed by 34 in the age group 35-49 years and lowest at 26 for the age group 20-34 years. The mortality rate was higher for both younger and older aged women than the middle aged women. The early neonatal mortality rate was 32 for newborns born to mothers of age below 20 years at the time of their first birth and the rate was 26 for mothers of age 20 and more years. There exists a negative relationship between mother's previous birth interval and rate of early neonatal mortality. With increasing years of previous birth interval, the mortality rate declines. When the previous birth interval was less than two years, the mortality rate was very high at 43 per thousand of live births. But when the interval increases to 2 to 3 years, the mortality rate sharply declines to 20 and for 4 and above years it further declines to 18 per thousand of live births.

Nutritional status of mother which is measured in terms of body mass index (BMI) and mother's anemic condition are also linked with early neonatal mortality (Kousar *et al* 2010) Mothers who were severe anemic, the early neonatal mortality was 41, whereas for mild and not anemic mothers it was 30 per thousand of live births. Child's biological characteristics at the time of birth has also significant impact on early neonatal deaths. It was found that early neonatal mortality rate was higher for male child (33) and lower for female child (26). The mortality rate was exceptionally higher in multiple types of births (146) compared with singleton births (28). The early neonatal mortality rate for low birth weight babies (<2.5kg) was 30, whereas for normal babies (>=2.5kg) it was only 12 per thousand of live

Table 6.6: Demographic and Biological Differentials in Early Neonatal Mortality Rate in India, NFHS-3 (2005-06)

Demographic and Biological Factor	*Number of Early Neo-Deaths*	*Number of Live Births*	*Early Neo-natal Mortality Rate*	*Confi-dence Interval (95%)*
Mother's Age at Child's Birth				
<20 yrs	507	11882	42.7	39.0-46.3
20-34 yrs	1098	42156	26.0	24.5-27.6
35-49 yrs	81	2400	33.8	26.6-41.1
Mother's Age at First Birth				<20 yrs
1081	33528	32.2	30.0-34.0	
>=20 yrs	605	22909	26.4	24.0-28.0
Previous Birth Interval				
<2yrs	471	10860	43.4	39.5-47.2
2-3 yrs	407	20677	19.7	17.8-21.6
>=4 yrs	141	7679	18.3	15.4-21.4
Body Mass Index				
Under weight	664	21031	31.6	29.2-33.9
Normal	956	33119	28.9	27.1-30.7
Anemia Level				
Severe	41	1003	40.9	28.5-53.0
Mild	942	31338	30.1	28.2-31.9
Not anemic	611	20706	29.6	27.2-31.8
Sex of the Child				
Male	977	29416	33.2	31.2-35.2
Female	709	27022	26.2	24.3-28.2
Type of Birth				
Single	1555	55541	28.0	26.6-29.4
Multiple	131	897	146.0	123.0-169.0
Birth Order				
First	658	17107	38.5	35.6-41.3
Second and Third	553	24429	22.6	20.8-24.5
Fourth and above	475	14902	31.9	29.1-34.7
Child's Birth Weight				
Low Birth Weight (<2500g)		123	4146	39.7
24.5-34.8				
Normal (2500 & above)	177	15104	11.7	10.0-13.4
Child's Birth Size				
Average/larger	1114	43866	25.4	23.9-26.9
Small	252	8363	30.1	26.5-33.8
Very Small	219	3402	64.4	56.1-72.6

births. Similarly, very small size babies have higher mortality rate (64) than small size (30) and average/larger size babies (25). Birth order also affects the rate of survival in early neonatal period. The first order births (38) and fourth and above order (32) have higher rate of mortality over second and third order births (23).

Programmatic and Newborn Care Differentials in Early Neonatal Mortality Rate

Table 6.7 shows the differentials in early neonatal mortality rate by programmatic factors. The mortality rate was lowest (15) for mothers who have visited at least three times for antenatal care during their pregnancy than those who have not visited at all (24). The early neonatal mortality rate was lowest for women who have visited for antenatal care during the first trimester (16) of their pregnancy than second and third trimester visit (19). Women who have taken IFA tablets for at least 90 days during their pregnancy had lowest rate of early neonatal mortality (16) compared with women who have not taken at all (22). Women who had taken at least two TT injections during their pregnancy, the rate of early neonatal mortality was lowest (17) compared with women who had taken only once (23) and who had not taken at all (28). Similarly, the rate of mortality was lowest (15) for those newborns whose mothers were taking full antenatal care compared with partial utilization (18) and no utilization at all (29).

The early neonatal mortality rate was more or less the same between the group of women having pregnancy complications (19) and another group of women without any pregnancy complication (18). In respect to place of delivery there was hardly any difference in early neonatal mortality rate between institutional and non-institutional delivery. (Table 6.7) But in case of hospital delivery there was large variations with respect to the duration of time spent in hospital after delivery. Those mothers and their newborns who had stayed in hospital less than one day after delivery, the early neonatal mortality was highest and lowest for those who had stayed at least one week and the rate was 28 for duration of stay between one day to less than one week. (Table 6.7) Therefore, it is not only the hospital delivery but also the duration of stay in the hospital is also very important for the survival of newborns during early neonatal period.

Table 6.7: Programmatic and Newborn Care Differentials in Early Neonatal Mortality Rate in India, NFHS-3 (2005-06)

Programmatic and Newborn Care Factor	*Number of Early Neo-Deaths*	*Number of Live Births*	*Early Neo-natal Mortality Rate*	*Confi-dence Interval (95%)*
Antenatal visit				
No visit	216	9035	23.9	21.0-27.0
1-2 visit	210	9706	21.7	18.8-24.6
>=3 visits	308	20602	15.0	13.3-16.6
Time of Antenatal Care Visit				
1st trimester	274	17416	15.7	13.9-17.6
2nd and 3rd trimester	249	12901	19.3	16.9-21.7
IFA Tablets Taken				
Not taken	327	14932	21.9	19.6-24.3
Less than 90 days	257	14457	17.8	15.6-19.9
90 days and more	146	9171	16.0	13.3-18.5
TT Injections Taken				
Not Taken	177	6396	27.7	23.7-31.7
Only Once	61	2647	23	17.2-28.6
Two and More	502	30259	16.6	15.1-18.0
Antenatal Care Utilization				
No Utilization	144	4987	28.8	24.3-33.6
Partial Utilization	487	27222	17.9	16.3-19.5
Full Utilization	111	7448	14.9	12.1-17.7
Pregnancy Complication				
No	306	16820	18.2	16.2-20.2
Yes	436	22790	19.1	17.4-20.9
Place of Delivery				
Non Institutional	1026	34549	29.7	27.9-31.5
Institutional	629	21821	28.8	26.6-31.1
Duration of Stay in Hospital				
<1 day	162	3921	41.3	35.0-47.5
1 day to <1 week	425	15421	27.6	24.9-30.1
1 week & above	39	2446	15.9	10.9-20.9
Blade/ delivery kits used				
No	38	985	38.6	26.5-50.6
yes	388	21514	18.0	16.2-19.8
During delivery: baby wiped dry and wrapped				
No	248	11920	20.9	18.3-23.4
Yes	179	10532	17.0	14.5-19.4
Initiation of breast feeding				
Within 1 hour of birth	229	12991	17.6	15.4-19.9
After 1 hour of birth	836	41885	20.0	18.6-21.3
Received nutrition from Anganwadi centre				
No	653	32035	20.4	18.8-21.9
Yes	90	7619	11.8	9.4-14.2

Receiving nutritional supplements from Integrated Child Development Scheme (ICDS) is negatively related with early neonatal mortality rate. If pregnant women have received food supplements from ICDS, results lower early neonatal mortality rate than those who have not received any supplements from ICDS (Table 6.7). At the time of home delivery if either a disposable delivery kit or a new blade is used for cutting the umbilical cord or baby wiped dry and wrapped without being bathed, then the rate of newborn survival is more than those who were not practicing such methods. In home deliveries where either disposable delivery kit or clean blade was used the early neonatal mortality rate was 18 and where not used the rate was 39 per thousand of live births. If a baby is wiped dry and wrapped without being bathed immediately after birth, the mortality rate was 17, whereas the rate was 21 in the absent of such practices. If breast feeding starts within one hour after birth results in lower early neonatal mortality rate (18) compared with breast feeding starting after one hour of birth (20).

6. Result from Multivariate Analysis: Determinants of Early Neonatal Mortality

Table 6.8 presents the result of the multivariate analysis which shows the net effect of each explanatory variable on early neonatal mortality in terms of odds ratio. Among the variables included in the model, caste, religion, education, drinking water, sex of the child, birth order, birth size, mother's age at child birth, antenatal care and place of delivery have significant impact on the survival of newborns during early neonatal period with expected direction except place of delivery. The chance of dying during early neonatal period was 32 percent lower for newborns born to scheduled tribe mothers (OR=0.682, p<0.05) compared with scheduled caste mothers. The odds of early neonatal deaths was 22 percent less for newborns born to Muslim mothers (OR=0.781, P<0.1) than Hindu mothers. The likelihood of dying was 40 percent less among newborns born to mothers having secondary and higher education (OR=0.601, P<0.01) compared with no educated mothers. The quality of drinking water used in the households also has significant impact on the survival of infants during the early neonatal period. The risk of dying was 28 percent more in households where no improved sources of drinking water was available (OR=1.281, P<0.05) compared with households available with improved sources of drinking water.

Of the demographic and biological factors, female infants have less chance of dying (OR=0.836, P<0.05) compared with male infants. Though the likelihood of dying was lower for all higher order births compared with first order births but it was lowest for second and third order births. The chance of dying among newborns of second and third order births (OR=0.590, P<0.01) and of fourth and above order births (OR=0.750, P<0.05) was low compared with first order births. The size of baby at the time of birth is an important factor influencing the survival of newborns. The chance of dying was nearly two and half times more among very small birth size babies (OR=2.456, P<0.01) compared with large/average/small size babies. Babies born to older women have higher chance of dying during the early neonatal period compared with very young age mothers. The chance of dying was one and half times more among newborns whose mothers were in the age group 35-49 years at the time of newborns birth (OR=1.496, P<0.05) compared with very young (<20 years) mothers.

Among the programmatic factors, the utilization of antenatal care in varying degrees also influences the chance of survival among newborns during early neonatal period. The likelihood of dying among newborns born to mothers utilizing partial antenatal care (OR=0.641, P<0.01) and full antenatal care (OR=0.541, P<0.01) were less compared with mothers not utilizing any antenatal care. In case of place of delivery the chance of dying was more in hospital deliveries (OR=1.480, P<0.01) compared with home deliveries. This contradictory result may be that in rural areas most of the high risk pregnant women go for hospital delivery at the last moment due to delivery complications where doctors cannot save the lives of the newborns. And in general in many cases the duration of stay in hospital after delivery is less than 24 hours, resulting higher chance of dying. This finding also goes with the finding of some previous studies where the chance of dying was more in hospital deliveries compared with home deliveries (Achyut 1997; James 2004).

Table 6.8: Odds Ratio and Predicted Probability for Early Neonatal Mortality from Binary Logistic Regression Analysis in India, NFHS-3 (2005-06)

Factor	*Category*	*Odds Ratio*	*Predicted Probability(P)*
Place of Residence	Rural®		31.3
	Urban	0.920	28.8
Caste of Mother	SC®		31.3
	ST	0.682**	21.5
	OBC	0.985	30.8
	General	1.013	31.7
Religion of Mother	Hindu®		31.3
	Muslim	0.781*	24.6
	Others	1.191	37.0
Mother's Education	No Education ®		31.3
	Primary	0.919	28.8
	Secondary & Above	0.601***	19.0
Mass-Media Exposure	No Exposure®		31.3
	Exposure	0.954	29.9
Wealth Index	Lower®		31.3
	Middle	0.983	30.7
	Upper	1.003	31.2
Source of Drinking Water	Improved®		31.3
	Not Improved	1.281**	39.7
Sanitation Facilities	Improved®		31.3
	Not Improved	1.194	37.1
Types of Cooking Fuel used in Household	Smoke Free®		31.3
	No Smoke Free	1.178	36.6
Sex of the Child	Male®		31.3
	Female	0.836**	26.3
Birth Order	First®		31.3
	2nd and 3rd	0.590***	18.7
	4th and above	0.750**	23.6
Birth Size	Large/Average/Small®		31.3
	Very small	2.456***	73.4
Mother's Age at Child's Birth	<20 yrs®		31.3
	20-34 yrs	1.001	31.3
	35-49 yrs	1.496**	46.1
Antenatal Care Utilization	No Utilization®		31.3
	Partial Utilization	0.641***	20.3
	Full Utilization	0.541***	17.2
Pregnancy Complication	No Complication®		31.3
	Complication	1.015	31.7
Place of Delivery	Home®		31.3
	Hospital	1.480***	45.6

(0=No Death , 1= Yes Death) ® Reference Category, Level of significance: * $p<0.10$, ** $p<0.05$, *** $p<0.01$

Note: Predicted Probability of Dying (P) is per thousand of live births

Table 6.8 also shows the predicted probability of dying for all categories of each factor after controlling other factors. The probability of dying was highest among very small birth size babies (73.4 deaths per thousand of live births), followed by newborns born to mothers in the age group 35-49 years (46.1), delivery taken place in hospital (45.6), households not having improved sources of drinking water (39.7) and improved sanitation facilities (37.1), women belong to other religion (37), and household not using improved cooking fuel (36.6). On the other side the predicted probability of dying was least among infants whose mothers were availing full antenatal care (17.2), followed by second and third order births (18.7), women having secondary and higher education (19), availing partial antenatal care (20.3), among scheduled tribe women (21.5), and in fourth and higher order births (23.4).

Conclusions

The present level of early neonatal mortality rate in India is very high and it has already reached to more than three-fourth of neonatal mortality rate. During the last three and a half decade the percentage reduction in early neonatal mortality rate was very slow than the reduction in post neonatal mortality rate and in late neonatal mortality rate. Among the bigger states the lowest percentage decline in early neonatal mortality was in Madhya Pradesh, Odisha and Rajasthan. Marked differences in early neonatal mortality rate are also observed between south and north Indian states and between rural and urban areas. Among some bigger states the percentage share of early neonatal mortality rate to neonatal mortality rate has already reached to more than ninety percent showing the increasing dominance of early neonatal mortality in neonatal mortality. The deaths during early neonatal period are unevenly distributed with the highest risk of dying in zero days (within first 24 hours of life) and this pattern has remained the same over the three rounds of NFHS. From this study it is found that newborns of very small birth size and born to old age mothers and living in unhygienic environment (lack of quality drinking water and sanitation facilities and households where solid cooking fuels are used) having the higher chance of dying. On the other hand, lower probability of dying was seen among newborns born to mothers who were taking full antenatal care and having secondary and above education.

From the point of view of policy implications it is quite evident that early neonatal mortality is an important component of infant mortality and particularly in neonatal mortality. Its slow rate of reduction and current substantial share in neonatal mortality urges policymakers to design exclusive programs for newborns in order to increase their chance of survival during early neonatal period with utmost care in the first twenty four hours of newborn's life. Focus should be given to different sub-groups of population where the probability of dying during these seven days is higher. Hygienic delivery and newborn care practices should be promoted in home deliveries and IEC programs on simple low cost hygienic delivery and newborn care should be strengthened. There is also a need to ensure full utilization of antenatal care to all pregnant women and in case of hospital deliveries the duration of stay in hospital should be increased to at least the first week of life for all newborns along with the serious one and if not possible then providing essential newborn care at home by community health workers and the ongoing maternal and child health programmes should also cater the needs of mothers and her newborns.

References

Achyut, P., S. Lahiri, and R. Acharya. (1997). "Non-biological Correlates of Early Neonatal Deaths: Evidence from Five Selected States of India," *Demography India* 26(2):241-260.

Aggarwal, A. K., R. Kumar, and P. Kumar. (2003). "Early Neonatal Mortality in A Hilly North Indian State: Socio-Demographic Factors and Treatment Seeking

Behaviours," *Indian Journal of Preventive Social Medicine* 34(1 & 2).

Araujo, B. F., M. C. Bozzetti, and A. C. A. Tanaka. (2000). "Early Neonatal Mortality in Caxias do Sul: a Cohort Study," *Jornal de pediatria* 76(3): 200-206.

Bang, A. T., R. A. Bang and H.M. Reddy. (2005). "Home Based Neonatal Care: Summary and Application of the Field Trial in Rural Gadchiroli, Maharashtra, India: 1993-2003," *Journal of Perinatology* 25:S108 S122.

Baqui, A. H. et al. (2005b). "Evidence Based, Cost Effective Interventions: How Many Newborn Babies Can We Save," *Lancet* 365: 977-88.

Baqui, A. H. et al. (2006a). "Rates Timing and Causes of Neonatal Deaths in Rural India: Implications for Neonatal Health Programs," *Bulletin of World Health Organization* 89 (9).

Bassani, D.G. *et al.*(2010). "Causes of Neonatal and Child Mortality in India: A Nationally Representative Mortality Survey," *Lancet* 376: 1853-60.

Chavan, Y. S. et al. (1992). "Causes of Early Neonatal Mortality," *Indian Pediatrics* 29: 781-783.

Chowdhury, Q. H., R. Islam, and K. Hossain. (2010). "Socio-economic Determinants of Neonatal, Post Neonatal, Infant and Child Mortality," *International Journal of Sociology and Anthropology* 2(6): 118-125.

Fernandez, A., J. Mondkar, and S. Mathai. (2003). "Urban Slum-Specific Issues in Neonatal Survival," *Indian Pediatrics* 40 :(1161-66).

Galjaart, P. (2008). "Early Neonatal Deaths in Sub-Saharan Africa," The Netherlands: KIT(Royal Tropical Institute) Vrije Universiteit Amsterdam.

Golestan, M., R. Fallah, and S. A. Karbasi. (2008). "Neonatal Mortality of Low Birth Weight Infants in Yazd, Iran," *Iranian Journal of Reproductive Medicine* 6 (4) : 205- 208.

Hill, K. and Y. Choi. (2006). "Neonatal mortality in the Developing World," *Demographic Research* 14(18): 429-452.

International Institute for Population Sciences (1992-93), "National Family Health and Survey-I", *Ministry of Health and Family Welfare,* New Delhi.

International Institute for Population Sciences. (1998-99). "National Family Health and Survey-II", *Ministry of Health and Family Welfare,* New Delhi.

International Institute for Population Sciences. (2005-06). "National Family Health and Survey-III", *Ministry of Health and Family Welfare,* New Delhi.

Kikhela, D. N. (1989). "Techniques of Collection and Analysis of Data on Perinatal Mortality in Kinshasa, Zaire," *International Development Research Centre,* 1-100.

Kumar, D., A. Verma, and V. K. Sehgal. (2007). "Neonatal Mortality in India," *Rural and Remote Health,* 7: 833.

Kumar, V. et al. (2008). "Effect of Community Based Behavior Change Management on Neonatal Mortality in Shivgarh, Up, India: a Cluster-Randomized Controlled Trial," *The Lancet,* 372(9644): 1151 - 1162.

Lawn, J. et al. (2005). "4 million Neonatal Deaths: When? Where? Why?" *The Lancet.*1-10.

Lawn, J., K. W. Ketende, and S. N. Cousen. (2006). "Estimating the Causes of 4 Million Neonatal Deaths in the Year 2000," *International Journal of Epidemiology, 35(706-718).*

Mavalankar, D. V., C. R. Trivedi and R. H. Gray. (1991). "Levels and Risk Factors for Perinatal Mortality in Ahmadabad, India," *World Health Organization* 69(4):435- 442.

Millennium Development Goals in India, (2010). A Civil Society Report.

Mosley, W. H. and L.C. Chen. (1984). "An Analytical Framework for the Study of Child Survival in Developing Countries," *A Supplement to Population and Development Review.* 10: 24-45.

Mufti, P., F. Senta, and K. Nazir. (2006). "Early Neonatal Mortality: Effects of Interventions on Survival of Low Birth Babies Weighing 1000-2000g," *Journal of Pakistan Medical Association* 56(4):174-176.

Ngoc, N. T. N. *et al.* (2006). "Causes of Still Births and Early Neonatal Deaths: Data from 7993 Pregnancies in Six Developing Countries," *Bulletin of the World Health Organisation* 84(9): 699-705.

Osrin, D. *et al.* (2005). "Effects of Antenatal Multiple Micronutrient Supplementations on Birth Weight and Gestational Duration in Nepal: Double Bind Randomised Controlled Trial," *Lancet* 365: 855-62.

PATH. (1999). *Clean Delivery Kit Workshop Report.* Nairobi, Kenya.

Registrar General of India. 1995-2009. "Sample Registration System Statistical Report," New Delhi: Registrar General of India.

Registrar General of India. (2009). "Compendium of India's Fertility and Mortality Indicators 1971-2007 Based on SRS," New Delhi: Registrar General of India.

Saksena, D. N. and J. N.Srivastav. (1980). "Biosocial Correlates of Perinatal Mortality," *Journal of Biosocial Science* 12: 69-81.

Saugstad, L. F. (1981). "Weight of All Births and Infant Mortality" *journal of Epidemiology and community Health* 35: 185-191.

Schoeps, D. *et al.* (2007). "Risk Factors for Early Neonatal Mortality," *Rev Saude Publica,* 41 (6).

Shah, U., A. K. Pratinidi, and P. V. Bhatlawande. (1984a). "Peri-natal Mortality in Rural India: Intervention through Primary Health Care. II Neonatal Mortality," *Journal of Epidemiology and Community Health* 38: 138-142.

Shah, U., A. K. Pratinidi, and P. V. Bhatlawande. (1984b). "Perinatal Mortality in Rural India: Intervention through Primary Health Care. I Stillbirths," *Journal of Epidemiology and Community Health* 38: 134-137.

Singh, M. and V. K. Paul. (1988). "Strategies to Reduce Perinatal and Neonatal Mortality," *Indian Pediatrics*, 25: 499-509.

Srivastava, J.N. (1992). "Correlates of Perinatal Mortality In Lucknow City: Repeat Study of a Hospital's Experiences," *The Journal of Family Welfare* 38(4): 43-52.

UNICEF, WHO. (2010). *Levels and Trends in Child Mortality Report 2010.*

WHO. (2006). *Neonatal and Perinatal Mortality: Country, Regional and Global Estimates.*

Differentials in Maternal Health Care Utilization in Odisha: An Inter-District Analysis

Ayusmati Das & Pratap C. Mohanty

Introduction

The maternal deaths mostly (99 percent) occur in the developing countries, India is not an exception. The rate of decline in maternal mortality is quite significant in South-Asia regions like India (*World Health Statistics 2011*). India has managed to reduce maternal mortality rate, but the interstate variation still persists. Odisha is one of the states which has high maternal mortality. The infant mortality has remained at very high level in Odisha. An important proximate determinant of maternal mortality is access to and use of quality healthcare services (McCarthy and Mine 1992; Bhatia 1995). Reviving maternal and child health services certainly can affect positively on family planning and health condition of mother and child in India (Mishra *et al* 1998). There is a substantial reduction in prenatal mortality due to the initial antenatal check up being availed by women as late as the third trimester of pregnancy (Ramachandran 1992). The improvement in the quality of services can further substantiate the service utilization of maternal care (Kumar *et al*.1997; Rao and Richard 1984). Of late, the focus has been shifted from supply to demand side in exploring under utilization of maternal health care. Several studies indicate the importance of the supply side variable in this regard (Sugathan *et al* 2001; Navaneetham and Dharmalingam 2000). Often, it is argued that the effects of inadequate access to services on underutilization of services is greater than the impact of socio-economic factors (Elo 1992), whereas other studies highlight factors such as the lack of motivation and its demand as the major root (Rao *et al* 1984).

The poverty level of Odisha has always been an alarming situation for India. Despite India's progress, large-scale interstate inequality in terms of socio-economic condition still prevails. The rising poverty and low performance in public health are the major backblocks for Odisha. Infant mortality rate (IMR) and maternal mortality rate continue to be very high in Odisha. In order to reduce both infant and maternal mortality, it is necessary to strengthen the maternal healthcare.

The study focuses on the pattern, determinants of maternal health care utilization which would be useful to identify the intervening areas to work out for the better maternal health situation in Odisha. By availing districts picture in this regard, the purpose would be better exercised.

Objectives

1. To analyze the pattern of antenatal care and safe delivery in Odisha and its districts.
2. To find out the determinants of antenatal care and institutional delivery across the districts.

Data Source and Methodology

Data from the District Level Household Survey (DLHS)-3 conducted during 2007-08 is used for the present analysis. This is the only large scale survey in India which gives detailed information on reproductive and child health at the district level. The survey provides basically information on the practice of family planning, maternal and child health and utilisation of health services provided to mothers and children. A multi-stage stratified systematic sampling was adopted in DLHS-3. This survey covers 34 states and union territories, and 601 districts in the country.

There are 7,203,20 household, 6,43,944 ever married women aged 15-49 and 1,66,260 unmarried women aged 15-24 in India. The present study is based on Odisha, where 33,172 households, 27,848 ever married women and 7,257 unmarried women were selected as sample from the population.

In order to achieve the objectives, both bivariate and multivariate techniques are used. However, simple frequency tables and crosstabs are used under the bivariate techniques and logistic regression is applied under the multivariate techniques by using SPSS software.

Odisha contributes three percent of population to the total population of India. The decadal growth rate of population in Odisha is four percent less than India. However, the growth rate of this in Odisha has been reduced by 2 percent since 2001. One of the impressive facts concerning Odisha is the sex ratio composition. The sex ratio exceeds the India's sex ratio (940) and various developed states the child sex ratio has fallen substantially from the preceding year. Around 73 percent people are literate in Odisha, within that the share of male is 82 percent.

Table-7.1: Some Background Characteristics of Odisha

Indicators	
Population[a]	41947358
Decadal Growth Rate	13.97
Sex ratio[a]	978
Density[a]	269
Child sex ratio[a]	934
Literacy Rate[a]Male[a]Female[a]	73.4582.4064.36
Infant mortality rate[b]	69.0
Maternal mortality ratio[c]	346

Source: [a] Provisional Population Totals, Census of India, 2011
[b] Sample Registration System, 2008
[c] Sample Registration System, 2006

Pattern of Maternal Health Care Utilisation

The full antenatal care (ANC) constitutes three antenatal visits, one tetanus Injection and 100 and more days of taking iron folic acid tablets mentioned in DLHS-3. Fig.7.1 and 7.2 explain Odisha's position in comparison to other states in terms of full antenatal care. Despite the fact that Odisha is comparable to Bihar in terms of poverty, the full ANC use is much better than Bihar and Uttar Pradesh. Odisha has exceeded some of the developed states like Punjab and Gujarat regarding the full antenatal care utilization. Around 23 percent of women in Odisha have used full antenatal care during their last pregnancy in the last three year preceding the survey. Around half of the women had a safe delivery for their last birth, three years preceding the survey. Odisha has large percentage of safe delivery than of Bihar, Uttar Pradesh, and Jharkhand etc. But contrary to full ANC, Odisha has less percentage of safe delivery compared to Punjab and Gujarat.

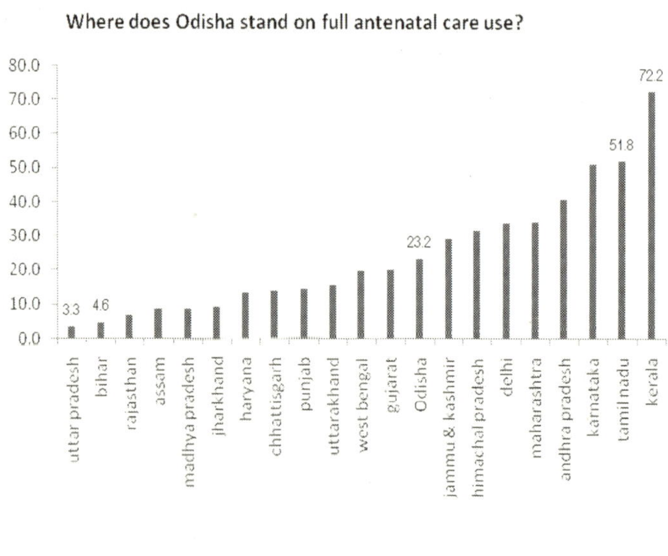

Fig.7.1: Where Does Odisha Stand on full Antenatal care Use?

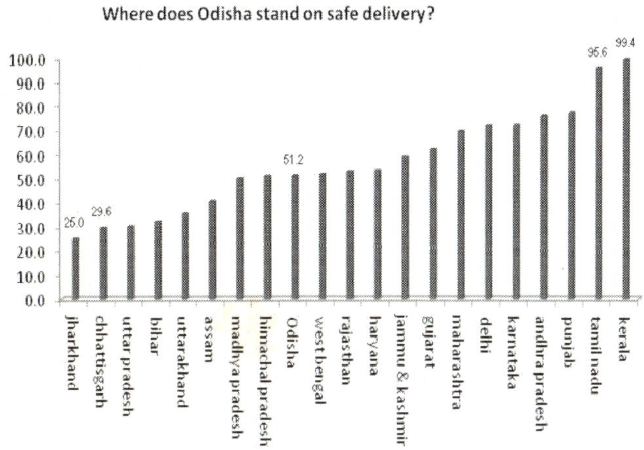

Fig.7.2: Where Does Odisha stand on safe Delivery?

Table-7.2 Some Maternal Health Care Utilisation Indicators and the Difference among Them by the Districts of Odisha, 2007-08

District	*Human Devt. Index*	*Full ANC*	*Safe Delivery*	*Gap between safe and full ANC*	*Gap between safe delivery and institutional delivery*	*who have got both delivery and full ANC*
Anugul	6	15.8	47.5	31.6	6.7	80.8
Balangir	21	30.0	62.1	32.1	10.3	75.0
Baleshwar	18	33.7	55.6	21.9	3.1	68.2
Bargarh	17	25.0	66.2	41.2	22.5	82.4
Baudh	23	26.6	37.8	11.1	9.0	52.9
Bhadrak	8	29.3	47.1	17.8	4.5	71.0
Cuttack	3	24.9	71.3	46.4	3.0	85.9
Debagarh	5	22.4	54.8	32.4	10.3	85.2
Dhenkanal	12	16.0	52.7	36.7	5.8	93.6
Gajapati	28	22.9	26.3	3.4	6.6	47.7
Ganjam	20	18.3	59.3	41.0	4.0	78.1
Jagatsinghapur	19	38.9	82.9	44.1	3.2	94.8
Jajapur	22	28.2	64.8	36.7	3.2	81.7

Jharsuguda	2	31.7	79.5	47.8	14.3	91.5
Kalahandi	11	26.6	42.5	16.0	15.1	39.7
Kandhamal	29	14.5	27.1	12.6	1.7	61.9
Kendrapara	10	24.6	57.8	33.2	10.9	77.8
Kendujhar	24	15.7	39.0	23.3	4.6	69.0
Khurda	1	23.1	77.3	54.2	6.5	91.5
Koraput	27	16.8	21.0	4.2	2.0	36.7
Malkangiri	30	13.0	15.3	2.3	0.5	33.3
Mayurbhanj	9	34.2	45.7	11.5	2.7	61.6
Nabarangapur	26	11.5	19.2	7.8	3.3	25.6
Nayagarh	15	14.7	48.7	34.1	4.7	75.0
Nuapada	14	29.5	45.5	16.1	16.6	65.0
Puri	7	19.5	69.3	49.8	5.6	76.8
Rayagada	25	13.6	21.3	7.7	3.1	38.3
Sambalpur	13	33.5	69.0	35.5	12.4	80.7
Sonapur	16	31.9	56.4	24.5	15.5	72.2
Sundargarh	4	26.6	52.4	25.8	6.9	72.6
Max		38.9	82.9	54.2	22.5	94.8
Min		11.5	15.3	2.3	0.5	25.6
Gap		27.4	67.6	51.9	22.0	69.2
Central Odisha		24.5	62.9	38.4	5.2	31.5
Northern Odisha		25.2	57.9	32.7	11.8	34.9
Southern Odisha		18.5	31.8	13.3	5.7	29.2

Source: DLHS-3

The determinants and pattern of maternal healthcare utilization of a state can be clear if the districts' situation could be analyzed. Table 7.3 presents full ANC, institutional and safe delivery utilization among the women during their last delivery, three year preceding the survey. The human development index rank is also presented for better exploration. The percentage of full antenatal care use is lowest in Nowrangapur, which is followed by Malkanagiri, Rayagada and Kandhamal. The same is high in Jagastingpur, Mayurbhanj and Balasore districts. As a whole most of the southern districts are getting less full antenatal care compared to central and northern districts of Odisha. Malkanagiri and Nowrangpur are at the bottom in terms of safe delivery utilization where as Jagatsinghapur, Khurda and Jharsuguda have better delivery facilities compare to any districts of Odisha. One of the notable observations is that all the southern districts except Ganjam have low percentage of safe delivery compared to northern and central districts. The association between development and geographical pattern is well observed in the Odishan context. The gap between full ANC and safe delivery use is very high among the northern and central districts, where as southern districts have less disparity in this regard, except Ganjam. The developed districts (based on HDI rank) have minimum percentage of antenatal care in comparison to safe delivery. However, antenatal care is much less than the developed districts. The percentage difference between antenatal and safe delivery care is very high among the developed districts compared to the undeveloped districts. Women in developed districts opt less antenatal care than safe delivery. All these go to show that both antenatal and safe delivery care levels are very low in undeveloped districts. In spite of the high level of maternal health care in developed districts less attention is paid towards antenatal care than safe delivery. Regarding the percentage of women who have got both the care is more visible in the developed districts than undeveloped districts. The women belonging to developed districts who have got antenatal care also go for safe delivery. However, a large percentage of women go for safe delivery without having proper ANC care. In the underdeveloped districts, the proportion of women who opt for both the care is unimpressive.

Determinants of Maternal Health Care Utilisation

Maternal healthcare utilization is sometimes considered as an abstract phenomenon so long as it is not defined with the help of its determinants. Nevertheless, the large scale survey like DLHS has covered a wide range of factors which may affect the problems of maternal healthcare utilization. Having a close observation of various literatures, it becomes possible to earmark some of the very important determinants, like age, education, wealth, religion and marital duration etc.

The following table presents the bivariate analysis of antenatal care and safe delivery with some of the implicative background characteristics. This process has again been divided according to three geographical regions of Odisha i.e. north, south and central.

It has already been clarified that the economical situation is highly linked with the geographical settings of Odisha. So it's very essential to segregate the level of maternal healthcare utilization and determinants across the three regions.

It is observed that the middle aged mothers, especially in the age of 21 to 30, receive highest attention towards Full ANC and safe delivery across the three regions. The Full ANC and safe delivery increase till the age of 30 and exceeding this age, women receive less attention. The level of education as a path of information and empowerment, really suffice the improving trend of Full ANC and safe delivery. With the higher education attainment, mothers get better attention in both the aspects across all regions. It is also noticed that mothers having 'no education' and 'with education' identified a clear departure from very meagre level of care to better degree of care. Educational attainment of mothers in the category '11 or more' have more than 90 percent safe delivery in all the three regions. So far as the education level of husband is concerned, there is an increasing trend of Full ANC and Safe delivery in all the regions with the higher educational attainment. Marital duration also matters for mothers' care. So long as the marital duration increases, the Full ANC and Safe delivery trends get lower in all regions. Mothers those who were working 12 months before the survey get lower care than those not working.

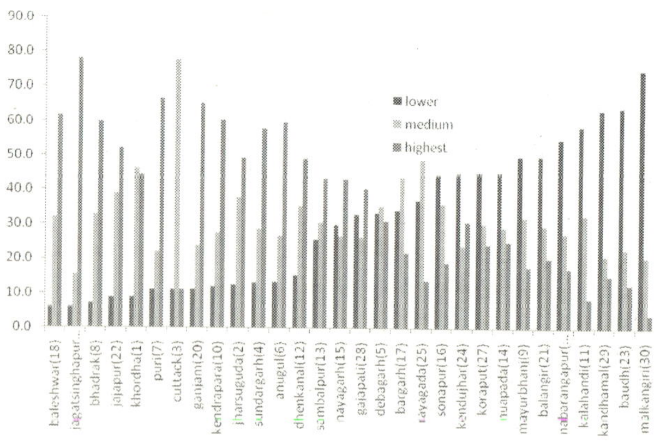

Fig.7.3: Utilisation of Full Antenatal Care by Wealth Index-Districts of Odisha

Table 7.3: Maternal Health Care Utilisation Indicators by Some Background Characteristics of Odisha, 2007-08

	Southern			*Northern*			*Central*			*Odisha*		
Background Characteristics	*Full ANC*	*Safe Delivery*	*No. of women*	*Full ANC*	*Safe Delivery*	*No. of women*	*Full ANC*	*Safe Delivery*	*No. of women*	*Full ANC*	*Safe Delivery*	*No.of women*
Age												
15 to 20	16.0	34.9	350	28.8	59.1	208	18.4	63.7	223	20.8	50.3	798
21 to 30	20.4	33.6	1636	25.6	60.5	1509	25.7	65.6	1882	24.5	54.2	5374
30 to 39	15.0	25.0	487	22.9	48.6	385	23.3	54.2	424	20.4	40.8	1371
40+	5.7	13.9	35	12.0	34.6	25	11.1	26.3	18	9.9	23.5	81
Education of respondent												
No schooling	12.5	20.2	1690	14.7	36.8	780	11.2	36.4	627	13.2	27.7	3136
less than 5	25.9	41.8	347	21.0	57.7	466	15.3	54.0	470	20.4	50.5	1377
6-8	23.9	56.6	176	24.6	66.3	264	19.6	59.9	409	21.9	60.1	939
9-10	35.9	64.4	217	34.2	74.9	398	31.9	81.6	684	33.6	76.3	1442
11 and more	54.3	90.1	81	56.0	93.1	218	52.4	91.3	359	53.2	91.5	730
Total children born												
1	21.1	52.1	658	36.1	78.9	724	33.6	81.7	1008	31.6	72.8	2576
2	25.3	33.6	607	28.1	60.5	631	24.1	64.5	780	25.5	53.6	2183
3+	13.7	20.1	1206	12.7	36.8	765	12.7	37.9	733	14.0	29.7	2863
Education of Husband												
No schooling	11.5	17.5	1156	13.9	37.4	439	11.5	39.2	358	12.5	26.3	1989
less than 5	18.9	30.1	576	18.4	50.4	561	13.1	44.7	542	17.5	41.2	1747
6-8	20.0	43.9	285	22.8	57.9	356	20.1	59.3	383	20.8	53.4	1087

Table contd....

Southern			*Northern*			*Central*			*Odisha*			
Background Characteristics	***Full ANC***	***Safe Delivery***	***No. of women***	***Full ANC***	***Safe Delivery***	***No. of women***	***Full ANC***	***Safe Delivery***	***No. of women***	***Full ANC***	***Safe Delivery***	***No.of women***
9-10	29.1	53.0	333	28.5	64.5	403	25.8	70.5	667	27.6	54.3	1554
11 and more	42.8	76.1	159	47.8	86.4	368	44.4	89.0	599	45.1	35.8	1248
Occupation												
Non worker	21.5	40.3	1303	28.6	62.7	1404	25.8	67.0	2166	26.1	58.6	5367
Professional	42.9	55.2	30	36.6	73.2	39	35.7	82.8	29	37.0	70.0	100
Services	36.0	40.0	26	32.1	64.2	53	30.0	33.3	28	31.5	48.1	108
Agricultural Labourer	16.0	26.7	404	13.9	41.7	266	13.5	34.6	150	14.9	34.0	826
Skilled and Un-skilled Labourer	12.7	17.7	708	18.5	48.3	358	13.6	38.6	148	14.7	28.4	1223
Worked 12 months before												
Yes	15.6	22.5	379	16.0	45.	231	18.5	40.0	54	15.4	32.2	671
No	21.4	40.3	1321	28.6	62.8	1401	25.8	67.0	2194	26.1	58.6	5359
Religion												
Hindu	19.1	32.6	2372	25.3	58.0	2025	24.6	63.3	2506	23.4	51.6	7303
Muslim	50.0	33.3	4	34.6	92.6	26	27.8	66.7	36	33.7	69.5	95
Christian	8.7	16.8	126	16.9	40.0	65	16.7	33.3	6	12.3	25.7	203
Other	.0	22.2	9	36.4	70.0	11	0	NA	0	18.2	45.5	22
Caste												
scheduled caste	19.7	36.9	498	21.1	57.7	469	16.8	56.0	529	19.6	49.7	1640
scheduled tribe	13.0	16.0	1195	15.9	41.9	656	16.6	28.8	362	14.4	26.0	2187
none of them/ others	28.4	57.6	204	39.2	78.3	372	31.5	75.6	880	33.2	72.1	1674

Source: DLHS-3

The utilization of full care across the wealth index furnishes an odd trend among the districts. In most of the developed districts (HDR scores) the poor women are utilizing less full ANC than the medium and highest wealth index women. But in the undeveloped districts, poor women are utilizing more maternal healthcare utilization than the middle and rich women. It might be due to the less representative sample from the middle and rich women.

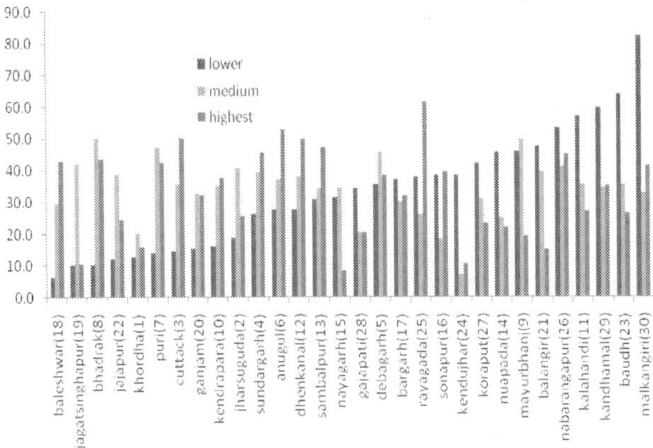

Fig. 7.4: Utilisation of Safe Delivery by Wealth Index-Districts of Odisha

Source: DLHS-3

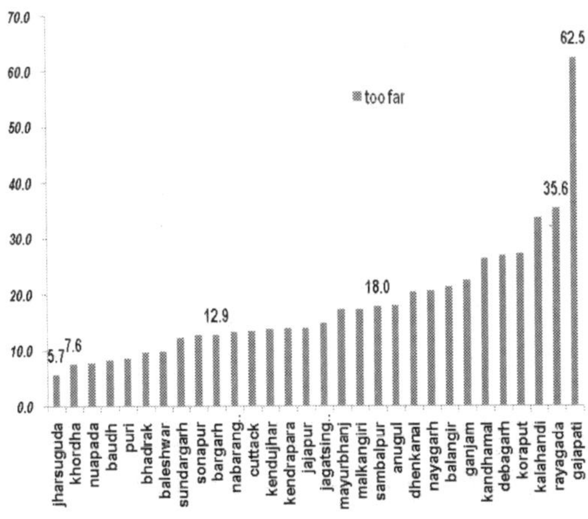

Fig. 7.5: Reason for Not Utilizing Health Facility for Delivery: The Time Factor

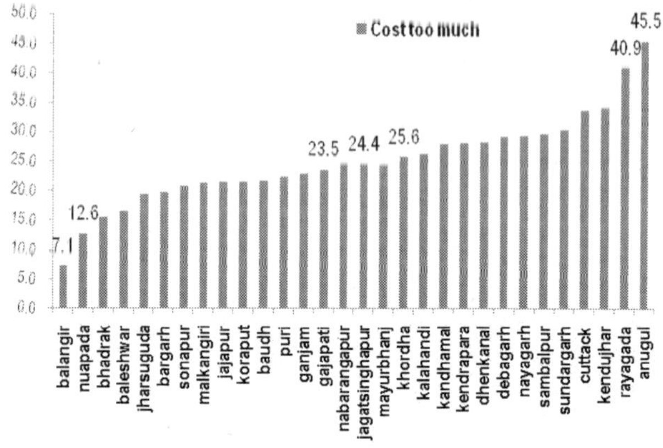

Fig. 7.6: Reason for not utilising health facility

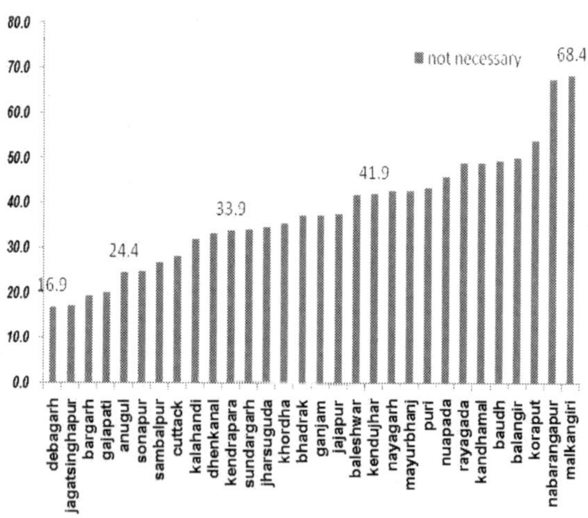

Fig 7.7: Reason for not utilizing Health Facility

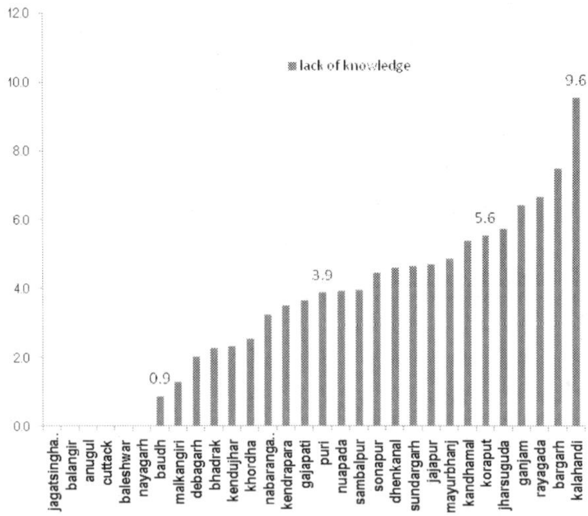

Fig 7.8: Reason for Not Utilizing Health Facility

The DLHS-3 includes some of the indicators in order to know the direct demand barriers in the access underutilisation of the services. Women in Malkanagiri, which is a backward district of Odisha,reported cost and accesibility as a cause for not utilising health facility. It may be concluded that not only supply factor but also the cultural stigma, myths, less awarness about maternal healthcare utilisation prevent them in utilising the health facilities for institutional delivery. However, the preventing factors like lack of knowledge and family opposition are less reported in Malkanagiri. In Nowrangpur, 21 percent women are not utilizing health facility due to better care at home. Although this district is ahead of other districts, but the level itself is very less. As expected most undeveloped districts have reported this as a reason.

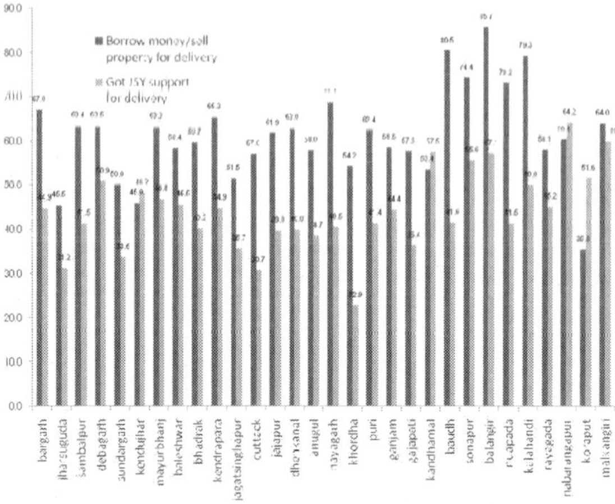

Fig. 7.9: Expenditure Burden of Delivery and Janani Surakhya Yojana(JSY) Support for Delivery in Odisha by Districts.

More than 70 percent women/households in Nupada, Sonpur, Khalahandi , Boudh and Balangir districts have borrowed or sold property for delivery. These districts are indeed poor districts which need government intervention for their financial support. Nowrangapur, Malkanagiri, Kandhamal and Balangir have high support from Janani Surakhya Yojana(JSY) in Odisha.

Multivariate Analysis

Table 7.4: Unadjusted and Adjusted Effects (Odd Ratio from Logit) Of Region Variable on the Likelihood of Getting Full ANC in Odisha: DLHS-3

Independent variable	*Unadjusted Odd ratio*	*Adjusted Odd ratio$*
Region		
Southern®		
Northern	1.48**	.971
Central	1.40**	.672**

Source: Computed from DLHS-3

Note. $Age, religion, caste, place of residence, woman's education, heard of ANC, husband education, wealth index, Number of children, Occupation and ever had a still birth

® Reference category, ** significant at 1percent

Table 7.5: Unadjusted and Adjusted Effects (Odd Ratio from Logit) Of Region Variable on the Likelihood of Getting Safe Delivery in Odisha: DLHS-3

Independent variable	*Unadjusted Odd ratio*	*Adjusted Odd ratio$*
Region		
Southern®		
Northern	2.98**	.770
Central	3.75**	.440**

Note: $Age, religion, caste, place of residence, woman's education, heard of ANC, husband education, wealth index, Number of children, Occupation and ever had a still birth
® Reference category, ** significant at 1 percent.
Source: Computed from DLHS-3

Tables 7.4 and 7.5 reveal both unadjusted and adjusted effects of region on full ANC and safe delivery respectively. The unadjusted odd ratio has not been controlled by any other variables, where the northern and central Odisha women are less likely to go for full ANC and safe delivery compared to southern women. The women of central Odisha have less possibility of getting full ANC and safe delivery facility as compared to the southern parts of the state.

In addition to the result, Table 7.6 presents the regression of full ANC and safe delivery with some other independent variables. Education is the most important variable in influencing both the dependent variables. Women with education are more likely to utilize health care than the uneducated. With growing wealth the probability of getting safe delivery also increases substantially. But this effect is not well-built where full ANC concern. The women who do not receive full ANC are 44 percent less likely to get safe delivery than the others who have received full ANC. Women with more children are less likely to get health care than women who have less number of children.

Table 7.6: Regression Analysis, Dependent Variable: Antenatal Care, Safe Delivery

Characteristics	*Full ANC*	*Safe Delivery*
BACKGROUND FACTORS		
Age(in years)	1.05	1.00
Religion		
Hindu®		
Muslim	1.28	1.18
Christian	.625	.613
Other*Caste*	1.10	2.08
SC®		
ST	.944	.544**
No caste	1.20	1.10
None of them	1.14	1.12
Place of Residence		
Rural®		
Urban	1.08	1.65**
DEMAND FACTORS		
Woman's education		
Illiterate®		
<5	1.40**	1.53**
6-8	1.31**	1.50*
9-10	1.99**	2.14**
11+	3.32**	3.50**
Wealth Index		
Poorest®		
Poorer	1.10	1.29**
Middle	1.27	1.82**
Richer	1.43*	2.51*
Richest	1.69**.	4.26**.
No. of children		
1	788**.	424**
2		
3+	495**	.260**
OTHERS		
Heard of antenatal message		
Yes®		
No	.493**	
Heard of institutional delivery message		
Yes®	--	.770
No	--	
Received any antenatal care		
Yes®	--	.440**
No		

Source: DLHS-3

® Reference category, ** significant at 1percent, * significant at 5 percent

Conclusion

Maternal health has become an inevitable issue for policy makers in the country since decades. Better facility of healthcare is surely the gateway to ensure better maternal health in India. Despite the fact that maternal health has been improved in India, interstate differences still persist. Odisha is one of the underdeveloped states in India having major proportion of people below poverty line. Infant mortality rate has been highest in Odisha. Only recently Madhya Pradesh took the top position in term of infant mortality. It is found that most of the southern districts are undeveloped than the central and northern ones. Further, women from northern and central part of the state receive better maternal health care than the southern part. Whereas in southern Odisha both the level of full ANC and safe delivery are low, the central and northern areas have more safe delivery than full ANC. There is an urgent need to improve both full ANC and safe delivery in the southern Odisha, while full ANC needs to be triggered in the developed districts.

References

Bhatia, J.C. and J. Cleland. (1995). "Determinants of Maternal Care in A Region of South India", *Health Transition Review,* 5(2):127-142.

Elo, I.T. (1992). "Utilisation of Maternal Health-Care Services In Peru: The Role of Women's Education", *Health Transition Review* 2(1):46-49.

McCarthy, J., & Maine, D. (1992). "A Framework for Analysing the Determinants of Maternal Mortality", *Studies in Family Planning,* 23(1):23-33.

Mishra, U.S., T.K.Roy and Irudaya Rajan. (1998). "Antenatal Care and Contraceptive Behaviour in India: Some Evidence from NFHS", *The Journal of Family Welfare,* 44(2):1-14.

Navaneetham, K and A. Dharmalingam, (2000). "Utilisation of Maternal Health Care Services in South India", Unpublished paper of CDS.

Ramachandran, Prema. (1992). Need for Organisation of Antenatal Care and intra-Partum Care in India. *Demography in India,* 21(2):179-93.

Rao, P.S. and J. Richard. (1984). "Socio-economic and Demographic Correlates of Medical Care and Health Practices", *Journal of Biosocial Science* 16(3):343-55.

Registrar General of India. *Census of India 2011, Provisional Tables.*

Sample Registration System. (2006). *Maternal Mortality India-1997-2003: Trend, Cause and Risk Factor,* Registrar General of India.

Sample Registration System. (2008). *SRS Bulletin,* vol. 44(1), Registrar General of India

Sugathan, K.S., V. Mishra, and R.D. Retherford. (2001). *Promoting Institutional Deliveries in Rural India: The Role of Antenatal-Care Services,* National Family Health Survey Subject Report No.20, Mumbai: International Institute for Population Studies, and Honolulu: East-West Center.

World Health Organization. (2011). *World Health Statistics*

Health Status of Tribes in Odisha: Reflection on Critical Issues and Problems

Sudhakar Patra & Kabita Kumari Sahu

Health is an important element and determinant of well-being of people in a society. Improved health is desirable to enhance the capabilities to work and to participate in economic development. Improved health and nutritional status also contribute to increase life expectancy by enhancing resistance to micro organisms. Good health may be thought of as an important livelihood asset and illness can be a major cause of impoverishment. In the context, every individual has the choice to lead a healthy and a reasonable life span and the state has to ensure this minimum requirement. The health of a Nation can best be judged by the health status of its people. General mortality, infant mortality and life expectancy at birth are considered as primary determinant in improving the health status. The development of health is a holistic process related to the overall growth and development of social, cultural, economic, educational, political and environmental factors. Health also depends on many supporting services such as water supply, sanitation, nutrition, public health and medical services and human resource development. Health policies are directly and indirectly influenced by the policies to these areas. Political forces/ ideology play a major role in determining the health policies of a state through decisions on resource allocations, manpower policies, choice of technology and degree to which health services are to be made available and accessible to the population.

Similarly, health is considered as a function not only of medical intervention but over all integrated development of a society. The value system, its philosophical and culture traditions and its social, political and economic organisations are increasingly related to the health of a society. The objectives of integrated development are to eliminate hunger and poverty, to spread education and enable poor, under privileged and particularly women and children to assert themselves. It is evident from the fact when the health situation of Odisha is analyzed with a closer looks. After almost half a decade of socialistic planning though substantial results have been achieved in terms of aggregate economic growth, at the same time these had admittedly been a relative, if unintended, neglect of social and human development as evident from evidence of emphasis on material resources and services infrastructure. Most specifically the health situation of the state remains unrelentingly depressing irrespective of organised activities and efforts.

India is the seventh largest country in the world and the second most populous country after China. A large part of its population lives on less than Rs 100/ a day. The standards of living and hygiene is very unsatisfactory, especially in rural areas. All these reasons, coupled with a sub tropical climate, make India a hot bed for diseased people. It is not just the poor who suffer but the rich suffers too. However, the difference is that the rich have money and therefore can afford expensive medical but the poor people have nowhere to go. At a time when medical costs are rising worldwide, India is emerging as a popular medical tourism destination for its relatively low cost and better success rates. However, it is a kind of paradox that the health care services still remain out of reach not only for the poor, but also the middle class people. Compounding the problem is the paltry number of beds and qualified doctors available to provide treatment. There are 178.7 hospital beds per 1,00,000 people in the urban areas, and an astonishingly low 9.87 beds per 1,00,000 people in rural areas.

Health infrastructure promotion and financing are the centre piece of capacity-building efforts in Odisha and India. It is essential to emphasize on quality-improvement on health promotion infrastructure and financing. There is a strong emphasis on sustainable financing in health sector for rising population in India. The investment in health in India was 3.33 percent of total budgetary expenditure in first V year plan which decreased to 3.01 percent in second plan, 2.63 percent in third plan, 2.13 percent in fourth plan, 1.93 percent in fifth plan, 1.87 percent in sixth plan, 1.69 percent in seventh plan, 0.6 percent in ninth plan and increased to 2.9 percent in tenth plan in India and family welfare expenditure increased but remained within 2 percent from 1951 to 2009. The health expenditure as percentage of GDP is above 8 percent in Australia, Brazil, Canada, France, Germany, Italy, South Africa but it is less than 5 percent in India, Bangladesh (3.8 percent), Nigeria (2.2 percent), Thailand (3.7 percent), and Uganda (3.9 percent). Surprisingly USA spends 13 percent of GDP on health. So developed countries spend a higher proportion on health infrastructure than LDCs. Health insurance coverage is substantially higher in DCs than LDCs and it is extremely low in India. Private health expenditure as percent of total health expenditure is 82 percent in India but it is 63 percent in Bangladesh, 59 percent in Brazil, 63 percent in Chin, 77 percent in Pakistan, 56 percent in USA. In India the percentage of Public expenditure is marginally increasing over time.

Odisha is abundantly rich in mineral and natural resources. It's cultural and social status are quite advanced. The people though diverse in caste, creed and religion enjoy a common principle of peaceful living in comparison to other states. It is increasingly ironic that in spite of development planning and fair utilization of both available human and material resources the pace of progress is somewhat not encouraging as desired. The vital statistics which are the basic yardsticks of measuring health, only except a few present a sordid picture of our development. Though we are in better position statistically in some of the National average, rate and ratio, however, the basic indicators of health, viz, infant mortality and maternal mortality remain high and Odisha occupies a dubious distinction in the health scenario of the country. In spite of our sincere and concerted attempt we do fail to yield the optimum result. It may be attributed to a series of factors.

Tribes in Odisha

Tribes live in forests, hills and isolated regions that are the most neglected section of the society. The problem of land alienation, exploitation, migration, bonded labour and deprivation are serious issues of tribes in India. Education and health status of tribals is very low compared to other sections of our society. Since the tribes are primarily forest dwellers, their productivity is very low which leads to poverty, unemployment, illiteracy, low standard of consumption and living. Odisha is a less developed state where the standard and status of tribals is relatively adverse. In this context the paper seeks to analyze the education and health status of tribes in Odisha.

The main tribes of the Odisha are Khadia, Mahali, Bathudi,Bhuyan, Munda, Kolha and Santhal .Even though there are minor cultural differences in rituals, clothing and food habit, the referred tribes are illiterate and superstitious, live in villages and have a patriarchal culture. The concentration of Bathudi is more in the Northern parts of Odisha particularly in the areas bordering the districts of Mayurbhanj and Keonjhar. They live in houses made of mud walls and thatched roofs.. They speak Oriya as their mother tongue. Munda tribe mainly inhabit in the region of Jharkhand, although they are well spread in the states of West Bengal, Chattisgarh, Odisha and Bihar. The common surnames used among the Mundas includes Topno, Bala, Aind, Hemrom, Guria, Herenge, Surin, Horo, Sanaga and Samad. Christianity is the main religion followed among the Mundas. The Mundas have their own religion known as Sarana. Sarana stress on the belief of one God. Mundas have remained hunters for centuries. But now they have been converted into settled agriculturists. Most of them don't have land of their own. They largely depend on the labor work in the fields of others to earn their livelihood. They have a separate language of their own but most of them use Oriya, Hindi as a subsidiary language.

The majority of Kolhas follow Hindu customs and rites. But they hold the Sajana tree, Paddy and the dog in special veneration. The Santal form a niche in the great museum of races in India and being one of the Pre-Dravidian tribes of the central belt of India. They live along with other tribes. The Santals have got their own dialect known as Santali which is said to be one of the oldest languages of India. The Santal society is well known for its division into 12 clans, the names of which are occasionally used as surnames such as Hansdah, murmu, Kisku, Hembrum, Baskey, Besra, Tudu, Soren, Marandi, Dandkar, Paunria and Chapiar.

Tribal Health Status in Odisha

The World Health Organisation (WHO) defines health as a State of complete physical, mental and social wellbeing and not merely the absence of disease or infirmity. The Article 21 of the Indian constitution requires that the State Government should ensure Health & Nutrition to all people. The health status in terms of health indicators and infrastructural availability is very poor in a less developed state like Odisha. The human development index of Odisha stands at 0.404 as compared to All India Human Development Index at 0.602 as per the human development report 2005. Despite substantial progress in the field of curative and preventive health, the substantial part of tribal population is suffering from serious health hazards. There are 635 tribal communities including 75 primitive tribal communities living in India. They constitute about 22.3 percent of State population of Odisha. There is consensus agreement among the researchers and academicians that the Health status of tribal population is worst because of their isolation , remoteness, and largely unaffected by the developmental process going on in our country. Several research studies have revealed that distinct health problems of tribals are governed by multi dimensional factors like their habitat, difficult terrain, illiteracy, poverty, isolation, superstition and deforestation. The Primary occupation of tribals are hunting, shifting cultivation to settle agriculture and rural crafts. The health status of tribals is also lower than other social groups in terms of infant mortality rate, fertility rate, nutrition and nourishment.

A majority of tribals need healthcare on account of malnutrition, lack of safe drinking water, poor hygiene, environmental sanitation and poverty. Although tribals live in close proximity with nature, mal nutrition and under nutrition are common among them who largely depend upon food which either they gather or raise by using simple methods. The poor nutritional status of women directly influences their reproductive performance and their infant survival, growth and development. Odisha Health Strategy 2003 has strongly recommended for improving the health status of tribal population by substantially reducing mortality and morbidity. The tribal people in Odisha and Mayurbhanj mostly suffer from malaria, tuberculosis, genetic disorders, sickle cell anemia and nutritional deficiency diseases. The health indicators of tribal population in Odisha are far below the national average. The infant mortality rate is 84.2 , under-five mortality rate is 126.6 , children underweight is 55.9 and anemia in children is 79.8 per 1000 . The children with acute respiratory infection is 22.4, women with anemia is 64.9 per thousand. The high incidence of malnutrition is also found in tribal dominated districts of Odisha, like Koraput, Bolangir, Phulbani, Sundargarh, Mayurbhanj and Malkangiri. National nutrition monitoring bureau (NNMB) has covered Odisha among 10 States and its report states that Odisha has second highest level of under nutrition among the 10 states . The chronic energy deficiency in adult men and women is highest in Odisha compared to 10 States. The malnutrition among the tribals leading to death is also highest in our State. The highest mortality rate among the tribes may be attributed due to infectious diseases. A study conducted in Bondo , Juanga and Kutia Kondha tribes of Odisha reveals that there is severe malnutrition upto 26.6 percent of population. The tribal population of Mayurbhanj and Sundargarh districts suffers more from malnutrition.

Current Scenario of Tribal Health in Odisha

Tribal health status is worse compared to scheduled caste and general population. Infant mortality for tribes is 78.7 where as it is only 65 for Odisha and 57 for general caste population. Under five mortality is 136.6 for tribes where as it is only 64.2 for general population. Similarly underweight is 54.4 for tribes which is highest compared to other groups. (Table 8.1)

Table 8.1: Health Characteristics of Tribes and other Social Groups in Odisha

Region/ Group	*Child mortality*	*Under 5 mortality*	*Anaemia (<11.0g/)*	*Stunted (height for age)*	*Wasting (weight for height)*	*Under- (weight for age)*
India	57	74	70	48.0	19.8	42.5
Odisha	65	91	65	45.0	19.5	40.7
Sc	73.7	91.8	63.5	49.7	19.7	44.4
ST	78.7	136.6	80.1	57.2	27.6	54.4
Others	53.1	64.2	58.2	33.6	12.8	26.4

Source: Govt. of Odisha. *Tribal health*, 2010-11

Odisha comprises of a total 118 tribal RCH sub-plan blocks. The vulnerability scoring states that there are 50 most difficult blocks out of which there are 46 most difficult tribal blocks. Our main focus is the tribal blocks in the most difficult areas. Apart from the difficult and inaccessible geographical locations, left wing's extremists act as hurdles in catering to the healthcare services. This also reflects into poor perceived health seeking behavior, resulting in poor utilization to healthcare services in tribal communities. These are also the reasons associated in poor institutional delivery and RCH outcomes as a whole. Maternity Waiting Homes are operational in Malkangiri and Gajapati. Institutional delivery against expected delivery in the year 09 - 10 in Malkangiri and Gajapati has reached from 35 to 37 and from 38 to 42 respectively. Establishment of other maternity homes in Rayagada, Koraput, Kandhamal, Nowrangpur and Nuapada districts are in process. Tribal Health Camps are being organised across all focused tribal districts to create increased awareness on health services on quarterly basis. Magico Religiuos Healers Meet is being organized to bring traditional healers into the mainstream of health care system, and also to act as an agent in improving health seeking behavior and utility pattern of health services.

Distribution of Scheduled Tribe Population in Odisha

Odisha has the second largest tribal population in India in terms of absolute size next to Madhya Pradesh. In percentage term, it has the highest tribal concentration in its population. As per the 2001 census tribal population is 22.13 percent of the total population in the state. As per Census data from 1981 to 2001 their decadal growth rate declined from 22.43 percent to 22.13 percent. It has also the largest variety of ethnic groups numbering 62 tribal races next only to Assam. More than one third of the area of the state is declared as "Scheduled area" with not less than 50% concentration of tribes. These areas include the entire district of Koraput, Mayurbhanj, Sundargarh and parts of Ganjam and Boudh, Kandhamal. The extent of this area is 68.579 sq.kms. Thus the tribal population in the state is spread over more than 44 percent of its geographical area. The details of tribal population in different district of Odisha are given in Table 8.2

Table 8.2: District wise distribution of Scheduled Tribe Population in Odisha in 2001

Sl.No	*State/ District*	*Total Population ('000 nos)*	*ST Population(in nos)*			*Percentage of ST population*
			Total	*Male*	*Female*	
	Odisha	36,804	8,145,081	4,066,783	4,078,298	22.1
1	Mayurbhanj	2,223	1,258,459	631,149	627,310	56.6
2	Sundargarh	1831	918,903	458,815	460,088	50.2
3	Keonjhar	1562	695,141	348,666	346,475	44.5
4	Koraput	1181	585,830	290,306	295,524	49.6
5	Nowrangpur	1026	564,480	282,472	282,008	55.0
6	Rayagada	831	463,418	224,908	238,510	55.8
7	Kalahandi	1335	382,573	188,646	193,927	28.6
8	Kandhamal	648	336,809	166,283	170,526	52.0
9	Sambalpur	936	322,770	161,756	161,014	34.5
10	Malkangiri	504	289,538	143,498	146,040	57.4

Table contd...

11	Balangir	1337	275,822	137,442	138,380	20.6
12	Gajapati	519	263,476	128,679	134,797	50.8
13	Bargarh	1346	260,691	131,145	129,546	19.4
14	Balasore	2024	228,454	116,193	112,261	11.3
15	Nuapada	531	184,221	90,901	93,320	34.7
16	Jharsuguda	510	159,757	80,760	78,997	31.3
17	Dhenkanal	1067	136,501	69,356	67,145	12.8
18	Angul	1140	132,994	67,386	65,608	11.7
19	Jajpur	1624	125,989	64,198	61,791	7.8
20	Khurda	1877	97,186	50,431	46,755	5.2
21	Deogarh	274	92,103	45,961	46,142	33.6
22	Ganjam	3161	90,919	45,843	45,076	2.9
23	Cuttack	2341	83,591	42,800	40,791	3.6
24	Sonpur	542	52,978	26,786	26,192	9.8
25	Nayagarh	864	50,836	25,778	25,058	5.9
26	Boudh	373	46,557	23,276	23,281	12.5
27	Bhadrak	1334	25,141	12,839	12,302	1.9
28	Jagatsinghpur	1058	8,640	4,605	4,035	0.8
29	Kendrapara	1302	6,822	3,550	3,272	0.5
30	Puri	1503	4,482	2,355	2,127	0.3

Source: Government of India. *Census of India, 2001*

As per the 2001 census data, Mayurbhanj has the second largest ST population i.e. 56.6 percent following Malkangiri with 57.4 percent. Puri has lowest percentage of ST population that is only 0.3 percent .In 2001, the population of Mayurbhanj district was 2,22,3456. Population growth was particularly sharp over the last two decades since 1981, when the district population increased rapidly from its 1981 level of 1,58,1873 to 1,88,4580 in 1991. This was indicating that the acceleration in population growth was and much the consequence of new migration as of high local birth rates.

Health and Human Development Index in Odisha

Human development refers to the process of widening the choices of people as well as the achieved levels of their wellbeing. It emphasizes on the building up of human capabilities through human health, knowledge and use of acquired capabilities for work. (UNDP 1990). It focuses on the three essential elements of human life such as longevity, knowledge and decent living standards. Three essential dimensions of human development are as follows:

(i) Ordinary citizens must have rights to participate in normal economic, social and political activities without discrimination.

(ii) There is need to enhance capabilities and expand opportunities of each citizen.

(iii) The removal of economic and social conditions of deprivation is necessary for a broad based equitable enhancement of capabilities and expansion of opportunities.

The overall HDI of a country / state reveals that different states and region have different levels of human development for which states specific policy can be framed and implemented. Human development, health and education index of tribals is very low in Odisha and particularly in tribal dominated Districts. Table 8.3 shows the human development index, education and health index in all districts of the State. The human development index of Odisha is 0.579 which is much lower than the HDI of India & many other states. The pattern and extent of variation in respect of HDI, EI, HI & GDI in different districts are shown in Table 8.3.

The health index in tribal dominated districts is 0.106 in Kandhamal (30th Position), 0.122 in Malkangiri (29th Position) and 0.173 in Gajapati (28th position) which shows adverse health scenario among tribes. The human development index is highest in Khurda district which is developed region and the state capital, Bhubaneswar is situated in it. It has highest education index, 4th rank in health index and 5th rank in gender development index.

Table 8.3 provides detail value & ranks of EOI, HI, GDI which have positive co-relation among them. Jagatsingpur, Puri and Kendrapara secure 2nd, 3rd and 4th rank in education index because they are all developed costal districts of the state. Malkangiri has the lowest EI and GDI rank and second lowest in HI ranks indicating extreme backwardness in health, education and gender discrimination. The trend reveals that tribal dominated districts in southern and western Odisha have low HDI, EI, HI and GDI compared to costal districts.

Table 8.3: Health and Human Development Index in Odisha in 2001

Sl.	Districts	HDI.	HDI Rank.	EI.	EI Rank.	HI	HI Rank	GDI	GDI Rank
1	Angul	0.663	06	0.760	12	0.481	12	0.637	04
2	Balangir	0.546	21	0.666	21	0.468	14	0.518	16
3	Balasore	0.559	18	0.770	10	0.442	10	0.519	14
4	Baragarh	0.565	17	0.727	16	0.449	17	0.528	13
5	Bhadrak	0.646	08	0.803	06	0.673	08	0.497	21
6	Boudh	0.536	23	0.688	20	0.423	20	0.509	19
7	Cuttack	0.695	03	0.813	05	0.686	07	0.618	07
8	Deogarh	0.669	05	0.698	19	0.776	02	0.647	03
9	Dhenkanal	0.591	12	0.773	09	0.468	15	0.531	12
10	Gajapati	0.431	28	0.561	26	0.173	28	0.401	27
11	Ganjam	0.551	20	0.718	17	0.404	21	0.518	15
12	Jagatsinghpur	0.557	19	0.833	02	0.288	25	0.491	22
13	Jajpur	0.540	22	0.786	07	0.333	24	0.386	28
14	Jharsuguda	0.722	02	0.773	08	0.635	09	0.687	01
15	Kalahandi	0.606	11	0.585	24	0.763	03	0.579	08
16	Kandhamal	0.389	29	0.645	23	0.106	30	0.372	29
17	Kendrapara	0.626	10	0.815	04	0.596	11	0.516	18
18	Keonjhar	0.530	24	0.704	18	0.340	22	0.504	20
19	Khurda	0.736	01	0.845	01	0.724	04	0.632	05
20	Koraput	0.431	27	0.535	27	0.218	27	0.415	26
21	Malkangiri	0.370	30	0.491	30	0.122	29	0.362	30
22	Mayurbhanj	0.639	09	0.647	22	0.782	01	0.621	06
23	Nowrangpur	0.436	26	0.516	29	0.340	23	0.422	25
24	Nayagarh	0.571	15	0.766	11	0.462	16	0.452	23
25	Nuapara	0.581	14	0.582	25	0.692	05	0.561	09
26	Puri	0.657	07	0.823	03	0.622	10	0.516	17
27	Rayagada	0.443	25	0.531	28	0.250	26	0.428	24
28	Sambalpur	0.589	13	0.742	13	0.436	19	0.560	10
29	Sonepur	0.566	16	0.731	15	0.474	13	0.543	11
30	Sundargarh	0.683	04	0.740	14	0.692	06	0.659	02
	Odisha	0.579	-	0.723	-	0.468	-	0.546	

Source: Govt. of Odisha, *Human Development Report*. PP. 281- 312

UNDP has categorized human development into high HDI as above 0.8, medium as between 0.5 to 0.8, low as between 0.4 and 0.5 and lowest as below 0.4. None of the districts In Odisha falls under the category of high HDI category of UNDP i.e. above 0.8. The present study has categorized human development into high HDI as above 0.6, medium as between 0.5 and 0.6 and low as below 0.5. Eleven districts have HDI value above 0.6 with Jharsuguda, Cuttack and Sundargarh securing 2nd, 3rd and 4th position with HDI values of 0.722, 0.695 and 0683 due to rapid industrialization. 13 districts have medium values of HDI between 0.5 and 0.6. There are six tribal dominated districts like Malkangiri, Kandhamal, Gajapati, Koraput, Nabarangpur and Rayagada having HDI less than 0.5 (Table 8.4). In Malkangiri has the lowest HDI of 0.370 which is least developed & naxalite affected area. These six districts are situated in southern part of state with majority tribal population and forest area.

Table 8.4:Levels of Human Development

Districts	*Levels of HD*
Khurda, Jharsuguda, Cuttack, Sundargarh, Deogarh, Angul, Puri, Bhadrak, Mayurbhanj, Kendrapara, Kalahandi (11)	High (> 0.6)
Dhenkanal, Sambalpur, Nuapada, Nayagarh, Sonpur, Bargarh, Balasore, Jagatsinghpur, Ganjam, Bolangir, Boudh, Keonjhar (12)	Medium (>0.5 & <0.6)
Rayagada, Nowrangpur, Koraput, Gajapati, Kandhamal, Malkangiri	Low (< 0.5)

There are many studies which indicate adverse health indicators for the tribes of Odisha in comparison to that of All Odisha and India. The demography data of Juanga tribes of Odisha revealed that the life expectancy at birth is only 35.9 years. The Unhygienic and primitive practices are mainly responsible for high maternal mortality among tribe. Malaria is the most important public health problem among the tribes of Odisha contributing 50 percent of malaria deaths in the country. More than 60 percent of tribal population of Odisha lives in high risk malaria area in the state. The tribes contribute 25 percent of total malaria cases in the state even if they constitute only 8 percent of the total population. Various epidemiology studies and malariometric survey carried out in tribal population indicate that there is high transmission of P. Falciferum in the forest regions of India and Odisha which is not attainable under health service of Govt. due to technical and operational problems. The tribal districts are more prone and endemic for malaria due to forest and hills and lack of health awareness. The respiratory disease is commonly prevalent among the tribes which account for a high infant mortality due to inadequate vaccination and lack of early diagnosis and prevention. This disease is 14.9 percent in percent Bondo, 13.6 percent in Kanda, 8.3 percent in Juango and 16.6 percent in Didayi. The infant mortality rate is high among tribals due to high incidence of respiratory infection especially among infants and children. Another major health problem among the tribes in Odisha is the skin problem like scabies mainly due to overcrowding and unhygienic living conditions and lack of health awareness. A research study made by Regional Medical Research Centre, Bhubaneswar reveals that 20.6 percent of Bond, 10.7 percent of Juango and 15 percent of Kuta Kandha tribes are affected by scabies. Other communicable diseases like Tuberculosis, Leprosy and Veneral diseases are commonly found in several major tribe population of Odisha. Sickle cell gene is widely prevalent among the tribal population of this state. Thalassaemia also contributes significantly to the health problems of tribes in Odisha. Intestinal parasitism is another major health problem in tribes of the state. About 44.6 percent of Bondo, 31.9 percent of Juanga and 41.1 percent of Kandha suffer from this health problem. Water bone communicable diseases like gastrointestinal disorder including acute diarrhea is very high among the tribals in Odisha. Poor sanitation unhygienic condition of living and lack of safe drinking water in the tribal area in the State is mainly responsible for the diarrheal diseases including cholera.

Suggestions and Conclusion

There is a consensus agreement that the health status of the tribal population is very poor and it is worst among the primitive tribes because of their isolation, remoteness and being largely unaffected by the developmental processes going on in the country. It is clear that the tribes in Odisha are suffering from many diseases and health problems relative to other social groups. Since they live in remote areas in forest and hills, it is not possible to provide them adequate health facilities. The following suggestions are put forward to improve the health status and proper management of health service in tribal area of Odisha.

(a) The primary health services and other health related services like nutrition, water and sanitation should be scaled and improved through participatory planning process involving the State Government, Panchayat raj institution, NGO and community representative.

(b) The private sector should encourage providing better health services and they should be encouraged to create a win-win situation. Health related intervention should be based on local needs aiming to reduce health disparities and improve service delivery.

(c) The regional and local plans on health services should address both supply side and demand side constraints keeping in view the location and geographic area requirement.

(d) The state Government should facilitate the growth of private, social and community insurance to improve affordability among the tribals in Odisha.

(e) Promoting demand side financing will help the targeted poor and tribals since resources will be transferred to beneficiaries to improve the accessibility.

(f) The self-help groups and Panchayat Raj institutions should be encouraged to deal with emergency transport facility for serious tribal patient and pregnant women in remote rural areas.

(g) The nurses, mid wives, health assistance and pharmacists should be trained properly to work in tribal areas.

It may be concluded that health and economic development are very closely related specially in tribal area of Odisha. Rapid economic growth of the state is not possible without improving the quality of life of the tribes of the state. The wide spread poverty, illiteracy, malnutrition, absence of safe drinking water and sanitary condition are responsible for higher maternal and child mortality rate among the tribes of the state. Ineffective coverage of National Health and Nutritional services is found in tribal areas which contribute to dismal health condition. Many of the infectious and parasitic diseases can be prevented by timely intervention, health awareness among the tribes. The health care delivery services among tribal people are still poor which need to strengthened to achieve the real goal of health in Odisha.

References

Balgir, R.S. (1998). Physical Growth , Health and Nutritional Status of Ashram School Children, Annual Report School Children, Annual Report, Regional Medical Research Centre, Bhaubaneswar ,PP-37 .

Basu, S.K. (1994). "Health Problems and Health care of the Tribal Population of India," in N. Mahanti (ed.), *Tribal Economy, Health and Wasteland Development,* Inter-India publications .New Delhi, PP-137.

Bulliya, G., Mohapatra, S.S.S., Kerketta, A.S. and Nayak, R.N. (2000). Assessment of Health and Nutritional Profile among Elderly Population of Odisha Primitive Tribes. Annual Report, Regional Medical Research Centre, Bhubaneswar, p.40,

Chakrabarty S, G Shukla and C.P. Suresh. (2007). "Tribal Welfare and Development in India," *Kurukshetra,* Vol 56, November, PP- 33-39

Government of Odisha. (2002). *Annual Reports,* Directorate of Health Services, Bhubaneswar.

Govt. of Odisha: Odisha Vision (2010). A Health Strategy - Odisha State Integrated Health Policy, Strategies and Action Points. Health and Family Welfare Department, 2003

Indian Council of Medical Research (1998). *Health of Tribal Population in India: Results of Some ICMR Studies,* New Delhi.

Panda, P.K. (2002). "Health Status of Odisha," A Background Paper for the Human Development of Odisha, Submitted to the Human Development Resource Centre, UND, New Delhi, May 6.

Pati, S. (2004). "Health Services in Odisha at Cross Roads," *Odisha Economic Journal,* Vol. XXXVI, PP.138-143.

Patra S. (1997). "Consumption Pattern of Tribals of Phulbani District of Odisha," in S.N. Tripathy (ed.), *Tribal Labour in India,* New Delhi: Mohit Publication, PP- 117-154.

Psachara P. George. (1988). "Education and Development: A Review," *The World Bank Research Observer,* 3(1), Jan., PP. 99-116.

Rizvi, S.N.H. (1989). "Health Practices of the Jaunsaris – A Socio-Cultural Analysis," in B. Chaudhuri (ed.), *Tribal Health: Socio–Cultural Dimensions,* New Delhi: Inter-India Publications, p.85.

Roy, A.K. and E.A. Rath. (1991). "Indian Tribal Fertility Patterns from Odisha", *Man in India,* PP- 235.

Dutt, Tara. (2001). *Tribal Development in India – with Special Reference to Odisha,* New Delhi: Gyan Publishing House, PP. 55-90.

Tripathy, S.N. ((1997). "Tribals in India: Problems and Policies," in *Tribal Labour in India,* New Delhi: Mohit Publication, PP. 48 – 56.

Health Status of Tribes in Odisha: A matter of Concern

Bijaya Kumar Panda

Introduction

Removal of regional disparities has been one of the important development strategies adopted by the Government of Odisha during the successive Five-Year Plans. However, due to several economic, social and institutional obstacles, all the regions in Odisha have not shared the gains of development in an equitable manner. Some regions continue to languish in abject poverty with poor health status. The district of Kandhamal forms one such region where incidence of poverty is one of the highest (71.4 percent) and health status is very poor among the districts of the state. This pocket of southern Odisha is also socially and economically depressed (Panda and Sarangi, 2004 and Hann and Dubey 2005)[1]. Heavy incidence and persistence of poverty and poor health status in this region has been a cause of concern for the State Government as well as the Government of India.

Odisha has the highest infant mortality rate in the country which is 98 per 1000 live births (Sample Registration System 1998) as against the all India average of 64. This translates into 95,000 infant deaths in the state every year. The main causes of infant death are due to low birth weight, diarrhea, pneumonia, malnutrition, birth injury etc. Maternal mortality rate is also the highest which is 740 per 100000 live births. Anemia, malnutrition and sepsis are the main reasons of maternal deaths. Malnutrition among children and mothers is rampant across the state and particularly it is more pronounced in the tribal areas. About 53 percent of children under four years of age suffer from malnutrition, of which 23 percent are severely undernourished. Young children aged 12-23 months are most vulnerable to malnutrition, with over two-thirds (68 percent) of children are suffering from moderate to severe malnutrition (UNICEF 2000). The crude death rate in the state is also the highest (10.4 percent) as against the all India average of 8.1 percent (Census 2001). Infectious and parasite disease account for more than 20 percent, and diseases of nervous system, respiratory system and digestive system accounts for another 20 percent while diseases like circulatory system itself accounts for nearly 20 percent of all deaths. Peri-natal deaths account for as much as 13 percent of all deaths (HDR, GoO, 2004).

Kandhamal, a tribal-infested hilly plateau, is one of the backward districts of the state. The plateau of Kandhamal is at a higher altitude with the height ranging from1700 feet to 3500 feet above the sea level. It is replete with undulating terrains, sharp gorges and rivers, hilly tracts, forests and inaccessible areas. The tribes of Kandhamal are the aboriginal or indigenous people of the state. They are called as the 'Kondh' representing one of the oldest ethnological group and are the original inhabitants of the district. Tribal communities are very backward and primitive with distinct tracts. They constitute the disadvantaged and vulnerable section of the society. These people inhabit in inaccessible jungle and hilly areas. The very nature of the economy is primitive, subsistence and stagnant. Their food is deficient in quantity and quality (Panda and Sarangi 2004).

In Kandhamal, the tribals are susceptible to a number of epidemic diseases, especially the children suffer from malnutrition and related diseases. Many tribal children die of malnutrition. Infant mortality rate is as high as 169 per thousand births. Malnutrition occurs owing to protein-calorie deficiency (HDR, GoO, 2004). The growth of children gets stunted and they become easily susceptible to various diseases. Because of unhygienic living, lack of health consciousness, ignorance and inadequate medical facility and above all, owing to low economic status, the tribals fall easy prey to killer diseases like malaria, meningitis etc. Sometimes the epidemic of meningitis takes a heavy toll of lives. Malaria also causes havoc taking a sizeable number of lives of the people. The sexually transmitted diseases like yaws and syphilis, skin diseases like scabies and anaemia etc. occur. In the event of illness the tribals do not prefer to consult doctors rather they take recourse to sorcery or *gunia* (village priests). The lack of health awareness accompanied with superstitions results in poor health for the tribals. Further, the habit of drinking saps all energy and vitality of the tribal people (Pothal 2005). This is evident from the lowest health index of 0.468 and reproductive index of 0.462 (HDR, GoO, 2004) in Kandhamal district. Under this backdrop, the study is an attempt to assess the health status and the extent of access to the available health care facilities by the tribals in Kandhamal district of southern Odisha.

Objectives of the Study

Some of the main objectives of this study are as follows:

1. To explore the living standards and problems of the tribals to know the social and regional dimensions of health status in southern Odisha.
2. To ascertain the nature of health services provided at secondary and tertiary level in term of infrastructure, personnel and quality of care provided to the tribals in the state.
3. To assess the general health condition of the tribals in the state vis-à-vis in the sample villages of Kandhamal district.

4. To examine the level of access to and utilization of available public health care facilities by the tribal and their quality of life.

Methodology

The study is based both on primary and secondary data. The secondary data sources of the study are the published information of Sample Registration System (SRS) Bulletin, National Family Health Survey-2 (NFHS-2), Human Development Reports and other reports. The National Family Health Survey provides information on a variety of health and nutritional indicators by levels of income, social class, education etc. to examine the social and regional inequality in health and nutritional status. To supplement the findings of the study, primary data have been collected from 218 households by census method from three sample villages, namely, Sunaponga, Munisigam and Khajurisahi in Tikabali Block of Kandhamal district of Odisha through a field survey conducted during the period from December 2004 to March 2005. All the three villages are purposively selected on the basis of concentration of tribal (ST) population and geographical location. Out of the three sample villages, Munisigaon is the largest village which is situated about 9 km away from the State Highway. The village consists of 115 households, out of which 72 (63 percent) are ST households, 29 (25 percent) are SC households and the rest 14 (12 percent) households are 'other' (or general) households. The sample village, Sonaponga, is situated at the foothills of hilly and mountainous terrain surrounded by forest, and is about 12 km away from the State Highway. It consists of 62 households out of which 42 (68 percent) are ST households, 15 (24 percent) are SC households and the remaining 2 (8 percent) are 'others' households. The other sample village, Khajurisahi is situated very close (2 km) to the State Highway. It has 41 households consisting of 18 ST (44 percent), 21 SC (51 percent) and 2 'others' (5 percent) households. Higher concentration of SC households as compared to ST households is found in this village.

Some Indicators of Health Status

Health can be seen as an important determinant of well-being in the broadest sense of the term. Improved health is desirable to enhance the capability to work and to participate in economic activities. Improved health and nutritional status also contribute to increased life expectancy. Good health may be thought of as an important livelihood asset and illness can be a major cause of impoverishment. In this context, every individual is supposed to lead a healthy life with a reasonable life span and the state is expected to ensure this minimum requirement. Despite this majority of the tribals in Kandhamal lack access to public healthcare facilities and their quality of life is poor (Pothal 2005).

Infant Mortality Rate of Tribals

The infant and child mortality rates are the important indicators of overall health status of a population. It is the most important indicator illustrating the level of human development of a nation or state. IMR below 10 indicates a high level of development and Kerala with an IMR of 14 is the only state which is approaching this level. Infant mortality rate continues to be the highest in Odisha followed by Madhya Pradesh, Uttar Pradesh and Rajasthan. The IMR was 100.2 in rural areas, 66 in urban areas and 96.7 for rural-urban combine in Odisha. It is higher for males (97.3) and little lower for females (96) in the state.2 It has declined by 25 percent i.e. at a rate of 1.6 percent per annum during the period from 1981-83 to 1995-97. The relative slow decline in IMR of the state can be partly explained in different components of IMR like neo-natal mortality rate (NNMR), peri-natal mortality rate (PNMR) and the Still Birth Rate (SBR). The figures for different components of IMR for the state in 1998-99 were 60 for NNMR, 61 for PNMR and 17 for SBR (SRS Bulletin, 2001). NNMR constituted 62.5 percent, PNMR constituted 63.5 percent and SBR constituted 17 percent of the IMR in the state. The state performs low in these indicators due to poor availability of professional attendants at birth, high percentage of low birth weight babies, lack of professional post-natal care and early marriage of girls.

Infant mortality rate and child mortality rate are also very high among the tribals in Orissa. In the sample villages, the average age at marriage is 15 years for ST girls and 16 years for SC and 'other' girls. But the age at marriage is 18 years for ST boys and 20 years for SC and 'other' boys. Marriage of girls at early age result in greater number of births and pregnancy complications which in turn cause high infant mortality rate. In Kandhamal more than 50 percent of girls get married before the age of 18 years. In addition to this, the other factors responsible for high IMR in the district are child malnutrition. Protein-calorie deficiency, superstitious beliefs, illiteracy, and ignorance give rise to defective antenatal and postnatal care. Sonaponga and Munisigaon villages do not have access to medical facilities. Children die of fatal diseases in the event of absence of preventive and curative measures and treatment at the doorstep.

Child Health and Child Mortality Rate

The child mortality rate (0-4 years) has shown a declining trend. The under-5 mortality rate and child mortality rate for the tribal population is about 19.6 percent and 52.7 percent higher than the corresponding figures for the state. The tribal children generally suffer from three common childhood diseases like respiratory infections, diarrhea and fever. It is surprising to note that the percentage of children suffering from the above three diseases was lower (21.2 percent) for ST population as compared to SC (48.1 percent) in the state of Odisha.

Women's Health

The health status of tribal women is not much worse when compared to their counterparts of other disadvantaged social group (SC) and the general population. However, the incidence of anemia among tribal women (74.7 percent) is significantly higher than SC women (66.3 percent) and the general category women (54.4 percent). It is 54.4 percent for all women in the total population. There are two indicators of maternal health viz., extent of antenatal check-up and delivery care. Around 37 percent of the tribal women do not have any antenatal checkup which is much higher than SC women (17.7 percent) and general category women (14.6 percent). It is 23.3 percent for all women in the total population. The percentage of tribal women who have undergone professional antenatal checkup is also much lower (30.7 percent) than SC women (51.3 percent) and women belonging to general category (77.1 percent). It is 66.1 percent for all women in the state. While institutional delivery is as low as (22.7 percent) in the state, it is much lower for tribal women (8.7 percent). Similarly, professional assistance during delivery is only 26.1 percent in case tribal women as against 42.3 percent for SC women and 56.6 percent for all women.

Incidence of Morbidity

It is generally noticed that there is an inverse relationship between overall mortality rate and the incidence of morbidity rate. With decline in mortality rate, life expectancy increases and the chance of survival improve; the propensity to fall increases more or less proportionally with the mortality rate (Johnsson 1991). Conversely, at a high mortality rate, morbidity rate tends to be less. In Odisha morbidity rate is significantly higher as compared to its neighbouring states like Bihar and Madhya Pradesh. It is 24.20 in rural areas and 24.38 in urban areas. The same is true for chronic ailment which is 2781 for rural areas and 2312 for urban areas per one lakh people.

Malaria, tuberculosis, gastroenteritis and vaccine preventable diseases have significantly contributed to morbidity. The state has witnessed about 62.8 percent of all malaria deaths in the country (NMEP Report 1999). There is also a marked endemic nature of malaria noticed in the districts of Kandhamal, Keonjhar, Sundargarh and Mayurbhanj. These four districts account for 50 percent of all PF malaria cases and 40 percent of the malaria deaths.

Tuberculosis also remains a major public health problem in the state. The prevalence rate of tuberculosis is 1.76 per 1000 persons in 2000-01. In 2003, the reporting cases of severe diarrhea were 1,44,672 resulting in 513 deaths with case fatality rate of 0.35 percent. The two major diseases malaria and tuberculosis have been a cause of concern for the state government. Apart from these, filariasis, leprosy, corneal blindness and goiter are the other major public health problems in Odisha.

The incidence of morbidity is high among the tribals in the state in general and in Kandhamal district in particular. To be specific the diseases from which the tribals suffer are malaria, meningitis, sickle-cell anaemia, anaemia, sexually transmitted diseases (STD), tuberculosis, various skin diseases, liver diseases etc. The causes for the occurrence of such diseases are: (i) malaria is due to the prevalence of high mosquito population, ignorance about sanitation, difficulty for DDT spray in inaccessible areas, illiteracy, superstitious belief, low economic status etc., (ii) sickle-cell anaemia, thalassemia, anaemia are due to hereditary-genetic causes, (iii) sexually-transmitted diseases (STDs) like syphilis, gonorrhea, yaws etc are owing to promiscuous sexual relations among the tribals, (iv) tuberculosis occurs because of low resistance of the body, low immunity status, ignorance, illiteracy, low economic status and superstitious beliefs, (v) skin diseases are due to the causes like uncleanliness, ignorance, illiteracy, unhygienic habitations, impure and insufficient water supply, low economic status, (vi) alcoholism, chronic ailing condition, and low economic status give rise to liver diseases.

In comparison to the females, the health condition of tribal males is worse. The male-folk are quite addicted to home-made liquor (made from Mahuwa flowers) and processed Salap[3]. Most of them suffer from diseases like chronic malaria, sexually transmitted diseases, anaemia, tuberculosis, scabies etc. They have low nutritional status. The health condition of the tribal females is little better than the males. However, they also suffer from low nutritional status. They are less alcoholic-addicted than men. Lack of adequate public healthcare facilities worsen the situation. Sorcery and the various kinds of herbs prescribed by the *gunia* (village priest) and quacks are the only means to fight against diseases.

Analysis of Health Status in the Sample Villages

Health status of the people in the sample villages of Kandhamal district presented in Table 9.1 reveals that 329 persons (26.2 percent of the sample population) were found to be in ill health. These persons are either suffering from diseases or are complaining of ill-health throughout the year. The health status of 501 persons (i.e. 39.9 percent of the sample population) was found to be moderately good. They are found to be suffering from diseases like malaria and other contagious diseases at least for a few days in a year. The remaining 426 persons (33.9 percent of the sample population) were found to be in good health. About 93 children (i.e. 26.42 percent of total children) in the age group of 1 to 14 are found to be in ill health and 148 children (40.05 percent of total children) are having moderately good health profile. For the other 111 children, which constitute 31.53 percent of total children are found to be in good health. About 28.54 percent adult males are found to be in ill health. Moderately good health is reported for 158 adult males (i.e. 37.26 percent) and the rest 145 adult males (i.e. 34.20 percent) possess good health. About 23.96 percent of total adult females are found to be in ill health and 195 adult females (40.63 percent of total adult females) are in moderately good health. The remaining 170 adult females (35.42 percent) are in good health. On the whole, the disappointing figure of 26 percent i.e. more than a quarter of total sample population was found to be in ill health. This indicates a low health profile of the people in the villages.

Table 9.2 reveals the incidence of morbidity of some common diseases which affect the people in the sample villages. Malaria and scabies were found to be the two main diseases from which the people suffered. During 2004-05, 342 persons (nearly 27.23 percent) suffered from malaria. Out of

Table- 9.1: Variation in Health Status among the Social Classes

Community	Good				Moderately Good				Bad			
	Adult		Child	Total	Adult		Child	Total	Adult		Child	Total
	Male	Female			Male	Female			Male	Female		
ST	78	116	67	261	84	98	85	267	81	58	45	184
SC	45	38	30	113	48	51	43	142	29	42	39	110
General	22	16	14	52	26	46	20	92	11	15	9	35
All households	145	170	111	426	158	195	148	501	121	115	93	329
Percent	11.5*	13.5*	8.8*	33.9*	12.6*	15.5*	11.8*	39.9*	9.6*	9.2*	7.4*	26.2*
	(34.2)	(35.4)	(31.5)		(37.3)	(40.6)	(40.1)		(28.5)	(24.0)	(26.4)	

Note: Figures in parentheses denote percentages of persons in their respective category.
* marked figures denote percentages of persons in total sample population

that 57 persons suffered from chronic malaria for a period of six months or more. About 181 persons (14.41 percent of the total sample population) are affected by scabies. Out of this, 43 suffered for a period of six months to one year. Other diseases which are found to be plaguing people are 12 persons from syphilis, 8 children from polio, 5 persons from jaundice, 5 persons from filarial, 23 persons from measles and 12 persons from chicken pox etc.

The people do not maintain hygiene because of the lack of awareness. They kept utensils clean but they do not know the fact that flies infect food. They fall prey to many diseases because of lack of cleanliness, malnutrition, lack of medical facilities for curative and preventive treatment and low economic status. Kandhamal is a malaria-prone district. Besides malaria, which takes a heavy toll of lives, infectious and contagious diseases like scabies are also prevalent. Moreover, it is found that owing to crude marital relations and promiscuity in sexual matters, venereal diseases like syphilis, yaws etc. are common among them.

Table 9.2:Duration of Suffering and the Number of Persons Affected in Malaria and Scabies, 2004-05

Sl. No.	*Period of suffering*	*Malaria*	*Scabies*
1	Less than one week	62	18
2	One week	57	32
3	Two weeks	44	41
4	One month	39	11
5	Two months	23	15
6	Three months	31	12
7	Four months	29	9
8	Six months	16	14
9	Eight months	23	11
10	One year	18	18
	Total	342	181
		27.23	14.41

Source: Computed from official data of PHC, Tikabali

Availability and Access to Public Healthcare Facilities

Access to healthcare is the basic requirement and an important aspect of public healthcare services. One can distinguish two types of access to health services viz., physical and economic. Physical access can be either population-based or area- based. The problem of physical access to healthcare facilities is compounded by two other factors such as condition of roads and transport connectivity. In Odisha, the population coverage per public health facility is better than its neghbouring states, but the area of coverage is very poor. On the contrary, economic access refers to direct cost of accessing the healthcare services provided. The extent of household expenditure on healthcare is a good indicator of economic access. Thus, the poor physical and economic access affects the proper utilisation of available public healthcare facilities. The state in 2003 had a network of 1701 government medical institutions with a provision 13,886 hospital beds. The medical institutions include 174 hospitals, 231 community health centres, 1282 primary health centres and 14 mobile health units. In addition to this, there are 5 ayurvedic, 4 homoeopathic hospitals and 522 ayurvedic and 480 homoeopathic dispensaries with 545 ayurvedic and 485 homoeopathic doctors in the state. The population served was about 21,923 persons and the area served was 92 sq. km per medical institution. The bed-population ratio is 1: 2,685 and doctor-population ratio is 1: 7,560. The 118 ITDA blocks of 12 tribal districts in the state had 567 medical institutions with 3,152 beds and area served per medical institution was123 sq. km.

The existing medical facilities available in the district of Kandhamal cover 21 hospitals and dispensaries, 34 primary health centres, 13 ayurvedic dispensaries, 16 homeopathic dispensaries. The number of beds per lakh of population in 2003 is 69 (GoI, 2005). Three Mobile Health Units (MHUs) were functioning in the district. Each MHU comprises of one medical officer, one pharmacist, one female health worker and one attendant. The MHUs hold health camps in the remote and inaccessible areas and supply medicine free of cost to patients. But there is a provision of distributing medicine worth Rs.1, 000/- per camp during their visit. However, the people in the sample villages are deprived of such MHU facilities. They have to depend on the PHC and the ayurvedic dispensary located at the Block headquarter, Tikabali. Since the two sample villages-Sunaponga and Monisigaon are far away from the Block headquarter, the villagers are deprived of public healthcare facilities available at Tikabali. They are either depending on quacks or village priest for health treatment. Table 9.3 depicts the community-wise medical facilities availed by the sample households. The figures in Table 9.3 reveal that 57 households (26.1 percent) depend on quacks, 42 households (19.27 percent) visit doctors, 94 households (43.1 percent) consult *gunias* (village priests), and 25 households (11.5 percent) do nothing in the event of illness and disease. That is nearly 54.6 percent of the households depend either on '*gunias*' and 'quacks' or do nothing when diseases befall. This is due to traditional culture of the tribals, superstitious beliefs, illiteracy and ignorance.

Table 9.3:Community-wise Medical Facilities Availed by the Sample Households

(No. of households)

Community	*Doctor*	*Quack*	*Gunia*	*Nothing*	Total
ST	24	32	64	12	132
SC	13	17	24	11	65
Others	5	8	6	2	21
Total	42	57	94	25	218
Percentage	(19.27)	(26.15)	(43.12)	(11.47)	(100.00)

Note: Figures in parentheses denote percentage of households in total number of households in sample villages.

The Family Welfare Programme is being implemented as a part of the National Production Control Programme. The programme is being implemented with full Central assistance covering both population control and maternal and child health services. Both the sterilization methods - tubectomy and vasectomy are adopted as a family planning measure but tubectomy is very popular in this region. The new technique for male sterilization, namely, 'No Scalpel Vasectomy' is being popularised with UNFPA assistance. The number of sterilised persons is about 0.89 lakh, and IUD, contraceptive and oral pill users as family planning measure are 1.42, 2.85 and 1.38 lakh respectively in the state as on March, 2004 (GoO, 2005). In the sample villages, out of 106 couples, 33 couples (31.1 percent) have undergone sterilisation, 28 couples (26.4 percent) have adopted tubectomy. Only 3 ST and 2 SC altogether 5 couples have resorted to vasectomy. Other methods of temporary family planning such as IUD, oral pill, contraceptive and medical terminations of pregnancy are not so popular among the ST and SCs (Table 9.4).

In the health sector also the tribal families are deprived of receiving the fruits of health delivery services and they remain marginalized on the outskirts of the society. They are still having a very low health profile.

Table 9.4:Methods of Family Planning Adopted in the Sample Population (in number of couples)

Methods	*ST*	*SC*	*Others*	*Total*	*Percentages*
Tubectomy	13	9	6	28	26.42
Vasectomy	3	2	0	5	4.72
Other temporary measures	2	5	4	11	10.38
Total	18	16	10	44	41.51
Percentages	16.98	15.09	9.43	41.51	

Note: Estimated from survey data. Percentage to the total no of 106 couples below 45 years in the sample villages.

Conclusion

Most of the CD blocks of Kandhamal are either 'backward' or 'very backward'. Tribal communities dominate this region. This region is rich in forest resources. The tribals have been depending on forests for their livelihood including other needs. Heavy incidence and persistence of poverty has been a cause of concern for policy makers. The major thrust of health policy is to achieve equity in healthcare by reducing the disparities across regions, gender, poor and the disadvantaged social classes (STs and SCs) and vulnerable groups such as the disabled and aged. However, the desired result is yet to be achieved.

The district is sparsely populated. About 51.5 percent of its population belongs to ST community and 18.2 percent to the SC category. Several socio-economic indicators reveal the backwardness of this region. The literacy rate at 52.7 is much lower than the state average of 63.1 percent. The female literacy rate 36.2 percent also compares unfavorably with the state average of 50.5 percent. Child mortality rate is the highest among the districts of the state. The population suffers from high morbidity on account of under nutrition as well as PH and endemic malaria and other localized diseases. Compared to national average of 36.8 percent of girls marrying below the age of 18 years, this percentage is as high as 60.6 in Kandhamal district. As against the national average of 48 percent users of family planning method, this is only 38.7 percent in Kandhamal district. The population coverage of public healthcare facilities is little better but the area coverage is lower than the KBK (undivided Kalahandi, Bolangir and Koraput) districts of the state. The number of hospital beds, bed-population ratio and doctor-population ratio are also far from satisfactory. Thus, the present health status of the tribals and the availability of healthcare service providers in tribal areas are not adequate in comparison to the state and national averages.

Notes

1. Sahu,1997; Panda and Sarangi (2004); Hann and Dubey (2003 and 2005); HRD, Government of Odisha, 2004 and many other studies estimated tribal poverty of the Odisha using different methodologies.

2. The IMR, Neonatal and Peri-Natal Mortality Rate figures are little higher in SRS Bulletin than NHFS-2 Reports. However, we have quoted the SRS Bulletin figures in the study.
3. 'Salap' is a juice collected from Salap trees generally located in Hill terrains. The juice is then treated with a root and kept it for some time to increase its concentration. It is a popular as a alcoholic drink among the tribals in Kandhamal.

References

Dutta, K.K. *et al.* (1980). "Health and Population," *Perspectives and Issues*, 3, p.282.

Government of India. (2001). Registrar General, Sample Registration System Bulletin, 25, April, pp. 126.

Government of India. (2002). *The Indian Child: A Profile*, New Delhi: Department of Women and Child, Ministry of Human Resource Development.

Government of Odisha. (1998). *Health Statistics of Odisha*, Bhubaneswar: State Bureau of Intelligence, Directorate of Health Services, Odisha.

Government of Odisha. (2004). *Human Development Report, Orissa*, New Delhi: Planning Commission.

Government of Odisha. (2005). *Economic Survey*, Bhubaneswar: Directorate of Economics and Statistics, Odisha.

Haan, A.D. and A. Dubey. (2005). "Poverty, Disparity, or the Development of Underdevelopment in Odisha," *Economic and Political Weekly*, XL (18), No22 & 23, pp. 2321-29.

International Institute of Population Studies. (2001). *National Family Health Survey-2* (1998-99), Mumbai.

Johansson, S.R. (1991). "The Health Transition: The Cultural Information of Morbidity during the Decline of Mortality," *Health Transition Review*, 1 (1).

Panda, B.K. and P. Sarangi. (2004). "Incidence of Poverty Among the Tribals in Odisha: An Empirical Analysis," *Studies in History and Culture*, 9 (2), pp. 81-93.

Panda, B.K. (1996). 'Consumption Pattern in Odisha: An Econometric Analysis,' Unpublished Ph. D. thesis, Berhampur University, Berhampur ,Odisha.

Panda, B.K., P. Sarangi and R.K. Panda. (2005). "Impact of Water Harvesting Structures on Cropping Pattern and Food Security," *Orissa Economic Journal*, XXXVII (1 & 2).

Pannikkar, P.G.K. (1972). "Economics of Nutrition," *Economic and Political Weekly*, 7, Annual Number.

Pothal, S.P. (2005). 'Levels of living of Tribals in Odisha,' Unpublished M.Phil Dissertation, Berhampur University, Odisha.

Radhakrishna, R. (2005). "Food and Nutrition Security of the Poor: Emerging Prospective," *Economic and Political Weekly*, XL (18), April-May, pp. 1817-1821.

World Bank. (2002). *Human Development Report*, New York: Oxford University Press.

Growth and Pattern of Healthcare Expenditure in Odisha

Hadibandhu Sahoo, Anuva Choudhary
& Amita Kumari Choudhary

Introduction

The imperfect nature of the market for health services is often cited as the reason to justify government intervention in health sector. Arrow (1963) has stated that for health services market has to approximate a perfectly competitive equilibrium and thereby to dispense with government intervention. Government intervention is warranted to balance the inequities that may arise in provision of health services left to the private sector. According to Human Development Report (2004) in Odisha the Crude Death Rate (CDR) was 10.4 and 9.8 in 2001 and 2002 respectively. Among all states infant mortality rate (IMR) continues to be the highest in Odisha. According to an estimate by Odisha Voluntary Health Association (1995), diarrhoea accounts for 28 percent, acute respiratory infection for 15 percent and tetanus for 6 percent of death of children below 5 years of age.

The underlying stimulus for the study stems from the fact that there exists paucity of healthcare spending in the state. Further, there exists considerable variation among states in terms of real per capita spending (Sahoo 2006). One would envisage that as per capita income increases the pressure on the state to provide better and varied health service increases (for example this may be due to increasing incidence of the life style diseases such as diabetes, cancer and cardiovascular diseases) and the government is required to spend more to meet this demand. The people in rural areas suffer due to lack of proper healthcare facilities. How far this phenomenon is reflected in Odishan context needs to be empirically tested.

The paper is organized as follows. Followed by the introduction, section II reviews briefly the existing literature. Section III presents materials and methods. Section IV is an analysis of health expenditure.

Literature Review

The issue of healthcare expenditure has been dealt earlier by many scholars. Using 1971 data Newhouse (1977) attempted to identity factors determining the quantity of healthcare services in thirteen developed countries. The role played by income in determining the pattern of healthcare expenditure has been analysed using cross section data drawn primarily from the OECD nations (Newhouse 1977, Leu 1986, Gerdtham *et.al* 1992a). The small sample size reduced the statistical reliability of the obtained estimates. Gerdtham *et.al* (1992_b) relied on pooled cross-section and time-series of OECD countries. Hitris and Posnett (1992) re-analysed the models of Newhouse and Leu using panel data for twenty OECD countries for the period 1960-1987. All these works centered on developed nations. It is necessary to review some of the studies which work on data from different states of India. Reddy and Selvaraju (1994) estimate that average healthcare spending of the major Indian states can be explained in terms of variation in real per capita income. Prabhu and Chatterjee (1993) using cross section data for 15 major Indian states observe that real per capita government revenue expenditure influenced educational attainment substantially where as in the health sector the availability of infrastructure played an important role. Purohit and Siddiqui (1994) estimate that the utilization of government facilities was higher in states incurring higher per capita spending on health

Materials and Methods

The study draws data primarily from *Finance Accounts* of Government of Odisha which spans over twenty-six financial years and the paper is built upon secondary data. The period of study is from 1974-75 to 2001-02. The reference materials of the study have been collected from the books, reports and journals available in the important libraries of the country. They include libraries of National Institute of Public Finance and Policy, New Delhi; National Institute of Health and Family Welfare, New Delhi; Jawaharlal Nehru University, New Delhi; Delhi University; M.K.C.G. Medical College, Berhampur; Central Library, Berhampur University; the P.G Department of Economics, Berhampur University; Municipality Library, Berhampur; State Institute of Health and Family Welfare, Bhubaneswar; Directorate of Health and Family Welfare, Bhubaneswar; Center for Youth and Social Development, Bhubenswar; Nabakrushna Choudhury Centre for Development Studies, Bhubaneswar; Reserve Bank of India, Bhubaneswar and others.

Growth models

The following models have been used for finding the growth rates of the variables: a. Linear trend model, b. Exponential growth model and c. Compound growth model.

Linear trend model

$$\tilde{O}_t = \hat{a}_1 + \hat{a}_2 t + u_t$$

In this model Y is regressed on time and the time t is known as trend variable. If the slope coefficient $\hat{a}_2$ is positive there is an upward trend in Y, where as if it is negative there is a downward trend in Y.

Exponential growth model

$$Y = \beta_1 e^{\beta_2 t} e^{ut}$$

which can be written as:

$\ln Y_t = \hat{a}_1 + \hat{a}_2 t + u_t$

The model describes the constant relative ($=\hat{a}_2$) or constant percentage ($100\hat{a}_1$) rate of growth (if $\hat{a}_2=0$) or decay (if $\hat{a}_2<0$) in the variable Y where Y represents variables such as expenditure, GNP and so on. The model is called exponential growth model.

Compound Rate of Growth Model

To find out the compound growth rate over a period of time of health expenditure data (at current and constant prices) the popular log-lin model has been used. In this model, regressand is logarithmic and the regressor is 'time'. In process, the logarithmic form of dependent variable is regressed with the independent variable. By taking the antilog of the estimated slope coefficients ($\hat{a}_2$) and subtracting 1 from it and multiplying the difference by 100, we get the compound growth over the period of time.

Healthcare Expenditure: Meaning and Definition

Health expenditures are defined as all expenditures or outlays for prevention, promotion, rehabilitation and care with specific objectives of improving health for both individuals as well as the society. It excludes expenditure on nutrition, food subsidy programmes, water supply and sanitation, which indirectly help to improve health. Healthcare expenditure may be classified into macro and micro aspects. Macro expenditure refers to the amount spent on health care by the central, state and union territory government. It includes medical (medical relief, medical education, training and research), Public health (control of communicable diseases, infrastructure etc.), water supply and sanitation, maternal and child health

(Immunization etc.), family welfare services, special nutrition programme and grant-in-aid for health programmes. Micro expenditure refers to the household expenditure for various health care services. It includes medicines, access costs (transportation etc), diagnostic and investigation costs (x-rays, pathological tests etc), doctor's fees, surgery, hospitalization, immunization, contraception, pregnancy, abortion and delivery expenditure, special nutrition (food during illness), municipal taxes for water supply and sanitation etc. Health expenditure can further be classified as gross domestic expenditures on health and gross national expenditures on health. While the former is the sum total of health expenditure and exports of medical services and goods, the latter is the sum of the total health expenditure and imports of medical services and goods.

In order to estimate the total healthcare spending at regional level six items have been included in our study. They are: (a) Medical care, (b) Family welfare, (c) Public health, water supply and sanitation, (d) Nutrition, (e) Child welfare, and (f) Welfare of the handicapped.

Healthcare Expenditure in Odisha

Healthcare and services in Odisha experience changes and transformations. Currently it covers revenue vs. capital, plan vs. non-plan, and curative, preventive, promotive and rehabilitative aspects. Simultaneously, it has other dimensions like medical, public health, family welfare, water supply and sanitation. The two, of course, have overlapping areas. Under medical and public health there are urban and rural categories in allopathic, homeopathic and other systems of medicines. Under family welfare and water supply and sanitation, rural and urban categories are also mentioned. All these broadly show the overall structure of health services with its significant elements.

Table 10.1: Definition of the Variables

Sl	*Name*	*Explanation/Definition*	*Units of measure-ment*
[1]	*[2]*	*[3]*	*[4]*
		(A) Dependent variables	
1	RHECUP	Revenue health expenditure at current price	❖
2	***RHECOP***	Revenue health expenditure at constant price	❖
3	CHECUP	Capital health expenditure at current price	❖
4	CHECOP	Capital health expenditure at constant price	❖
5	THECUP	Total health expenditure at current price	❖
6	THECOP	Total health expenditure at constant price	❖
		B) Independent variables	
7	NSDCUP	Net state domestic product at current price	❖
8	NSDCOP	Net state domestic product at constant price	❖
9	PSDCUP	Per capita state domestic product at current price	◆
10	PSDCOP	Per capita state domestic product at constant price	◆
11	TTRCUP	Total tax revenue at current price	❖
12	TTRCOP	Total tax revenue at constant price	❖
13	NTRCUP	Non tax revenue at current price	❖
14	NTR COP	**Non tax revenue at constant price**	❖
15	GTRCUP	Grand total revenue at current price	❖
16	GTRCOP	Grand total revenue at constant price	❖
17	GIACUP	Grant-in-aids at current price	❖
18	GIACOP	Grant-in-aids at constant price	❖
19	ENBOYS	Enrollment of boys at primary schools	·
20	ENGIRL	Enrollment of girls at primary schools	·
21	ENTOTL	Enrollment of total student at primary schools	·
22	RTHCUP	Revenue received from health sector at current price	❖
23	INMORT	Infant mortality rate	◆

[1]	[2]	[3]	[4]
24	MCHCUP	Expenditure on maternity and child health at current price	❖
25	MCHCOP	Expenditure on maternity and child health at constant price	❖
26	FWCUP	Expenditure on family welfare at current price	❖
27	FWCOP	Expenditure on family welfare at constant price	❖
28	TENCUP	Total expenditure on nutrition at current price	❖
29	TENCOP	Total expenditure on nutrition at constant price	❖
30	RHSCUP	Expenditure on rural health services at current price	❖
31	RHSCOP	Expenditure on rural health services at constant price	❖
32	UHSCUP	Expenditure on urban health services at current price	❖
33	UHSCOP	Expenditure on urban health services at constant price	❖
34	CWCUP	Expenditure on child welfare at current price	❖
35	CWCOP	Expenditure on child welfare at constant price	❖
36	HWCUP	Expenditure on handicapped welfare at current price	❖
37	HWCOP	Expenditure on handicapped welfare at constant price	❖
38	PHWSCUP	Expenditure on public health and water supply at current price	❖
39	PHWSCOP	Expenditure on public health and water supply at constant price	❖
40	MCCUP	Expenditure on medical care at current price	❖
41	PECUP	Public expenditure at current price	❖
42	PECOP	Public expenditure at constant price	❖

Note: § Rupees in crore ❖ Rupees • Numbers • Number of death of infants under one year of age for every 1000 live births during one year

Table 10.2: State Expenditure on Health Care in Odisha (Rs. in crore)

Sl	*Year*	*THECUP*	*THECOP*	*TPECUP*	*TPECOP*	*NSDCUP*	*NSDCOP*	*% of col.3 to col.5*	*% of Col.3 to Col.7*
[1]	[2]	[3]	[4]	[5]	[6]	[7]	[8]	[9]	[10]
1	1974-75	21.02	83.75	223.51	890.55	1692	6741.57	9.40	1.24
2	1977-78	25.71	96.43	341.03	1279.09	2111	7917.64	7.54	1.22
3	1980-81	59.44	161.67	546.85	1487.42	3443	9364.88	11.06	2.11
4	1983-84	104.72	230.02	782.91	1719.70	5253	11538.46	13.37	1.99
5	1986-87	136.49	254.84	1247.95	2330.09	6748	12599.42	10.94	2.02
6	1989-90	190.27	284.51	1846.11	2760.46	9917	14828.72	10.31	1.92
7	1992-93	313.06	339.16	3048.88	3303.12	13416	14534.74	10.27	2.33
8	1995-96	512.28	421.28	4697.81	3863.33	23822	19590.46	10.90	2.15
9	1998-99	766.41	544.71	6816.89	4844.98	31211	22182.66	11.24	2.45
10	2001-02	793.28	491.80	9881.73	6126.30	37834	23455.67	8.03	2.10

Note: Variables are defined in Table 10.1

Source: Financial Accounts, Government of Odisha, various issues.

3822 19590.46 10.90 2.15

Table 10.2 reveals the trend of expenditure on health services in Odisha both at current and constant prices. It began with a small sum of Rs 21.02 crore in 1974-75 in nominal terms. In 2001-02 the figure rose to Rs.793.28 crore by 38 times. At constant prices the rise has been sliced down to six times. The rise has been gradual in the mid-Seventies and early-Eighties. Thereafter, it is more visible. We can compare these figures with total state expenditure and net state domestic product at current prices (NSDCUP). The share of health expenditure in the NSDCUP has increased from 1.24 percent in 1974-75 to 2.10 percent in 2001-02. Surprisingly, total health expenditure at current prices (THECUP) as a percent of total public expenditure at current prices (PECUP) has decreased from 9.40 percent in 1974-75 to 8.03 percent in 2001-02. However, the relative importance of health spending with reference to NSDCUP continues to rise.

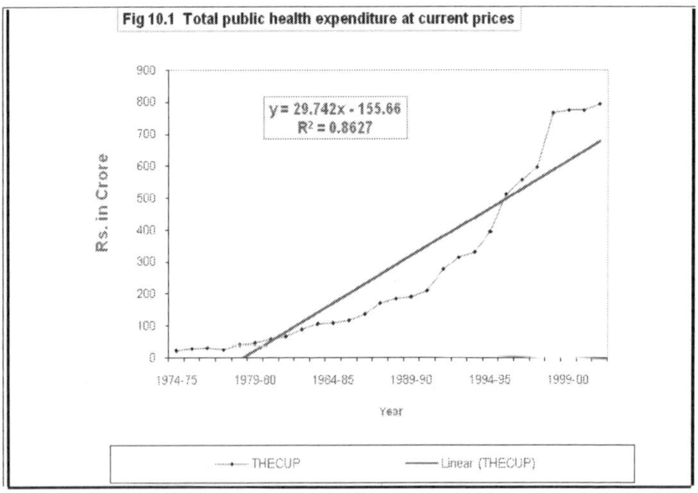

Fig 10.1 Total public health expenditure at current prices

The trend picture of total public health expenditure in money and real terms is evident from Figs. 10.1 and 10.2.

Both the figures depict government expenditure on health over the period from 1974-75 to 2001-02. As was noticed in Table 10.2 total expenditure has increased faster in money terms than in real terms. The slope of the trend line for total health expenses is 29.74 in money terms and 16.29 in real terms (Figs. 10.1 and 10.2).

Fig. 10.2 Total Health expenditure at constant prices

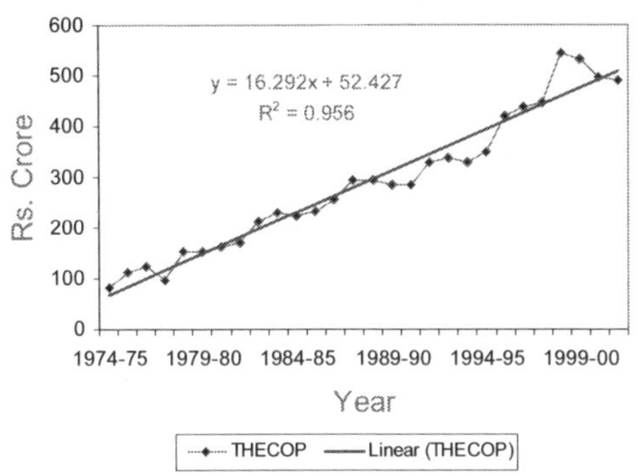

The Reserve Bank of India (R.B.I) has been classifying budget heads into functional categories such as developmental and non-developmental categories of expenditure. All expenditures under revenue and capital account are categorized into general services, social services and economic services. Expenditure on social services and economic services constitute developmental expenditure while those on general services are covered under the category of non-developmental expenditure. The state government resorted to economic-cum-functional classification of public expenditure quite for sometime (GOO 1975). This is a dimension, which shifts the pattern of expenditure. Table 10.3 makes this point clear. It may be observed from the Table that the expenditure on general services ranged from 30 to 49 percent during 1974-75 to 2001-02. Since 2000-01, it was a major component of total public expenditure. The percentage of expenditure on social services declined from 38.88 percent in 1974-75 to 32.99 percent in 2001-02. From 1974 through 2001-2002 spending on social services by and large exceeds that of spending on economic services. It ranged between 30-49 percent during this period. Expenditure on general services comes first. Spending on economic service ranks third. However, it fluctuates over the years. The share of expenditure on economic services also declined from 29.80 percent in 1974-75 to 15.38 percent in 2001-02.

Table 10.3: Classification of Public Expenditure in Odisha (Rs. in Crore)

Sl	*Year*	*General services*	*Social services*	*Economic services*	*Other services*	*Total expenditure*
[1]	[2]	[3]	[4]	[5]	[6]	[7]
1	1974-75	68.13 (30.49)	86.91 (38.88)	66.62 (29.80)	1.85 (0.83)	223.51 (100)
2	1977-78	97.77 (28.66)	134.35 (39.40)	105.78 (31.02)	3.13 (0.92)	41.03 (100)
3	1980-81	136.28 (24.92)	236.45 (43.24)	170.47 (31.17)	3.655 (0.67)	46.85 (100)
4	1983-84	231.19 (29.53)	338.9 (43.30)	208.28 (26.59)	4.53 (0.58)	782.91 (100)
5	1986-87	390.61 (31.29)	511.42 (40.98)	339.34 (27.19)	6.58 (0.54)	1247.95 (100)
6	1989-90	630.29 (34.14)	773.76 (41.91)	434.53 (23.54)	7.53 (0.41)	1846.11 (100)
7	1992-93	1013.24 (33.23)	1195.29 (39.21)	826.88 (27.12)	13.47 13.47	3048.88 (100)
8	1995-96	1603.21 (34.13)	1834.62 (39.05)	1247.10 (26.55)	12.88 (0.27)	4697.10 (100)
9	1998-99	2756.46 (40.43)	2720.44 (39.91)	1316.22 (19.31)	23.77 (0.35)	6816.89 (100)
10	2001-02	4933.22 (49.92)	3259.46 (32.99)	1549.40 (15.38)	149.56 149.56	9891.64 (100)

Note: Figures in bracket indicate the percentage of total expenditure
Source: As in Table 10.2.

Expenditure on Health, Education and Social Services: A Comparison

Tables 10.4 and 10.5 reflect the total expenditure of Government of Odisha on health and family welfare. Division of public money into different components of social services gives revealing picture. It is disheartening to note that the growth of spending on health services programme is slower than the same for education. It claims higher amount from 1999 onwards. Table 10.5 gives a synoptic view of the state's expenditure on education and health. When about 20.5 percent of total social service expenditure is devoted to education in 1974-75, the proportion decreased to 17.5 percent in 2001-02. In the same period 8 percent of total social service expenditure is devoted for giving health status to the state populace.

Table 10.4: Public Expenditure on Health, Education and Social Services in Odisha (1974-75 to 2001-02) (Rs in crore)

Sl	*Year*	*Education*	*Health*	*Social services*
1	1987-88	288.59	170.02	587.52
		(20.50)	(12.08)	(41.74)
2	1988-89	339.27	183.51 (	646.21
		(20.45)	(11.06)	(38.36)
3	1989-90	414.98	190.27	773.76
		(22.48)	(10.31)	(41.91)
4	1990-91	451.75	210.33	842.20
		(20.62)	(10.06)	(38.45)
5	1991-92	548.48	276.62	1040.18
		(20.82)	(10.50)	(39.47)
6	1992-93	620.09	313.06	1195.29
		(20.34)	(10.26)	(39.21)
7	1993-94	688.16	330.13	1326.66
		(19.78)	(09.49)	(38.07)
8	1994-95	815.24	394.03	1489.77)
		(20.20)	(09.76)	(36.92)

Sl	*Year*	*Education*	*Health*	*Social services*
9	1995-96	942.48 (20.06)	512.28 (10.90)	1834.62) (39.05)
10	1996-97	1066.10 (20.83)	56.30 (10.87)	2015.36 (39.38)
11	1997-98	1208.39 (21.83)	595.20 (10.75)	2211.57 (39.950
12	1998-99	1479.69 (21.71)	766.41 (11.24)	2720.44 (39.91)
13	1999-00	1920.07 (22.82)	774.13 (09.15)	4002.11 (47.31)
14	2000-01	1741.58 (19.72)	773.37 (08.75)	3115.96 (35.27)
15	2001-02	1733.34 (17.54)	793.28 (08.03)	3259.46 (32.99)

Note: Figures in brackets indicate percentage of total public expenditure
Source: As in Table 10.4

Table 10.5:Share of Spending on Health, Education and in Social Services in Odisha

Sl	*Year*	*Education(% of Col.5)*	*Health (% of Col.5)*	*Social services (Rs. in crore)*
[1]	[2]	[3]	[4]	[5]
1	1987-88	49.12	28.94	587.52
2	1988-89	52.50	28.40	646.21
3	1989-90	53.63	24.59	773.76
4	1990-91	51.64	24.97	842.20
5	1991-92	52.73	26.59	1040.18
6	1992-93	51.88	26.19	1195.29
7	1993-94	51.95	24.92	1326.66
8	1994-95	54.72	26.45	1489.77
9	1995-96	51.37	27.92	1834.62
10	1996-97	52.89	27.60	2015.36
11	1997-98	54.64	26.91	2211.57
12	1998-99	54.39	28.17	2720.44
13	1999-00	48.23	19.34	4002.11
14	2000-01	55.89	24.82	3115.96
15	2001-02	53.18	24.34	3259.46

Source: As in Table 10.2

Healthcare Expenditure in Odisha by Functional Categories

By functional categories health expenditure in Odisha can be classified into: (a). medical care (b). family welfare (c). public health, water supply and sanitation (d). child welfare (e). welfare of the handicapped and (f). nutrition. It is interesting to note that spending on medical care has increased significantly after the mid-eighties. It was Rs 10.28 crore in 1974-75 which increased to Rs 386.77 crore in 2001-02. The main reasons are reorientation of medical education, creation of additional posts in medical college hospitals, provision of twenty-four hour medical services in capital hospital and in all district headquarters hospitals, payment of non-practicing allowance to doctors, education and training of criminal investigation and vigilance. The mounting expenditure is also attributed to more expenditure on medical relief, tribal area sub-plan, expansion of hospital and dispensary, primary health center, and community health centers.

Though family welfare is a centrally-sponsored scheme, the state's participation cannot be ignored. Public spending on family welfare rose from Rs. 1.91 crore in 1974-75 to Rs 62.78 crore in 2001-02. This may be due to expansion of rural family welfare services, payment of more compensation, mass education, maternity and child health care, tribal area sub-plan, direction and administration, research and evaluation and other services and supplies. On the other hand, expenditure on public health and water supply and sanitation increased by 37 times due to more expenditure on prevention and control of diseases drug control, health statistics and evaluation, rural and urban water supply programme, prevention of air and water pollution and sanitation services and assistance to local bodies and municipality etc. Spending on medical and public health rose by 38 times over the period. All these are indicative of the state's spending priority on creation of healthy environment. Further, it is understandable from Cols. 6, 7 and 8 (Table 10.6) that there has been a slow rise in expenses on child welfare, welfare of handicapped and nutrition (Table 10.6).

Table 10.6: Health Care Expenditure by Functional Categories (Rs. in crore)

Sl. No.	Year	MC CUP	FW CUP	PH WS	CWC CUP	HW CUP	TEN CUP	Total
[1]	[2]	[3]	[4]	[5]	[6]	[7]	[8]	[9]
1	1974-75	10.28	1.91	6.77	2.05	0.01	–	21.02
2	1977-78	12.50	4.49	8.25	0.45	0.02	–	25.71
3	1980-81	26.70	6.42	25.60	0.65	0.07	–	59.44
4	1983-84	40.49	13.84	49.19	0.89	0.31	–	104.72
5	1986-87	54.74	17.22	61.48	2.24	0.81	–	136.49
6	1989-90	93.48	28.49	51.26	3.50	1.29	12.25	190.27
7	1992-93	138.07	37.27	104.38	11.83	2.25	19.26	313.06
8	1995-96	204.06	61.32	133.19	19.86	3.03	90.82	512.28
9	1998-99	323.29	83.82	255.19	24.39	4.11	75.61	766.41
10	2001-02	386.77	62.78	251.01	41.52	4.62	46.58	793.28

Note: Variables are defined in Table 10.1
Source: As in Table 10.2

Revenue and Capital Health Expenditure in Odisha

There are two major heads under which state government's healthcare expenditure is classified: revenue expenditure and capital expenditure. Revenue expenditure deals with the expenditure on goods and services for current consumption while capital expenditure deals with the expenditure on acquisition or creation of durable assets as well as certain financial investment. Revenue expenditures on health consist of the expenditure on personal health services including curative, preventive and promotive services given inside and outside the hospitals, public health services, teaching, training and research. Capital expenditures, on the other hand, consist of expenditure on health care infrastructure: construction of building, purchase of equipments and other durable goods.

Revenue expenditure on health can be examined under two heads (a) category wise i.e. proportion spending on salaries/wages and supplies (b) sector wise i.e. primary, secondary and tertiary sectors. Primary health sector includes

Table 10.7: Revenue and Capital Expenditure on Health in Odisha

Sl	*Year*	*Revenue expenditure*							*Capital expenditure*				
		MC CUP	*FW CUP*	*PHWS CUP*	*CW CUP*	*HW CUP*	*TEN CUP*	*Total*	*MC CUP*	*FW CUP*	*PHWS CUP*	*Total*	*Grand Total*
[1]	[2]	[3]	[4]	[5]	[6]	[7]	[8]	[9]	[10]	[11]	[12]	[13]	[14]
1	1974-75	10.21	1.91	6.04	2.05	0.01	-	20.22	0.07	-	0.73	0.80	21.02
2	1977-78	11.27	4.49	6.48	0.45	0.02	-	22.71	1.23	-	1.77	3.00	25.71
3	1980-81	25.11	6.48	23.64	0.65	0.07	-	55.63	1.59	-	2.22	3.81	59.44
4	1983-84	39.70	13.84	44.62	0.89	0.31	-	99.36	0.79	-	4.57	5.36	104.72
5	1986-87	53.17	17.22	56.44	2.24	0.81	-	129.88	1.57	-	5.04	6.61	136.49
6	1989-90	91.63	28.48	49.09	3.50	1.29	12.25	186.24	1.85	0.01	2.17	4.03	190.27
7	1992-93	134.28	37.22	88.11	11.83	2.25	19.26	292.95	3.79	0.05	16.27	20.11	313.06
8	1995-96	193.61	61.22	110.45	19.86	3.03	90.82	478.99	10.45	0.10	22.74	33.29	512.28
9	1998-99	317.69	83.82	218.70	24.39	4.11	75.61	724.32	5.60	-	36.49	42.09	766.41
10	2001-02	358.65	62.78	176.61	41.52	4.62	46.58	690.76	28.12	-	74.40	102.52	793.28

Note: Variables are defined in Table 10.1
Source: As in Table 10.2

primary health centers, family welfare, preventive and promotive programmes and the national disease control programmes. The secondary sector consists of the community health centers and the district headquarter hospitals. The teaching institutions and the hospitals affiliated to them are considered as the tertiary sector.

The division of public money into revenue and capital components under health care, medical care, nutrition and welfare of child and handicapped reveals interesting scenarios. Medical care expenditure rises faster than public health, water supply and sanitation. The rise in family welfare expenses is also noticeable. The nutrition has also claimed large expenses since late 1980s onwards. However, it is deplorable to note less capital expenses on medical care, family welfare and water supply which in turn indicate that there is less emphasis on health infrastructure (Table 10.7).

Plan and Non-plan Expenditure on Health Services in Odisha

Plan expenditure refers to expenditures on annual plan projects; programmes and schemes approved by the Planning Commission and is time based. They include centrally plan schemes, centrally-sponsored plan schemes routed through state budget with or without matching state expenditure. Non-plan expenditures refer to all expenditures of government not included in its annual plan programmes. Once the plan period is over, items of plan revenue expenditure become the items of non-plan expenditure.

Table 10.8 records state expenditure through plans. The significant addition to expenditure is well evident in case of medical care and public health, water supply and sanitation. The non-plan expenses grab a bulk amount in comparison to plan expenditure. However, health care has been emphasized in the National Programme for Minimum Needs (GOO, 1975). The objectives set in the plan documents of the state are clear in conformity with the guidelines of National Health Policy. Primary health centers, maternity and child health centers

Table 10.8: Plan and Non-plan Expenditure of Odisha on Health Services

Year		*Medical care*		*Family welfare*			*PHWSS*		
	Plan	*Non-plan*	*Total*	*Plan*	*Non-plan*	*Total*	*Plan*	*Non-Plan*	Total
[1]	[2]	[3]	[4]	[5]	[6]	[7]	[8]	[9]	[10]
1974-75	1.11	9.17	10.28	1.91	-	1.91	4.64	2.13	6.77
1977-78	2.49	10.01	12.50	4.49	-	4.49	5.30	2.95	8.25
1980-81	6.80	19.90	26.70	6.21	0.21	6.42	18.48	7.12	25.60
1983-84	11.68	28.81	40.49	13.83	0.01	13.84	40.58	8.61	49.19
1986-87	13.36	41.38	54.74	17.22	0.02	17.22	49.44	12.04	61.48
1989-90	26.64	66.84	93.48	28.49	0.09	28.49	38.06	13.20	51.26
1992-93	30.17	107.90	138.07	37.27	0.07	37.27	88.35	16.73	105.08
1995-96	53.47	150.59	204.06	61.32	0.02	61.32	111.02	22.17	133.19
1998-99	77.13	246.16	323.29	83.82	0.02	83.82	219.40	35.79	255.19
2001-02	114.90007	271.80	386.70	62.78	0.08	62.78	214.10	36.91	251.01

Source: As in Table 1**Rural and Urban Distribution of Health Care Expenditure in Odisha**

were set up in rural areas as an effective instrument of rural health services. The state government's keen consideration for these programmes to achieve "health for all" is well reflected in the budget speeches of finance ministers (GOO, 1975). All expanding health activities are carried out through the budgetary operation of the state government.

Table 10.9: Rural and Urban Distribution of Healthcare Expenditure in Odisha (Rs. in crore)

Sl	*Year*	*Rural*	*Urban*	*Total*	*% of Col.2 to Col.4*	*% of Col.3 to Col.4*
1	*2*	*3*	*4*	*5*	*6*	*7*
1	1987-88	31.04	32.06	63.10	49.19	50.81
2	1988-89	35.77	34.55	70.32	50.87	49.13
3	1989-90	39.85	37.70	77.55	51.39	48.61
4	1990-91	47.92	42.86	90.78	52.79	47.21
5	1991-92	70.62	49.01	119.63	59.03	40.97
6	1992-93	78.27	53.57	131.84	59.37	40.63
7	1993-94	88.20	57.85	146.05	60.39	39.61
8	1994-95	117.12	67.96	185.08	63.28	36.72
9	1995-96	139.06	82.28	221.34	62.83	37.17
10	1996-97	142.73	89.50	232.23	61.46	38.54
11	1997-98	177.57	96.71	274.28	64.74	35.26
12	1998-99	220.14	134.34	354.48	62.10	37.90
13	1999-00	229.45	153.56	383.01	59.91	40.09
14	2000-01	243.68	171.84	415.52	58.64	41.36
15	2001-02	260.34	182.19	442.53	58.83	41.17

Source: As in Table 10.2

An attempt is made to make a division between rural and urban healthcare expenditure in Odisha for appreciating the social justice aspect of health expenditure. Since details of data are not available, the expenditure on medical care, family welfare and public health and water supply and sanitation are taken to indicate the trend. Table 10.9 records the relevant information. Splitting public money on health services into rural and urban categories is quite a difficult task. There is no clear-cut demarcation between the two. The overlapping zone is so thick, even reason guessed is risky. But a division, however arbitrary it may be, is worthwhile. Further, the split is necessary to appreciate social justice aspects of health expenditure. Since details of data are not available, family welfare, water supply and health services are items taken to indicate the trend also reflect on rural and urban family welfare services.

Expenditure on rural health items as totals and in relation to total health expenditure are more than those of the urban items (Sahoo 2006). This is quite understandable when we take into account population and area belonging to both. But the fact that rural-urban dichotomy is found to be relevant in health service is suggestive of rural bias, hence for egalitarianism. This is corroborated by the policy statement of the Government of Odisha.

We can move a step ahead if we could locate particular spending items that are clearly oriented for rural mass. The plan document spells out that rural areas require higher attention in health services (GOO 1985). Maternity and child health care, prevention of communicable disease and medical relief are unambiguously meant for the less privileged people in society. There is an item: "Other systems of medicine" which refers to the treatment of Homeopathic and Ayurvedic system (GOO 1990). They are meant for the rural people who show preferences for such treatment because of traditional belief and cheapness of medicines.

Preventive and Curative Healthcare Expenditure in Odisha

Table 10.10 divides public money on health services according to purposes for which these are incurred. It is our supposition that curative expenses have significant impact on health status of people. Further, preventive and promotive expenses like water supply and sanitation, family welfare, etc. have greater egalitarian bias. Preventive care includes control and prevention of epidemic and communicable diseases to which the general mass of the people particularly the poor are afflicted. It also includes drug control, health publicity and so on (GOO 1997).

Resources devoted to preventive and curative aspect in the state of Odisha was 18.74 percent and 68.55 percent respectively in 2001-02. The increased allocation on curative aspect may be due to the tilt towards urban sector allocation. In the mid-seventies preventive expenditure was Rs 5.65 crore. In percentage terms towards the late Nineties there has been a slowing down, apparently because most of the dreaded epidemic disease like cholera, small pox, and tuberculosis has been controlled except on occasions, when such diseases appeared in vulnerable areas. Curative expenses, however, depict a positive rise both in absolute figures and in relation to total expenditure on health services. Preventive and curative spending together constitutes 87.29 percent of aggregate health expenditure in 2001-02 (Table 10.10).

Table 10.10 Preventive and Curative Expenditure on Healthcare in Odisha (Rs. in Crore)

Sl	*Year*	*Preventive*	*Curative*	*Others*	*Total*
1	2	3	4	5	6
1	1974-75	5.65(26.87)	13.02(61.98)	2.15(11.15)	21.02(100)
2	1977-78	6.55(5.48)	22.18(60.79)	3.53(13.73)	25.71(100)
3	1980-81	15.41(25.92)	36.98(62.22)	7.05(11.86)	59.44(100)
4	1983-84	25.49(24.34)	64.54(61.63)	14.69(14.03)	104.72(100)
5	1986-87	37.01(27.12)	87.41(64.04)	12.07(8.84)	136.49(100)
6	1989-90	44.96(23.63)	128.43(67.50)	16.88(8.87)	190.27(100)
7	1992-93	68.12(21.76)	204.77(65.41)	40.17(12.83)	313.06(100)
8	1995-96	114.49(22.35)	348.40(68.01)	49.39(9.64)	512.28(100)
9	1998-99	159.57(20.82)	514.72(67.16)	92.12(12.02)	766.41(100)
10	2001-02	148.67(18.74)	543.79(68.55)	100.82(12.71)	793.28(100)

Source: As in Table 10.2

Promotive Expenditure

It is our assumption that promotive expenditure includes expenditure on family welfare, public health, medical education and nutrition. Of late, economists have stressed on the relationship between economic development and population growth. The demography situation in the state is a matter of concern and has serious implications for overall socio-economic development. In other words, the excessive population corresponding to the productive resources lowers down the quality of living standard and ultimately hits the process of economic growth. In the current five-year plans the family welfare programme has been accorded a significant place and a well-planned strategy has been evolved. In pursuance to the National Population Policy, the Government of Odisha has adopted the welfare approach to the population growth and family planning has been redesigned as family welfare programme since 1977. It is being implemented by the state government as a part of national population control programme and to bring down the high infant mortality rate by promoting universal immunization under the family welfare programme. The programme seeks to promote responsible parenthood with focus on one child norm. The Government of Odisha has also introduced several incentives for providing special privileges in the sphere of education, employment, allotment of land, house etc for green card holders. Expenditure on family welfare comprises the expenditure on rural and urban family welfare services, maternity and child health, transport, compensation, mass education, training, research and evaluation and direction and administration. It is observed that expenditure on family welfare increased by about 83 times over the period from 1974-75 to 2001-02. (Sahoo 2006)

It covers the expenditure on public health establishments, prevention and control of diseases, prevention of food adulteration, drug control, and manufacture of vaccine. Health education is an essential tool of community health. It is the very foundation of every successful public health programmers. The medical profession has played an important role in determining the health status of the people. However, the number and types of health professional, recruitment, training and research for various functions at various levels must be primarily determined by the actual problems of health, the prevailing pattern of disease and available health technology. All these harp on human and financial resource of the state. The state's spending on medical education comprises of allocating resources for Allopathic, Homeopathy, Ayurveda, and Tribal Area Sub-Plan (TASP). It is observed that, financing allopathic education claims a significant amount of public money (Sahoo 2006).

Nutritional status affects morbidity and mortality. Low nutrition may lead to increased illness, low life expectancy at birth and high infant mortality. Special nutrition programme has been launched to provide nutrition to the vulnerable group. This group consists of pre-school children, nursing and expectant mothers below poverty line. The Government of Odisha had spent Rs 6.01 crore in 1987-88, which mounted to Rs 20.27 crore in 2001-02. Mid-day meals programme has been launched in primary school. In 1974-75 public expenditure on nutrition was Rs 12.38 crore, which rose to Rs 46.58 crore in 2001-02. The government allocation was only Rs. 6.01 crore for this in 1987-88. However, it went up by three times in 2001-02. Mid-day meal programme constitutes about five percent of total expenditure on nutrition (Sahoo 2006).

Growth rate of Aggregate Healthcare Expenditure in Odisha

This section analyses the growth rate of aggregate and different components of health care expenditure variables which are presented in Table 10.1. Table 10.11 reveals the exponential, linear and compound growth rate of aggregate health expenditure from 1974-75 to 2001-2002. It is observed that the exponential growth rate of Odisha's total health care expenditure is 13.92 percent at current price for the whole period. The growth equation yielded a high value for coefficient of determination. Aggregate public health care expenditure of Odisha at constant price has grown at the rate of 6.28 percent. A high value of R^2 is observed from the regression equation. The linear growth rate of total health care expenditure in nominal term is found to be higher when

Table 10.11: Linear, Exponential and Compound Growth Rate of Aggregate Revenue, Capital and Total Health Expenditure in Odisha From 1974-75 to 2001-02 At Current and Constant (1993-94) prices

Sl	*Variables*	*Linear* *Growth rate*	R^2	*Exponential* *Growth*	R^2 *rate*	*CGR* *Growth rate*	*Mean*	*SD*	*CV*
[1]	[2]	[3]	[4]	[5]	[6]	[7]	[8]	[9]	[10]
1	RHE CUP	27.116	0.8583	13.77	0.9841	14.76	254.17	240.76	94.72
2	RHE COP	14.707	0.9333	6.13	0.9300	6.32	268.17	125.22	46.69
3	CHE CUP	2.626	0.6807	15.78	0.9173	17.09	21.43	26.18	122.18
4	CHE COP	1.585	0.7614	8.14	0.7536	8.48	20.50	15.91	77.64
5	THE CUP	29.742	0.8627	13.92	0.9882	14.93	275.59	263.40	95.57
6	THE COP	16.292	0.956	6.28	0.9502	6.48	288.66	137.01	47.48

Source: Computed and estimated from secondary data using M.S. Excel, 2000 Software

compared to the compound growth rate of 14.93 percent. The value of goodness of fit is high for the whole period. The state's linear growth rate of health care expenditure in real terms is 16.29 percent from 1974-75 to 2001 02 at constant prices. The compound growth rate in real terms is estimated at 6.48 percent. The coefficient of determination is also higher for linear growth rate. The Exponential Growth Rate (EGR) of revenue health care expenditure of Odisha at current price is found to be 13.77 percent. The explanatory power of regression is also very high (0.9841).

The exponential growth rate (EGR) of revenue health care expenditure in real terms is 6.13 percent which is lower than nominal terms. However, the value of goodness of fit is high. The linear growth rate of revenue health care expenditure is found to be 27.11 percent in monetary terms and 14.707 percent in real terms. The values of the goodness of fit are high in both the cases. The compound growth rate of health expenditure for the whole period 1974-75 to 2001-02 is 14.76 percent in money terms and 6.32 percent in real terms. The exponential growth rate of capital health care expenditure at current price is higher compared to the growth rates of aggregate revenue health care expenditure. It is 2.626 percent in monetary terms and 1.58 in real terms. The linear growth rate in case of capital expenditure at current price and constant price is found to be much lower compared to the same in case of both aggregate as well as revenue health expenditure. In money terms it is 2.626 percent and 1.5852 in real terms. The values of goodness of fit are high in both cases. The mean expenditure RHECUP, CHECUP and THECUP are Rs.254.17 crore, Rs.21.43 crore and Rs.275.59 crore respectively. The coefficient of variation of CHECUP is 122.18 percent, which is highest among all variables. It implies that there is wide fluctuation in CHECUP.

Table 10.12 Linear, Exponential and Compound Growth Rate of Selected Health Expenditure Variables in Odisha from 1974-75 to 2001-02 at Current and Constant (1993-94) Prices.

Sl.	*Variables*	*Linear Growth rate*	*Linear R^2*	*Exponential Growth*	*Exponential R^2 rate*	*CGR Growth rate*	*Mean*	*SD*	*CV*
[1]	[2]	[3]	[4]	[5]	[6]	[7]	[8]	[9]	[10]
1	MC CUP	13.557	0.8552	13.88	0.9926	14.89	124.26	120.59	97.04
2	MC COP	7.4301	0.9483	6.24	0.9621	6.44	129.75	62.76	48.37
3	FW CUP	2.9860	0.9057	12.99	0.9533	13.87	30.96	25.81	83.36
4	FW COP	1.5159	0.8520	5.35	0.7721	5.49	34.38	13.51	39.29
5	PHWS CUP	8.7445	0.8290	12.88	0.9372	13.75	86.40	78.93	91.35
6	PHWS COP	4.2039	0.7647	5.08	0.7366	5.21	95.15	39.54	41.56
7	WH CUP	0.196	0.901	23.23	0.9099	26.15	9.93	12.01	120.90
8	WH COP	0.1387	0.8981	15.59	0.8212	16.87	9.18	7.34	79.94
9	CW CUP	1.2759	0.7642	17.12	0.8627	18.67	1.70	1.70	100
10	CW COP	0.7666	0.7383	9.48	0.6778	9.94	1.62	1.20	74.17
11	TENCUP	5.0149	0.5285	15.71	0.7226	17.01	41.70	30.85	73.97
12	TENCOP	2.5211	0.3036	8.09	0.441	8.43	34.68	20.46	58.99

Source: As in Table 10.11

Growth Rates of Selected Health Expenditure Variables

In this section an attempt has been made to regress selected health expenditure variables on time. The results obtained from the semi-log models are presented in Table 10.13. The exponential growth rate (EGR) of public expenditure on medical care at current price is higher (13.88 percent) than that in constant price (6.24 percent). Nearly 99 percent of the variation in MCCUP is explained by time. It means over the period of twenty-eight years MCCUP has increased significantly. In case of MCCOP, 96 percent variation has been noticed. In case of FWCUP exponential growth is 12.99 percent, LGR is 2.98 percent and CGR is 13.87. On the other hand, EGR, LGR and CGR of FWCOP are 5.35, 1.515 and 5.49 percent respectively. The values of R^2 are 0.9533 and 0.7721. Exponential, linear and compound growth rates of PHWSCUP are 12.88, 8.74 and 13.75 percent respectively. The R^2 in case of EGR is 0.9372and LGR is 0.829. On the contrary, in case of PHWSCOP the EGR, LGR and CGR are 5.08 percent, 4.20 percent and 5.21 percent respectively. The values of goodness fit in case of EGR and LGR are 0.7366 and 0.7647. In case of HWCUP the EGR is 23.23, LGR is 0.196 and CGR is 26.15 percent. The R^2 is 0.9099. On the contrary EGR, LGR and CGR of HWCOP are 15.59 percent, 0.13 percent and 16.87 percent. The R^2 is 0.8981. The exponential, linear and compound growth rates of CWCUP are found to be 17.12 percent, 1.27 percent and 18.87 percent. The value of goodness of fit is 0.7642. In case of CWCOP the linear growth rate seems to be lower than exponential growth rate. The exponential growth rate is 9.48 percent. The values of R^2 are 0.8627 (EGR) and 0.7642 (LGR). The compound growth rate is 9.94 percent. The exponential, linear and compound growth rates of TENCUP are 15.71 percent, 5.01 percent and 17.01 percent respectively. Compared to these, growth rates of TENCOP are relatively lower. The values of goodness of fit in case of TENCOP are much lower. It is found to be 0.441. The mean, SD and CV of MCCUP are Rs.124.26 crore, Rs. 120.59 crore and 97.04 percent respectively. In case of expenditure on CWCUP the mean and

Table 10.13: Linear, Exponential and Compound Growth Rate of Health Expenditure Variables from 1974-75 to 2001-02 at Current and Constant (1993-94) Prices

Sl	*Variables*	*Linear*		*Exponential*		*CGR*	*Mean*	*SD*	*CV*
		Growth rate	R^2	*Growth rate*	R^2	*Growth rate*			
[1]	[2]	[3]	[4]	[5]	[6]	[7]	[8]	[9]	[10]
1	PHCUP	2.132	0.8915	9.88	0.9552	10.38	25.05	18.53	73.97
2	PHCOP	0.592	0.5828	2.13	0.5491	2.15	30.61	6.38	20.85
3	RHSCUP	17.82	0.9663	16.31	0.9784	17.71	128.14	81.05	63.25
4	RHSCOP	8.686	0.9692	8.66	0.9707	9.05	105.99	39.52	37.28
5	UHSCUP	10.926	0.9046	13.14	0.9869	14.04	85.73	51.37	59.92
6	UHSCOP	4.308	0.7942	5.52	0.8350	5.76	73.02	21.62	29.61
7	CHSCUP	20.662	0.8667	14.17	0.9926	15.22	192.14	186.94	97.09
8	CHSCOP	9.367	0.6874	6.45	0.8795	6.66	198.12	100.13	50.54
9	PHSCUP	6.414	0.8888	13.49	0.9701	14.44	60.51	53.09	87.75
10	PHSCOP	2.685	0.7967	5.87	0.8465	6.04	65.89	26.92	40.84
11	MCHCUP	0.069	0.3539	21.78	0.4955	24.33	0.65	0.78	121.33
12	MCHCOP	0.047	0.2745	14.18	0.2957	15.23	0.62	0.61	98.88
13	PCHCUP	8.243	0.8859	12.21	0.9860	12.99	83.29	72.04	86.49
14	PCHCOP	3.891	0.9448	4.57	0.9166	4.68	92.47	32.93	35.61

Source: As in Table 10.11

standard deviation are equal so the coefficient of variation is found to be 100 percent. (Table 10.12)

Table 10.13 unfolds growth rate of some selected health expenditure variables relating to public health, maternity and child health, and rural and urban health etc. The exponential growth of public health spending in real terms is 9.88 percent and in money terms it is 2.13 percent. The linear and compound growth rates are 2.13 percent and 10.38 percent in money terms, whereas 0.592 and 2.15 percent in real terms. Further, the growth rate of rural health services is higher both in money and real terms than the urban health services. This may be due to population and area difference. The linear growth rate of maternity and child health expenses is negligible. On per capita basis, the EGR, LGR and CGR are 12.21, 8.243 and 12.99 percent respectively in money terms. The same is 4.57, 3.89 and 4.68 percent in real terms. Looking into coefficients of variation, it can be stated that CV is prominent in case of expenditure at current price than expenditure at constant price. The exponential, linear and compound growth rate of spending on curative health services is higher than that of preventive health services both in real and nominal terms.

Conclusion

The research problem hovers round the central theme of growth and pattern of public healthcare spending in Odisha over the period of 1974-75 to 2001-02. Public health expenditure in Odisha rose rapidly both in real and nominal terms. There have been multiplicities of people's programmes indicating clear strategy for giving health services to the common men and women. The range and varieties of programmes reflect Odisha government's concern for the distressed and deprived categories of people. Both the exponential and the compound growth rate of public spending on healthcare in Odisha are found to be lower in real terms in comparison lower in real terms in comparison with nominal terms. In it is, there is an imperative need to substantially raise the level of spending on healthcare, particularly on public health, rural healthcare infrastructure and primary healthcare.

References

Arrow, K. (1963). "Uncertainty and the Welfare Economics of Medical Care", *American Economic Review*, 53(1), pp.941-69.

Duggal, R. (1986). "Political Economy of State Health Financing", *Radical Journal of Health*, 1(3), pp.79-85.

Gerdtham, U.G., J.Sogaard, J.F. Andersson, and B.Jonsson. (1992a). "An Economic Analysis of Health Expenditure: A Cross Sectional Study of the OECD Countries", *Journal of Health Economics*, 11, pp.63-84.

Gerdtham, U.G., J. Sogaard, J.F. Anderseson, and B. Jonsson (1992b). "A Pooled Cross Section Analysis of the Health Care Expenditure of the OECD Countries", in P. Zweifel and H. Frech. (eds). *Health Economics Worldwide*, Kluwer Academic Publishers, Dordrecht.

Hitris, T.J. Posnet. (1992). "The Determinants and Effects of Health Expenditure in Developed Countries", *Journal of Health Economics*, 11, pp.53-74.

Leu, R.E. (1986). "The Public-Private Mix and International Health Care Costs", A.J.Culyer and B.Jonsson. (eds). "*Public and Private Health Services: Complementarities and Conflicts*", Blackwel, Oxford and New York.

New House, J.P. (1977). "Medical Care Expenditure: A Cross National Survey", *Journal of Human Resources*, 12, p.p.115-125.

Rao, Mohan and V.Ravishankar. (1989), *India: Government Expenditure on Social Services*, 1976-77 to 1986-87, New Delhi: World Bank.

Ready, K.N. and V.Selvaraju. (1994). *Health Care Expenditure by Government of India: 1974-75 to 1990-91*, New Delhi: Government of India.

Sahoo, H. (2006). 'Public Expenditure on Health Services in Odisha,' Unpublished Ph.D. thesis, Berhampur University.

World Bank. (1993). *World Development Report: Investing in Health*, Washington, D.C.: Oxford University Press.

Addressing Health Issues in Rajasthan: A Critical Review

Alpana Kateja

Introduction

It is a well known fact that health is one of the important components of human development. In fact, it is much more than just a component in some human development index. The other two attributes of human development viz. education and income are considerably dependent on this, the third one - health. All wisdom derived from sincerely pursued education or all income earned may be totally in vain if the person does not enjoy good health. The scope of livelihood and income opportunities, the degree of efficiency, with which the works are performed, and the ability to endure the strains of labour thus expended, all depend much on the health conditions of the involved persons. At the same time, the sense of fulfillment and joy of accomplished work are notions meaningful only in good health.

Promoting and protecting health is essential to human welfare and sustained economic and social development. This was recognized more than thirty years ago by the Alma-Ata Declaration signatories, who noted that Health for All would contribute both to a better quality of life and also to global peace and security. Significance of health in human well-being was again reiterated in the Millennium Declaration, adopted by United Nations (United Nations, 2000), which laid maximum weight to health related goals in the eight Millennium Development Goals (MDGs). They are the most broadly supported, comprehensive and specific goals the world has ever agreed upon. These time-bound goals provide concrete, numerical benchmarks for tackling maternal and child mortality and diseases. The eight MDGs break down into twenty one quantifiable targets that are monitored by sixty indicators. Out of eight, following three are directly health related; (i) reduce child mortality (ii) improve maternal health and (iii) Combat HIV/AIDS, malaria and other diseases. However, all the goals are closely intertwined and cannot be dealt independently. For example, hunger leads to malnutrition. Poverty (Goal - 1), lack of education (Goal 2) or even improper sanitation (Goal -7) may lead to poor health.

The present study primarily seeks to examine the ground reality in Rajasthan with respect to health parameters. It is an attempt to examine the progress made so far and to draw attention to the slow pace towards achieving MDGs. For the purpose it synthesizes and analyses the existing body of information to reach its conclusions and recommendations. It also explores the extent of inequality in health outcomes among different districts. The Paper also delves upon the issue of declining health expenditure in the state.

The present paper is organized into five sections. Section II briefly summarizes level and trend of some of the important health outcomes in Rajasthan and discusses the deplorable situation of malnutrition; Section III examines evidences of health inequalities. Section IV presents an overview of the issue of health expenditure. Finally, Section V offers some concluding remarks.

Table 11.1 Major States Ranked on the Basis of Health Status

States	*Health Expenditure as % of Total Expenditure*	*Per Capita Health Expenditure*	*Life Expectancy at Birth*	*Infant Mortality Rate*	*Maternal Mortality Ratio*	*Crude Death Rate*	*Crude Birth Rate*	*Child Mortality Rate*	*Total Fertility Rate*	*Under 5 Mortality Rate*
	2005	*2005*	*2008*	*2008*	*2008*	*2008*	*2008*	*2008*	*2008*	*2008*
1	2	3	4	5	6	7	8	9	10	11
Andhra Pradesh	5	7	8	8	5	11	6	7	3	7
Assam	15	13	14	12	15	13	11	13	11	12
Bihar	11	15	11	10	11	8	14	10	15	10
Gujarat	7	9	9	7	6	5	9	8	9	8
Haryana	14	6	4	9	7	6	10	9	10	9
Karnataka	10	11	6	6	9	9	7	6	6	6
Kerala	4	1	1	1	1	2	1	1	1	1
Madhya Pradesh	8	12	15	15	12	14	13	15	12	15
Maharashtra	2	5	3	3	3	3	5	3	7	3
Odisha	13	10	13	14	10	15	8	12	8	13
Punjab	12	2	2	5	8	7	3	5	4	5
Rajasthan	9	14	10	11	13	4	12	11	13	11
Tamil Nadu	6	4	5	2	2	10	2	2	2	2
Uttar Pradesh	1	8	12	13	14	12	15	14	14	14
West Bengal	3	3	7	4	4	1	4	4	5	4

Source: Computed by author **Trends in Health Outcomes**

Table 11.2: Health Outcomes in Rajasthan: Targets and Achievements

Indicator	*Millennium Development Goals (MDGs)*	*National Population Policy (by 2010)*	*Medium Term Goals for Rajasthan*	*Status in Rajasthan 32 per 1000 live*
Infant Mortality Rate 2011)	30 per 1000 live births	Below 30 per 1000 live births	32 per 1000 live births (by 2012)	59 per 1000 live births in 2009 (SRS
Under-five Mortality Rate	Reduce by two thirds, between 1990 and 2015, the under-five mortality rate			80 per 1000 live births in 2008 (SRS 2011)
Maternal Mortality Rate (SRS 2008)	Reduce by three quarters between 1990 and 2015.	Below 1 per 1000 live births	1.48 per 1000 live births (by 2012)	3.88 per 1000 live births in 2004-06
Crude Birth Rate		21	22.6	27.5 in 2009 (SRS 2011)
Total Fertility Rate		2.1	2.1	3.3 in 2008 (MOH & FW)

Rajasthan was never well-known for good health status of its people. Even after six decades of planned development, it remains one of the *BIMARU* states (also known as EAG or priority states); one of the unhealthiest states in the country. It is evident from the Table 11.1 that the state does not fare well in any of the health parameters. It is also a big concern that in the modest performance in human development, though income and education indices are showing signs of better performance, health indices have low values (IDS 2008).

Though Health outcome targets proposed for the state are not very ambitious, most of them remain out of reach (Tab. 11.2). It may also be pointed out at this stage that even if these targets are achieved, the state will continue to lag behind the national averages in most of the indicators (if the national targets too are achieved at the same time).

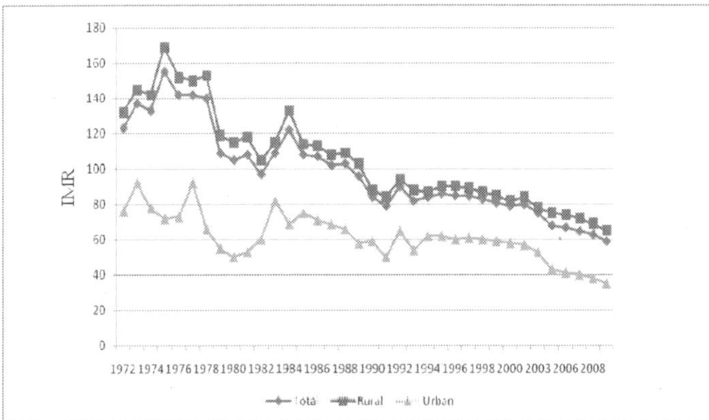

Figure 11.1: Infant Mortality Rate in Rajasthan (1972- 2009)

Sources: Various SRS Bulletins

In 2008, Infant Mortality Rate (IMR) in Rajasthan was fourth highest among Indian states (SRS, 2011). It has just achieved the level what Kerala had reached forty years ago. The pace of decline in IMR has been very slow. IMR in Rajasthan is not only high but also quite fluctuating. Kateja and Ramkrishnan

(2008) reveal that Neonatal Mortality Rate (NMR) and Perinatal Mortality Rate (PMR) contribute largely to the infants deaths. As far as the trend in IMR in rural and urban areas is considered, the IMR in rural areas declined more swiftly from 132 in 1972 to 65 in 2009 vis-à-vis urban counterpart from 76 in 1972 to 35 in 2009. As a result urban rural mortality differential has become smaller to some extent (Fig. 11.1), still pervasive rural urban differentials continue to prevail.

The average maternal mortality rate (MMR) for the year 2004-06 is estimated to be 388 by SRS (2009), which is the highest in India next to Uttar Pradesh and Assam. All other states, including states lagging behind in development like Odisha and Bihar are much ahead of Rajasthan in this respect. Actual MMR may be even higher due to notorious under-reporting. Such high MMR manifests actual crtical condition of maternal health prevailing in the state. NFHS-3 data indicate that majority of women have reproductive health and pregnancy related problems, but only 16.6 percent of all mothers received ante-natal care (ANC), 32 percent of all deliveries took place in institutions and only 29 percent received postnatal care. In the light of low coverage of ANC and even lower coverage of institutional deliveries and the great diversities prevailing therein according to caste, religion, media awareness, nutrition awareness, educational status and work status, it seems premature to talk of the possibility of attaining MDG (Goal 5) (Kateja, 2008).

The achievement of the state in terms of nutritional status among women and children is however better than its achievement in terms of IMR and MMR. Children's nutritional status in Rajasthan has improved substantially since NFHS-2, but 40 percent of children under age five years are still underweight. Among children under age three years (the age group for which nutritional status data are available in NFHS-2), stunting decreased from 59 percent to 40 percent between NFHS-2 and NFHS-3 and underweight decreased from 47 percent to 37 percent. However, because stunting improved more rapidly than underweight, the prevalence of wasting actually increased during that period (from 16 to 23 percent). Despite the improvements over time in stunting and underweight, undernutrition is still a major problem in Rajasthan. More than half of women in Rajasthan (53 percent) have anaemia, including 35 percent with mild anaemia, 15 percent with moderate anaemia, and 3 percent with severe anaemia. Anaemia is particularly high for women from scheduled tribes and women in the lowest wealth quintile. More than 60 percent of women who are pregnant or breastfeeding are anaemic. Anaemia is more widespread among women than it was seven years ago at the time of NFHS-2, having risen by 5 percentage points among ever-married women and 11 percentage points among pregnant women. However, the anaemia level among children age 6-35 months has declined marginally (by 2 percentage points).

Annual rate of decline in IMR and CBR has been lower in Rajasthan than the national average levels at all the points of time. In the state, as also observed in national averages, slightly faster rates of decline (1981-08) have been registered in rural areas. However, the gap still persists, since the absolute level was much higher in rual areas. In the pre reform period, faster rates of rural infant mortality decline contributed more to total decline rate while in post reform period faster decline in urban areas have contributed more. In post reform period, decline in IMR could not be sustained in rural areas in the state. If the rate of decline could be maintained at pre reform period, IMR would have significantly come down bringing the MDGs within reach. In Rajasthan, NMR, CMR and U5MR have actually increased substaintially during NFHS- 1 & 2. While during the same period national averages have been quite satisfactory. During NFHS- 2 & 3 all these outcomes in the state have been observed declining at slightly rapid rate, resulting in overall (1992-05) decent decline rates. In spite of declining mortality levels and narrowing rural-urban differentials in mortality, maternal health remains area of concern. Among the fifteen major states, Rajasthan ranks thirteenth with respect to MMR

Table 11.3: Mortality Decline in Rajasthan vis a vis National Average

Sl. No.		Annual Rate of decline (%)	Rajasthan Rural	Rajasthan Urban	Rajasthan Total	India Rural	India Urban	India Total
1.	IMR	1981-91	-2.881	-0.566	-2.685	-2.984	-1.846	-2.727
		1991-08	-1.050	-1.412	-1.191	-1.961	-1.887	-1.985
		1981-08	-1.538	-1.048	-1.543	-1.971	-1.652	-1.919
2.	CBR	1981-91	-0.601	-0.288	-0.566	-1.320	-1.00	-1.298
		1991-08	-1.176	-1.320	-1.261	-1.237	-1.404	-1.336
		1981-08	-0.919	-0.914	-0.958	-1.165	-1.166	-1.213
3.	CDR	1981-91	-3.291	0.132	-2.937	-2.263	-0.897	-2.16
		1991-08	-1.998	-1.222	-1.922	-1.443	-0.994	-1.441
		1981-08	-2.063	-0.731	-1.943	-1.541	-0.902	-1.511
4.	U 5 MR	1992-98	2.876	2.992	2.698	-2.192	-2.569	-2.196
		1998-05	-3.818	-2.588	-3.614	-2.989	-2.581	-3.101
		1992-05	-1.083	-0.263	-1.016	-2.409	-2.361	-2.463
5.	CMR	1992-98	2.763	13.657	3.205	-2.13	-2.30	-2.05
		1998-05	-6.288	-7.743	-6.416	-5.14	-5.33	-5.31
		1992-05	-2.672	-1.282	-2.64	-3.4	-3.53	-3.45
6.	NMR	1992-98	5.52	1.825	4.75	-1.95	-1.173	-1.78
		1998-05	-1.83	0.188	-1.48	-1.28	-1.442	-1.45
		1992-05	1.24	0.955	1.17	-1.51	-1.263	-1.52
7.	PMR	1992-98	0.28	-0.82	-0.10	-2.90	-5.00	-3.18
		1998-05	-4.35	-2.70	-4.12	-3.71	-2.23	-3.66
		1992-05	-2.25	-1.76	-2.25	-2.99	-3.15	-3.06
8.	MMR	1997-04			-3.37			-5.169

Source: Computed by author based on data from SRS (Various Bulletins) and NFHS (1-3).

reflecting poor condition of women in the state. The majority of the deaths could be prevented if women had access to adequate health services (either proper prenatal care or referral to appropriate health care facilities) (Jeejebhoy and Rao 1995).

Regional Disparties in Rajasthan

What has been achieved at the state/ aggregate level is not really happening at the district or lower level. There are wide inter-district variations and variations according to caste, sex, residence and so on. Table 11.3 presents relative position of different districts of Rajasthan based on parameter- specific ranking of total 593 districts studied in the country by Ram and Chander Shekhar (2006). Columns 3-6 show ranks of districts in individual parameters viz. percentage of women having three and more children, contraceptive prevalence rate, under 5 mortality rate (U5MR), three or more antenatal care visits (ANC). In Col. 7 overall rank of district in the country has been given; it presents distressingly dismal scenario. The best performer district Kota ranks as low as 213 amongst total 593 districts. It is followed by Ganganagar, Hanumangarh, Jaipur, Jhunjhunu, Ajmer and Sikar. On the other extreme, the worst performers are arid districts Jaisalmer and Barmer. As expected, other arid districts like Jalore and tribal districts including Dungarpur and Banswara also secure bottom positions.

Most of the districts are far behind in ANC visits. Overall rank of desert and border districts like Jaisalmer, Barmer, Bikaner, Ganganagar, Hunumangarh and Jhunjhunu has been worsened by poor performance in the parameter ANC visits. While the southern districts and districts which have higher percentage of tribal population namely Dungarpur, Udaipur, Bhilwara, Chittaurgarh and Rajasamand are characterized by higher U5MR. Only two districts Bikaner and Jhunjhunu have secured rank within hundred that too only in U5MR. However, pretty good performance in U5MR is inexplicable in view of not so good performance in other indicators including ANC visits, IMR, women having three or more children etc. Except Dholpur and Karauli all the districts have secured comparatively better ranks in the parameter percent of women having three and more children.

Table 11.4: Ranking of Districts

S. No.	*Districts*	*% of Women having 3 and more children*	*Contra-ceptive Preva-lence Rate*	*U-5 MR*	*3 or more ANC Visits*	*Overall Rank in Country*
1	Ajmer	331	382	411	342	336
2	Alwar	337	333	304	478	457
3	Banswara	482	402	409	576	558
4	Baran	391	386	463	352	392
5	Barmer	515	561	407	556	581
6	Bharatpur	442	371	354	509	518
7	Bhilwara	345	438	537	317	398
8	Bikaner	337	461	087	472	454
9	Bundi	338	421	428	379	376
10	Chittaurgarh	293	459	554	374	447
11	Churu	323	398	203	524	437
12	Dausa	387	325	388	452	473
13	Dholpur	540	463	475	537	574
14	Dungarpur	509	469	582	426	540
15	Ganganagar	202	120	130	441	244
16	Hanumangarh	179	102	101	456	244
17	Jaipur	281	158	294	320	276
18	Jaisalmer	496	551	332	538	586
19	Jalore	462	491	485	503	561
20	Jhalawar	313	324	394	375	404
21	Jhunjhunu	234	229	98	325	286
22	Jodhpur	404	378	249	435	413
23	Karauli	481	450	419	477	542
291	Kota	291	280	206	302	213
25	Nagaur	336	390	287	390	464
26	Pali	430	420	563	378	394
27	Rajsamand	363	394	519	400	426
28	Sawai Madhopur	408	366	496	419	507
29	Sikar	286	392	124	365	364
30	Sirohi	424	497	482	385	481
31	Tonk	361	343	516	372	466
32	Udaipur	383	408	536	420	444

Source: Ram F and Chander Shekhar 2006.

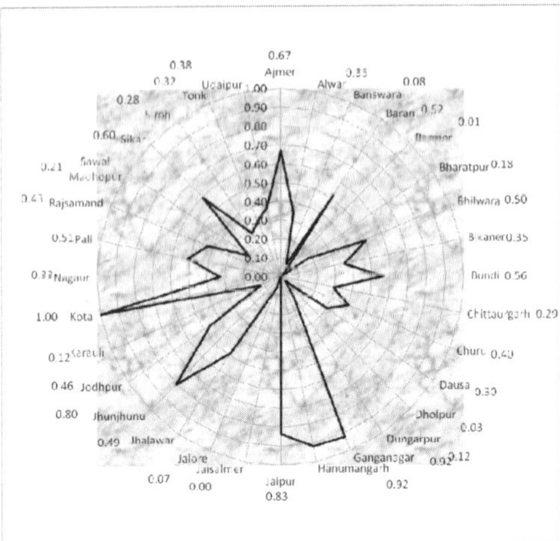

Fig. 11.2: Inter-District Differences in Health Index

Note: Based on Table 11.3

Inter-district disparity based on overall health index can be presented on radar, (Figure 11.2). The values shown on the radars have been computed using Range Equalisation Method (REM) to locate the gap each district has to travel to catch up the best performer district in the state. The vast differences in health status among the districts warrant government intervention.

Issues in Health Expenditure

Share of public spending on health has been declining over the years (Fig. 11.3), yet it is the highest among the low income states of India (Sen *et al* 2009). Though it is indicative of the high priority acccorded to the health sector by the state government, it is also true that it has not been reflected in the health outcomes. One of the reasons of which is that expenditure on health and family welfare in the state is skewed towards the tertiary health care services (Sen et al 2009). While the National Health Policy suggests a ratio of 55:35:10 towards primary, secondary and tertiary services, the state spends in the proportion of 43:28:29 in these services. The low share of expenditure towards primary and secondary health care facilities is mainly due to relatively larger coverage of urban health facilities in camparison to rural health facilities. The existing rural health facilities in the state are not even equipped with baisic infrastructure like electricity, water supply and telephone connectivity. In the state, like most other states, the salary component of health budget exceeds three-fourth of the total (Banerjee *et al* 2004). This has the implication that there will be inadequate provision for drugs and the reasons for the underutilization of public health facilities are the shortage of medicines and other supporting services. Besides, due to widely scattered villages inhabited by low density population, the radial distance covered by different categories of rural health facilities in the state is much larger than the normative radial distance as per the national norms (Rao and Choudhury 2008). Distances to health facilities are particularly high in desert and border districts of Barmer, Jaismalmer and Bikaner (Kateja 2007). And the adverse effect is clearly mirrored in low percentage of institutional deliveries and high IMR & MMR. There is no denying the fact that these poor health outcomes could also result from different socio-economic variables. There are many factors affecting health. Some lie outside the confines of the health sector. The "circumstances in which people grow, live, work and age" strongly influence how people live and die (WHO 2008). Education, housing, food and employment all impact on health. Redressing inequalities in these will reduce inequalities in health. Also, Underfunding alone is not reason for poor health services in most of the states. Expenditure efficiency is equally important.

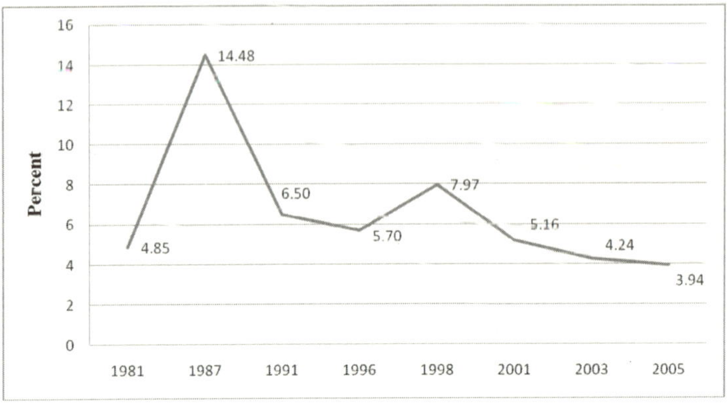

Figure 11.3: Health Expenditure as Percentage of Total Expenditure

Source: GoI (2006)

Concluding Remarks

The most important purpose of the MDGs is to focus attention on gaps that remain in achievement and on the changes needed to enable the fulfillment of rights for all especially those who are the poorest and the most vulnerable. Official claims regarding decline in mortality rates and estimates about the prospects of achieving MDGs appear reasonably optimistic. It's also true that in the last decades, the life expectancy of the population has shown remarkable improvement. Yet a huge toll on the lives of women and newborns persists and there is evidence that women and children are still vulnerable. As long as high levels of mortalities persist, a reflection of the poor health of the society, the fruits of development will always remain questionable. The slow decline in Rajasthan's child mortality rate calls for new approaches to the problem of child mortality. Future child health policies should build on past lessons from child health programmes, sustain the achievements that have already been made, enhance quality and efficiency and address specific gaps in neonatal care. Existing vast inter district differences in infant and child mortality levels demand stratified child health policies that take into account area-specific epidemiological and demographic patterns and key determinants. There are some issues that the health sector needs to address immediately. First, Infant and child mortality in Rajasthan has declined substantially over the past forty years. According to SRS, during last three decades infant mortality declined at the rate of 1.54 percent per year. Last two decades have witnessed comparatively slower decline, as a result the infant mortality rate is increasingly departing from the longer term trend. The present record does not assure achievement of millennium development goals. Under-five mortality declined by about 1.02 percent per year between NFHS - I and NFHS - II. Decline in both the vital rates in Rajasthan has been slower than the average rates of the country. The overall progress of Rajasthan in terms of outcomes on RCH, Public Health and Diseases surveillance programme leaves ample scope of improvement. There is a need to improve programme management at the Block and the District levels and to respond to the demand for basic services especially among women, children, socio-economically under-privileged people and population living in hardship. Secondly, the scant attention paid to women's health needs to change if there is to be any improvement not only in maternal health but also in child health and the health of population as a whole. Third, instead of targeting an increase in the level of health on an average at the state level, health policy should explicitly aim at reducing inter district inequalities and rural-urban differentials. Last but not the least, progress in achieving the MDGs requires considerable expansion in coverage of essential services and core infrastructure. Reduction in the proportion of unattended deliveries through health education and effective training of traditional birth attendants would go a long way. Scaling up promising and successful approaches to the provision of basic services and infrastructure is imperative for the achievement of the MDGs. While the state appears to be close to meeting the national population norms on rural health infrastructure, these are not proper equipped. Besides, the average radial distances covered by rural health facilities are much larger than what ought to be under the National norms. However, target specific interventions for districts with sparse population like Barmer, Bikaner and Jaisalmer would help in tackling the problem of low access. Mobile health centres, provision of ambulance services at PHCs may also take care of the problem of long distances. It is an urgent need to make the health care system more reliable, transparent and efficient. The Journey has certainly come a long way but it has still a long way ahead if a presentable rank is to be attained in terms of some standard Health Indicator.

References

Banerjee, Abhijit, Angus Deaton, and Esther Duflo. (2004). "Healthcare Delivery in Rural Rajasthan", *Economic and Political Weekly*, 39(9): 944-9.

Government of India. (2006). "Review of Healthcare in India", New Delhi: Ministry of Health and Family Welfare.

IDS. (2008). "Human Development Report Rajasthan (An Update)", Institute of Development Studies and Government of Rajasthan.

Jeejebhoy, Shireen J. and Saumya Ramma Rao. (1995). "Unsafe Motherhood: A Review of Reproductive Health", in Monica Das Gupta, Linclon C. Chen and T.N. Krishnan (Eds.) "*Women's Health in India: Risk and Vulnerability*", Bombay : Oxford University Press.

Kateja, Alpana. (2007). "Healthcare Services in Rajasthan", *Research Journal*, Vol. 15, No. 1.

Kateja, Alpana. (2008). "Maternal Health in Rajasthan", *Rajasthan Economic Journal*, Vol. 32, No. 2.

Kateja, Alpana and Ramakrishnan, Sandhya K. (2008). "Causes, Trends and Levels of Infant Mortality: A Compartative Study of Rajasthan and Kerala", *Demography India*, Vol. 37, No. 2.

NFHS-II. (2002). "National Family Health Survey II - 1998-99", International Institute of Population Science (IIPS) & ORC MACRO, Deonar, Mumbai.

NFHS-III. 2005-06. "National Family Health Survey III - 2005-06", International Institute of Population Science (IIPS) & ORC MACRO, Deonar, Mumbai.

Ram F and Chander Shekhar. (2006). "Ranking and Mapping of Districts-Based on Socio-Economic and Demographic Indicators", International Institute of Population Sciences, Mumbai.

Rao, M. Govinda and Choudhury, M. (2008). "Interstate Equalisation of Health Expenditures in Indian Union", National Institute of Public Finance and Policy, New Delhi.

Sen, Tapas K., H. K. Amarnath, M. Choudhury and Surjit Das. (2009). "Rajasthan: Fostering Economic and Human Development Concurrently", Monograph, National Institute of Public Finance and Policy, New Delhi.

SRS (Sample Registration System), Various Bulletins, Registrar General of India, GOI.

United Nations. (2000). United Nation General Assembly Resolution, A/ 55/ 2.

World Health Organization. (2008). "Closing the Gap in Generation – Health Equity through Action on the Social Determinants of Health", Geneva, (http:/ / whqlibdoc.who.int/ hq/ 2008/ who_IER_CSDH_08.1_eng.pdf, accessed on 27 June 2010).

Trends in Health Status in Punjab

Bharati Kapur & Vipla Chopra

Health is an important ingredient of development. It supports development process, spurs economic growth and is a good measure of human wellbeing. Enhancement of health of the people is one of the major objectives of the process of development. It improves the productivity and skills of the people and reduces absenteeism from work. It thus increases income of poor people. Health directly improves the socioeconomic conditions of people in many ways. Improving health status of people is one of the basic goals of development. Health is not only an end product but it is also a major contributor to economic development. Health gives capability and brings the capacity for personal development, with economic wellbeing; it is a critical input for poverty reduction and economic development. It is a component of capability and human resource. Improving health condition not only improves wellbeing but also increases income earning capacity. It acts as a means to enhance one's capability to work and earn more. Income, health and education act together and improve individual capability and induce overall development of a country. "Health is more than the well-being of an individual. The health of an individual or group affects the well-being of communities and nations through economic productivity, school attendance and performance by children and long-term prospects for the development of a country's human resources" (WHO 2003).

Good health and prosperity tend to support each other. Healthy people can more easily earn an income and people with a higher income can more easily seek medical care, have better nutrition and have the freedom to lead healthier lives (Sen 2000). Health gain increases life expectancy and quality of life, reduces morbidity, mortality and fertility. These are the signs of development of a nation. "Improvements in health are important in their own right, but better health is also prerequisite and a major contributor to economic growth and social cohesion. Conversely, an improvement in people's access to health technology is a good indicator of the success of other development processes" (WHO 2003). Health and development of a country are interlinked. Health plays a crucial role in the economic development and poverty reduction.

One of the major objectives of India's planned economic development has been to raise the standard of living and subsequently health status of its population. For achieving this objective the provision of healthcare services to all, besides other things like education, adequate food etc. play significant role. An overview of health indicators in India over a period of time has been presented in Table 12.1. It reveals that crude death rate fell sharply from 12.5 (per 1000) in 1981 to 7.4 (per 1000) in 2008, showing a net drop of 40.8 percent. This rapid fall may be due to the technological advances and improved quality and coverage of health care. In contrast, the reduction in crude birth rate has been less steep, declining from 33.9 (per 1000) in 1981 to 22.8 (per 1000) in 2008, depicting a decline of 32.74 percent. The total fertility rate (TFR) declined from 4.5 in 1981 to 2.7 in 2007 i.e. a decline of 40 percent. This fall in fertility rate in India is a result of socio-economic development as well as the intense implementation of family planning programmes. But there are huge variations in the level of fertility in rural-urban areas. During 1991-2001, TFR in rural areas i.e. 3.1 was higher than that of urban areas i.e. 2.3. The urban fertility rate remains lower than rural fertility rate probably because urban women are more educated, enjoy higher incomes and have better access to family planning services. India's maternal mortality rate (MMR) was

437 in 1992-93 which decreased to 254 in 2004-06 showing a net drop of 41.87 percent. The high rate of maternal mortality rate in India is the result of poor health status of women and lack of adequate health facilities during pregnancy and child birth. The infant mortality rate (IMR) declined significantly from 110 (per 1000) in 1981 to 53 (per 1000) in 2008, showing a decline of more than 50 percent. The female infant mortality rate (55) was found to be higher than the male infant mortality rate (52) during 2008. Moreover, infant mortality rate in rural areas has remained higher than those in urban areas throughout the period due to inadequate health facilities, illiteracy and poverty etc. in rural areas. Life expectancy at birth for males moved up from 55.4 years in 1981-85 to 63.5 years in 2002-06 while it increased from 55.7 to 64.2 for females during the corresponding period, thereby showing a greater increase in life expectancy for females. The life expectancy has increased as a result of an overall decline in mortality caused by general improvement in medical services, check on epidemics, spread of immunization programmes etc.

Punjab occupies an extremely important place in India (Punjab- Human Development Report, 2004). It is one of the richest states of India whose per capita gross state domestic product (GSDP) in 2009-10 was US$ 1423.6. It grew at a compound annual growth rate of 9.8 percent between 2001-02 and 2009-10. According to the Planning Commission, the state ranks amongst the top five states in terms of per capita income (IBEF, 2010). It has the lowest incidence of poverty (8.4 percent) as against the all India incidence (27.5 percent) (Ahluwalia 2010). Given these impressive economic performance, the health status of population of Punjab need to be critically examined as health is recognized as an important component of social sector development.

Table 12.1. India – Selected Health Indicators

S.No.	*Parameter*	*1981*	*1991*	*Current Level*
1.	Crude Death Rate(CBR) (per 1000 population)	12.5	9.8	7.4 (2008)
2.	Crude Birth Rate(CDR) (per 1000 population)	33.9	29.5	22.8 (2008)
3.	Total fertility Rate(TFR) (per women)			2.7 (2007)
	Rural	4.5	3.6	3.1 (1991-2001)
				2.3 (1991-2001)
4.	Maternal Mortality Rate) (MMR (per 1,00,000 live births)	NA	437 (1992-93)	254 (2004-06)
5.	Infant Mortality Rate(IMR) (per 1000 live births)	110	80	53 (2008)
	Male	–	–	52 (2008)55
	Female			(2008)
6.	Life Expectancy at birth (in Years)	(1981-85)		(1989-93)
(2002-06)				
	Total	55.5	59.4	63.5
	Male	55.4	59.0	62.6
	Female	55.7	59.7	64.2

Source: Ministry of Health and Family Welfare/RGI.

The health status is generally measured in terms of life expectancy at birth, infant mortality rate, birth rate, death rate etc. The indicators of health like birth rates and death rates are more reflective of the demographic changes taking place in the country. The life expectancy rate and infant mortality rates are better indicators of the health status of the population.

In this paper an attempt has been made to determine the progress in health status of the people of Punjab on the basis of improvements made in health indicators like birth rate, death rate, infant mortality rate, life expectancy etc., over the period 1981-2008 (i.e. almost three decades). This period has been further disaggregated into three time periods i.e. (i) First period- 1981-90, (ii) Second period-1991-2000, (iii) Third period-2001-08. An attempt has also been made to highlight some of the morbidity patterns in Punjab as revealed by surveys undertaken during different rounds of the National Sample Survey Organization (NSSO) and the health surveys undertaken by the National Council of Applied Economic Research. (NCAER).

Birth Rate

Birth rate is the number of births per 1000 persons per year. The birth rate is an item of concern and policy for a number of national governments. High birth rates are associated with health impairments and low life expectancy, low living standards, low status of women and low levels of education. There are claims that as countries go through economic development and social change, birth rate declines. Birth rates ranging from 10-20 births per 1000 are considered low, while rates from 40-50 births per 1000 are considered high. There are problems associated with both an extremely high birth rate and an extremely low birth rate. High birth rates can cause stress on the government welfare and family programmes to support a young population. Additional problems faced by a country with high birth rate include educating a growing number of children, creating jobs for these children when they enter the workforce, and dealing with the environmental effects that a large population can produce. Low birth rates can put stress on the government to provide adequate welfare systems for seniors and also the stress on the families to support the elders themselves. There will be less children or working age population to support the constantly growing aging population. The data regarding birth rates, death rates and natural growth rate of the population in Punjab has been presented in Table 12.2. The birth rate has declined from 30.3 births per 1000 population to 17.3 births per 1000 population during 1981 to 2008, showing a net drop of 42.90 percent. During the first period, the birth rate for the state of Punjab declined from 30.3 to 27.6, i.e. a decline of 8.91 percent, during the second period it reduced from 27.7 to 21.5, i.e. a decline of 22.38 percent and finally during the third period, it declined from 21.2 to 17.3,

Table 12.2: Area-wise Birth Rate, Death Rate and Natural Growth Rate in Punjab (per 1000 population per annum)

Year	*Birth Rate*	*Death Rate*		*Natural Growth Rate*					
	Rural	*Urban*	*Com-bined*	*Rural*	*Urban*	*Com-bined*	*Rural*	*Urban*	*Com-bined*
1981	30.8	28.5	30.3	10.0	7.1	9.4	20.8	21.4	20.9
1985	29.1	27.6	28.7	9.9	6.7	8.9	19.2	20.9	19.8
1990	28.4	25.6	27.6	8.5	5.8	7.8	19.9	19.8	19.8
1991	28.5	25.6	27.7	8.5	5.7	7.8	20.0	19.9	19.9
1995	26.0	20.8	24.7	7.8	6.1	7.3	18.2	14.7	17.4
2000	22.6	18.5	21.5	7.8	5.8	7.3	14.8	12.7	14.2
2001	22.1	18.7	21.2	7.2	6.4	7.0	14.9	12.3	14.2
2002	21.7	18.1	20.8	7.4	6.2	7.1	14.3	11.9	13.7
2003	21.5	17.9	20.6	7.3	6.0	7.0	14.2	11.9	13.6
2004	19.3	17.6	18.7	6.9	5.6	6.4	12.4	12.0	12.3
2005	18.8	17.0	18.1	7.2	5.8	6.7	11.6	11.2	11.4
2006	18.4	16.8	17.8	7.4	5.8	6.8	11.0	11.0	11.0
2007	18.3	16.4	17.6	7.7	5.9	7.0	10.6	10.5	10.6
2008	18.0	16.1	17.3	8.0	6.0	7.2	10.0	10.1	10.1

Source: *Statistical Abstract of Punjab*, Various Issues

indicating a decline of 18.40 percent. Thus, maximum decline in birth rate has been witnessed during the second period. Further, area-wise analysis depicts a declining trend in both rural and urban areas during the period 1981-2008. The percentage decline in birth rate during the first and second period was higher in the urban areas (i.e. 10.18 percent and 27.73 percent respectively) as compared to those of rural areas (i.e. 7.79 percent and 20.70 percent respectively), but during the third period, the rural areas showed a greater decline (18.55 percent) as compared to that of urban areas (13.90 percent). However, the birth rate per 1000 in rural areas remained higher than that of urban areas throughout the period.

Diminishing birth rate in Punjab points towards a new environment of reproduction where modifications in the reproductive strategy of couples reflect preference for progressively smaller families. The substantial decrease in birth rate in Punjab, despite some of the key social indicators, such as strong son preference, sizeable presence of a socially backward population and relatively higher infant mortality, being against the decline, is a manifestation of the primacy of intervention by selected development factors, namely, the family planning programme, female literacy and prosperity at the household level.

Death Rate

Death rate has declined from 9.4 per 1000 population to 7.2 per 1000 population during the period 1981 to 2008, showing a fall of 23.40 percent. During the first period, it declined from 9.4 to 7.8 (i.e. 17.02 percent), during the second period, it went down from 7.8 to 7.3 (i.e. 6.41 percent) and during the third period, it further declined from 7.0 in 2001 to 6.4 in 2005 (i.e. 8.57 percent) and thereafter increased to 7.2 in 2008.

Further, area-wise analysis depicts a declining trend in both rural and urban areas during the period 1981-2008. On comparing the percentage decline in death rate in rural and urban areas, it has been observed that during the first period, death rate declined sharply in urban areas (18.31 percent) as compared to the rural areas (15 percent). During the second period, it declined by 8.24 percent in rural areas while in urban areas fluctuations have been observed. During the third period, instead of declining, death rate went up. The figures of rural areas reveal that death rate declined from 7.2 to 6.9 during 2001-04 but later increased from 7.2 to 8.0 during 2005-08. In the urban areas, death rate went down from 6.4 to 5.6 during 2001-04 but increased from 5.8 to 6.0 during 2005-08. The recent rise in death rate in Punjab, in spite of advanced medical facilities is really worrisome. Diseases like cancer have been killing many in Punjab, especially in parts of Malwa. Besides, death rate due to heart and other diseases have also gone up. Even diseases like dengue have taken the lives of many. Besides diseases, road accidents have also become a big killer.

Natural Growth Rate

Birth and death rates are the dominant factors in determining the natural growth rate of population. The natural growth rate of population in Punjab declined from 20.9 to 10.1 during 1981-2008, showing a net drop of 51.67 percent. During the period 1981-90, it reduced from 20.9 to 19.8, depicting a decline of 5.26 percent, during 1991-2000, it went down from 19.9 to 14.2, showing a decline of 28.64 percent and during 2001-08, it reduced from 14.2 to 10.1, indicating a decline of 28.87 percent. On comparing the natural growth rate in rural and urban areas, it has been found that during the first and second period, the percentage decline in natural growth rate of population was lower in rural areas of Punjab (i.e. 4.33 percent and 26 percent respectively) as compared to those of the urban areas (i.e. 7.48 percent and 36.18 percent respectively), while during the third period, the percentage decline in natural growth rate of population was lower in the urban areas (17.88 percent) as compared to that of the rural areas (32.89 percent).

Infant Mortality Rate

Infant mortality rate is seen as an indicator of child health and the well-being of a society. The causes of infant mortality are correlated to structural factors like economic development, general living conditions, social well-being and the quality of the environment, that affect the health of entire population. Infant mortality rate is widely accepted as good indicator of health status by governments and also international organizations like World Health Organisation. It is one of the most telling indicators on the health services, health awareness and satisfactory health practices. Table 12.3 manifests data regarding the infant mortality rate in Punjab during the period 1981-2008.The infant mortality rate in Punjab has been steadily declining since 1981. It dropped significantly from 81 per 1000 live births to 41 per 1000 live births during 1981-2008, depicting a decline of 49.38 percent. During the first period, it declined from 81 to 61 (24.69 percent), during the second period, it declined very slightly from 53 to 52 (1.89 percent) and during the third period it declined from 52 to 41 (21.15 percent). It shows that the fall in infant mortality rate has slowed down during the second period.

Table 12.3: Area-wise Infant Mortality Rate in Punjab (per 1000 population per annum)

Year	Infant Mortality Rate		
	Rural	Urban	Combined
1981	88	51	81
1985	78	51	71
1990	66	45	61
1991	58	40	53
1995	58	39	54
2000	56	38	52
2001	55	37	52
2002	55	35	51
2003	53	34	49
2004	50	36	45
2005	49	37	44
2006	48	36	44
2007	47	35	43
2008	45	33	41

Source: Statistical Abstract of Punjab, Various Issues

The infant mortality rate went down both in rural and urban areas during the study period; but still there exists wide area-wise differences. The percentage decline in infant mortality rate during the first period was quite high in rural areas (25 percent) as compared to that of urban areas (11.76 percent), while during the second period the percentage decline in urban areas was higher (5 percent) as compared to that of the rural areas (3.45 percent). During the third period, the percentage decline in infant mortality rate was higher in rural areas (18.18 percent) as compared to that of the urban areas (10.81 percent). It has also been observed that the infant mortality rate has remained higher throughout the study period in rural areas than that of the urban areas. In fact, lack of rural bias is one of the reasons why Punjab has had a much slower decline in infant mortality. It indicates the need for more health facilities in rural areas. For a greater achievement in infant mortality reduction in Punjab, there is a need to concentrate more on rural areas where two-thirds of the population resides.

The infant mortality rate has shown a declining trend mainly because most of the causes of infant mortality have been prevented through immunization. The control over the main infant killer diseases like measles, diphtheria, tetanus, poliomyelitis and pertusis have helped to reduce the deaths among infants. Since the 1980s the government has focused special attention on the prevention of infant deaths. Some of the effective ways to fight infant mortality can be removal of gender bias, strengthening of the Child Survival and Safe Motherhood (CSSM) Programmes under the Reproductive and Child Health (RCH) umbrella, screening mothers-to-be for ante-natal check-up and nutritional intake, reduction in the share of non-institutional births, adequate provision for emergency obstetric services, introduction of nutritional programmes especially for anaemic mothers, proper immunization and nourishment for the new born, strengthening the sub-centre, subsidiary health centres and primary health centres, and making women doctors available for female clients, particularly at selected centres in remote rural areas and wider community involvement.

Life Expectancy

Life expectancy is closely connected with health conditions, which are in turn an integral part of development. The unprecedented increase in human longevity reflects gain in public health and in access to primary health care services. It is thus, a basic indicator of health and social development. Improvements in living conditions and health have helped to reduce overall mortality levels across all sections of the society and this has resulted in, on an average, a longer life-span of individuals in Punjab. The data on expectation of life at birth in Punjab between 1981-85 and 2006-10 has been presented in Table 12.4. It shows that expectation of life at birth in Punjab has undergone a significant change from 63.1 years during 1981-85 to 70.2 years during 2006-10, registering an increase of more than 7 years. The expectation of life at birth for females was 63.6 years during 1981-85 and it increased to 71.6 years during 2006-10. For males, expectation of life was 62.6 years during 1981-85 which increased to 68.7 years during 2006-10. Life expectancy in Punjab increased 8 years for females and 6.1 years for males during the corresponding period. Besides, it has been observed that life expectancy of females has always remained higher than that of males during the study period.

Table 12.4 Life Expectancy at Birth by Sex, Punjab (in years)

Period	*Life Expectancy*		
	Male	*Female*	*Total*
1981-85	62.6	63.6	63.1
1986-90	64.7	66.9	65.8
1991-95	66.1	68.4	67.3
1996-00	67.1	69.2	68.2
2001-05	68.1	70.1	69.1
2006-10	68.7	71.6	70.2

Source: *Economic Survey, Punjab, 2009-10.*

Fertility Rate

Total fertility rate of a population is the average number of children that would be born to a woman over a lifetime if she were to experience the exact current Age-Specific Fertility Rates (ASFRs) through her lifetime, and she were to survive from birth through the end of her reproductive life. It is obtained by summing the single-year-age specific rates at a given time. High fertility is associated with increased risk of maternal morbidity and mortality. In most settings, women who have several children find it difficult to work outside the home, thus having fewer opportunities to improve their economic and social status and that of their families. Low income households with many children often find it more difficult to get out of poverty than those with less children, and high fertility societies face greater demand from their youthful populations. The changes in the population age distribution resulting from declining fertility are, for a period, beneficial for economic growth. As fertility declines, the proportion of children in the population falls and the proportion of population of working age increases, resulting in a lower dependency ratio. Provided jobs are available for the increasing population of working age, a country can reap the benefits of increased production and lower the costs associated with the decreasing proportion of dependents. This "demographic bonus" can thus contribute significantly to economic growth and poverty reduction. As a result of socio-economic development and family planning intervention Punjab has undergone substantial transformations in its fertility profile. Table 12.5 shows the fertility rates in Punjab during 1981 to 2008. It reveals that there has been a sustained decline in fertility in the state. It declined from 4.0 to 1.9 during 1981-2008, i.e. a net drop of 52.50 percent. During the first period, it declined from 4.0 to 3.2 in (20 percent), during the second period it reduced from 3.1 to 2.4 (22.58 percent), and during the third period it went down from 2.4 to 1.9 (20.83 percent). The maximum decline in fertility rate was observed during the second period. Further, it has been observed that fertility declined in both rural and urban areas during the study period. During the first period, the rate of decline in fertility was found to be higher in rural areas (17.07 percent) as compared to that of urban areas (14.71 percent), while during the second period, the percentage decline in fertility was higher in urban areas (25 percent) as compared to that of rural areas (18.75 percent). During the third period, the percentage decline in fertility was higher in rural areas (20 percent) as compared to that of the urban areas (14.29 percent).

Table 12.5: Area-wise Fertility Rate in Punjab

Year	*Fertility Rate*		
	Rural	*Urban*	*Combined*
1981	4.1	3.4	4.0
1985	3.6	3.1	3.5
1990	3.4	2.9	3.2
1991	3.2	2.8	3.1
1995	3.1	2.4	2.9
2000	2.6	2.1	2.4
2001	2.5	2.1	2.4
2002	2.4	2.0	2.3
2003	2.4	2.0	2.3
2004	2.3	2.0	2.2
2005	2.2	1.9	2.1
2006	2.1	1.9	2.1
2007	2.1	1.8	2.0
2008	2.0	1.8	1.9

Source: Sample Registration System (SRS), Registrar General, India, Various Volumes.

Declining fertility rate indicates that the people prefer to have smaller family size. It is extensive in the state and is not confined to any specific region or community. Rural and urban areas in each district have been experiencing transition in fertility in different ways depending on changes in local conditions, which often act as important inducements for the determination of family size.

Immunization

Following the Alma Ata Declaration, immunization was taken up on a war footing the entire world over. The 1990s saw a massive programme launched by the Government of India, with many international aid agencies and the state governments, to universalize immunization of children and expectant mothers. The basic immunization programme covers children against the major killer and debilitating diseases. The progress of immunization in Punjab for the period 1981-82 to 2008-09 has been presented in Table 12.6. It shows that the achievements in immunization in case of expectant mothers increased rapidly from 213122 in 1981-82 to 450445 in 2008-09, with a growth rate of 33.35 percent per annum. The growth rate was maximum during the first period (9.93 percent per annum) while during the second and third periods it declined to negative, i.e. -0.32 and -0.98 per annum respectively. In case of infants, it has been found that the achievement in immunization increased from 333882 in 1981-82 to 425422 during 2008-09, with overall growth rate of 1.25 percent per annum. The maximum growth rate (4.06 percent per annum) was witnessed during the first period while the growth rate reduced to 0.05 percent per annum during the second period and later turned negative (-1.71 percent per annum) during the third period. The achievement in immunization in case of children increased from 272378 in 1981-82 to 444787 in 2008-09, showing a growth rate of 2.33 percent per annum. Just as in case of expectant mothers and infants, the growth rate was again recorded to be maximum during the first period i.e. 6.66 percent per annum. The growth rate then turned negative (-0.26 percent per annum) during the second period but later showed an improvement and increased to 2.02 percent per annum during the third period. The analysis also reveals that the targets of immunization in case of infants and children have not only been met but even exceeded for most of the years during the study period.

Table 12.6 Progress of Immunization in Punjab

Year	Expectant Mothers (T.T)			Infants (D.P.T) 0-2 years			Children (D.T.) 3-8 years		
	Target	Achieve-ment	Percent Share	Target	Achie	Percent vement	Target Share	Achieve	Percent ment
1981-82	200000	213122	106.58	750000	333882	44.52	250000	272378	108.95
1982-83	300000	228418	76.14	600000	349602	58.27	300000	257676	85.89
1983-84	350000	251498	78.86	450000	411476	91.44	300000	314570	104.86
1984-85	350000	275675	78.76	400000	435743	108.95	400000	312864	78.23
1985-86	350000	227079	79.16	400000	353482	88.37	300000	344661	114.89
1986-87	400000	299690	74.92	400000	366015	91.5	300000	330719	110.24
1987-88	500000	373657	75.53	403000	434550	107.83	300000	412205	137.4
1988-89	491000	414033	81.31	397033	453155	113.39	391000	387953	99.22
1989-90	477100	466766	93.83	370700	476518	128.55	364900	453932	124.40
1990-91	459440	464548	101.1	429786	516823	120.25	367837	463245	125.94
1991-92	552000	551020	99.8	517000	543722	105.17	378800	592733	156.48
1992-93	595954	576103	96.7	545746	566900	103.88	378800	495033	130.68
1993-94	607185	622350	102.5	556003	607678	109.88	385787	498199	129.14
1994-95	612200	632477	103.3	559700	607996	108.63	451200	532803	118.09
1995-96	599000	613531	102.4	548600	601678	109.6	456100	492497	107.9
1996-97	589300	608548	103.2	540000	571211	105.78	462400	527770	114.[illegible]4
1997-98	*	556272	-	*	574957	-	*	482050	-
1998-99	570000	565362	99.2	520000	570311	109.68	530000	436051	82.87
1999-00	603006	581734	96.5	520028	592325	113.9	538087	581207	108.01
2000-01	583800	570388	97.7	502060	569497	113.43	544960	548383	100.53

Year	Expectant Mothers (T.T)			Infants (D.P.T) 0-2 years			Children (D.T.) 3-8 years		
	Target	Achievement	Percent Share	Target	Achie	Percent vement	Target Share	Achieve	Percent ment
2001-02	565400	510900	90.3	486760	532832	109.47	549860	460864	83.81
2002-03	582000	485977	83.5	501000	517023	103.21	552000	435013	78.81
2003-04	594920	503630	84.7	512713	497124	96.96	561936	535044	95.21
2004-05	595074	520826	87.5	513386	518144	100.90	586908	546451	93.11
2005-06	591082	534156	90.4	509942	531806	104.3	578682	612307	105.8
2006-07	592604	537810	90.8	512333	536117	104.6	601496	623594	103.7
2007-08	544035	471736	86.7	472322	498503	105.5	608304	567743	93.3
2008-09	535061	450445	84.2	465017	425422	91.5	618102	444787	72.0
Compound Annual Growth Rate (in percent)									
1981-82 to 2008-09		33.35			1.25			2.33	
1981-82 to 1990-91		9.93			4.06			6.66	
1991-92 to 2000-01		-0.32			0.05			-0.26	
2001-02 to 2008-09		-0.98			-1.71			2.02	

Note: *No Target Allocated by Government of India.
Source: *Statistical Abstract of Punjab*, Various Issues

Prophylaxies against Nutritional Anaemia

The progress of prophylaxies against nutritional anaemia in Punjab state for the period 1981-82 to 2008-09 has been presented in Table 12.7. It shows that achievement in prophylaxies in case of children showed a steady increase from 365382 in 1981-82 to 1064776 in 2005-06 but dropped consistently thereafter, and finally settled at only 43739 in 2008-09, showing a negative growth rate of -1.87 percent per annum during the study period. The growth rate was 4.45 percent per annum during the first period and 2.75 percent per annum during the second period but during the third period it turned negative (-37.26 percent per annum). Thus, the maximum progress was observed during the first period.

The achievement in prophylaxies for expectant mothers increased from 336169 in 1981-82 to 597534 in 2005-06 but declined thereafter and settled at 234398 in 2008-09, showing a negative growth rate of -2.97 percent per annum during the study period. The growth rate was 4.81 percent per annum during the first period but later it turned negative during the second (0.87 percent per annum) and third period (-24.72 percent per annum). Data also reveal that targets have been met in a better way for the expectant mothers as compared to the children because for most of the years the targets could not be met for children, while in case of expectant mothers targets have been met and even exceeded for most of the years. It has also been observed that during the recent years i.e. from 2006-09, the achievement rate of prophylaxies have been very low for both children and expectant mothers.

Incidence and Prevalence of Morbidity

The NSS 28th round defines morbidity as sickness that includes injury and poisoning which ultimately is a deviation from the state of physical and mental wellbeing. The chronic events were not treated as morbidity in this survey. It estimated both the incidence rate (frequency of morbidity commencing during the reference period, started and ended during the reference period) and prevalence rate (frequency of morbidity

Table 12.7: Progress of Prophylaxies against Nutritional Anaemia in Punjab

Year	*Children*			*Expectant Mothers*		
	Target	*Achievement*	*Percent Share*	*Target*	*Achievement*	*Percent Share*
1981-82	300000	365382	121.79	300000	336169	112.06
1982-83	300000	362962	120.99	300000	381899	127.30
1983-84	300000	515816	171.94	300000	560552	186.85
1984-85	400000	587942	146.9	400000	533408	133.30
1985-86	450000	577179	128.2	450000	572199	127.10
1986-87	500000	625827	125.6	500000	649950	130.00
1987-88	532000	728213	136.8	510000	764049	149.81
1988-89	500000	464891	92.10	510000	545336	106.93
1989-90	500000	571017	114.2	510000	590692	115.82
1990-91	663800	560826	84.5	347600	504315	145.1
1991-92	750000	705752	94.1	507000	583467	115.08
1992-93	1049600	673264	64.1	595954	664804	111.55
1993-94	N.A.	N.A.	-	N.A.	N.A.	-
1994-95	1078576	1053862	97.7	612200	885159	144.59
1995-96	1186700	956015	80.5	599000	683758	114.15
1996-97	1470000	906027	61.6	589300	590310	100.17
1997-98	*	886123	-	*	593566	-
1998-99	1050000	762054	72.6	570000	617019	108.2
1999-00	1522089	982321	64.2	603006	748652	124.2

Year	*Children*			*Expectant Mothers*		
	Target	*Achievement*	*Percent Share*	*Target*	*Achievement*	*Percent Share*
2000-01	1540050	958924	62.3	583800	584997	100.2
2001-02	1553960	882543	56.8	565400	580667	102.7
2002-03	927000	819107	88.4	582000	500733	86.0
2003-04	1453704	943017	64.9	594920	535008	89.9
2004-05	1145267	1492074	65.1	595074	570445	95.9
2005-06	1395036	1064776	76.3	591082	597534	101.0
2006-07	1699880	262587	15.4	592604	223675	37.7
2007-08	1719120	49825	2.8	544035	25041	4.6
2008-09	1749810	43739	2.4	535061	234398	43.8
Compound Annual Growth Rate (in percent)						
1981-82 to 2008-09			-1.87			-2.97
1981-82 to 1990-91			4.45			4.81
1991-92 to 2000-01			2.75			-0.87
2001-02 to 2008-09			-37.26			-24.72

Note: * No Target allocated by Government of India.
Source: Statistical Abstract of Punjab, Various Issues.

prevailing in the reference period). The survey revealed that Punjab had higher incidence and prevalence rates of morbidity than the all-India level both for rural and urban areas. No variations by residential status of households were reported in the incidence and prevalence rates of morbidity at the all-India level, but greater morbidity (both incidence and prevalence) was reported in rural than in urban areas of Punjab (Table 12.8).

Table 12.8: Incidence and Prevalence Rates of Morbidity per thousand Persons

State/Country	*Incidence Rate*		*Prevalence Rate*	
	Rural	*Urban*	*Rural*	*Urban*
Punjab	19.3	16.7	27.5	24.6
All India	12.6	13.5	22.5	22.8

Source: NSS 28th Round, *Sarvekshana*, Volume IV, No. 1& 2, 1980.

Table 12.9: Prevalence Rate of Illnesses by Socio-economic Characteristics (per 1000 Persons)

Socio-economic Characteristics	*Rural Areas*		*Urban Areas*	
	Punjab	*India*	*Punjab*	*India*
Sex				
Males	58.4	105.3	61.2	88.1
Females	23.9	59.8	34.0	46.6
Boys	47.4	93.9	79.4	90.8
Girls	7.1	45.7	33.4	40.5
Annual Income				
Low income (less than 12000)	25.0	87.4	67.1	77.2
Middle income (12500-56000)	48.8	65.7	43.4	63.1
High income (more than 56000)	18.0	47.2	45.7	57.6
Education				
No Formal education	27.8	74.9	25.9	69.7
Primary	25.2	84.8	50.1	65.4
Secondary	56.3	79.1	60.5	70.0

Socio-economic Characteristics	*Rural Areas*		*Urban Areas*	
	Punjab	*India*	*Punjab*	*India*
Graduate and others	52.3	78.6	53.2	66.6
Occupation of the head of household				
Cultivators	41.6	71.2	32.4	67.2
Wage earners	28.0	94.0	79.9	66.3
Salary earners	50.8	79.0	51.3	68.2
Professionals	40.3	73.7	55.5	69.3
Artisans	0.0	84.3	45.2	62.5
Petty shopkeepers	79.4	91.0	47.3	67.9
Businessmen	139.3	97.4	18.2	60.1
Others	0.0	73.1	6.3	78.0
Total	37.7	79.1	49.7	67.7

Source: NCAER, *Household Survey of Medical Care*, May-June 1990

Household Survey of Medical Care (NCAER, May-June 1990) covered a sample of 8,417 households from 34 villages in 12 districts to study morbidity patterns in Punjab. It classified illnesses by various socio-economic characteristics of the households, such as sex, income, education and occupation. Classification of all household illness-episodes revealed that the prevalence rate was higher among males and boys than among females or girls in both rural and urban areas of Punjab and India. All-India trend show a declining morbidity with increase in income, while no such trend was observed for Punjab. Similarly, education did not have much impact on morbidity patterns, except that reporting of illnesses was less among the illiterates, or not formally educated, in both rural and urban areas of Punjab. In rural areas, businessmen, including petty shopkeepers, reported maximum morbidity than the other occupational groups. Urban areas did not show any such trend (Table 12.9).

NCAER (1995) survey of healthcare utilization and expenditure also measured the prevalence rate of illnesses. It revealed that the prevalence rate of illnesses per 1000 persons was much higher in Punjab than the national average. The survey also indicated sex-wise rural-urban differentials. For instance, the prevalence rate of illnesses was much higher among rural males in Punjab than in India (155.8 per 1,000 as against 105.5 per 1,000). It was also much higher for both males and females in urban areas of Punjab than the national average. The percentage of illness episodes treated was also much higher in Punjab than in India (Table 12.10).

Table 12.10: Prevalence Rate and Treatment of Illness by Area and Sex (per 1000 Persons)

Sex	*Rural Areas*				*Urban Areas*			
	Punjab		*India*		*Punjab*		*India*	
	Preva-lence of Illness	*Percent Treated*	*Preva-lence of Illness*	*Percent treated*	*Preva lence of illness*	*Percent treated*	*Preva-lence of illness*	*Percent* treated
Males	155.8	100.0	105.5	88.1	120.6	95.0	98.2	92.4
Females	106.4	98.2	108.1	88.4	175.4	94.2	108.4	90.9
Total	132.0	99.3	106.7	88.2	175.4	92.3	103.0	91.7

Source: NCAER, *Household Survey of Health Care Utilization and Expenditure*, March1995.

Classification of Illnesses

NSS 28th round survey revealed that more people suffered from chronic diseases with increase in age in both the rural and urban areas of Punjab. Such chronic morbidity was more common among males in rural areas and among females in urban areas. The common chronic diseases suffered by the people of Punjab in both rural and urban areas were asthma, piles, rheumatism, bronchitis, tuberculosis, epilepsy, kidney stone or kidney trouble and high blood pressure.

The prevalence rates of illness have been classified under serious communicable diseases, acute illness and chronic diseases in rural and urban areas in Punjab and India. According to NCAER (1995) survey the prevalence rate of communicable diseases was lower in rural areas and higher in urban areas of Punjab as compared to India, which might have been due to influx of migrants from backward states. The prevalence rate of acute illness was higher in both rural and urban areas of Punjab than in India, which might have been due to greater awareness and prompt reporting. There were fewer patients with chronic diseases in rural areas and additional patients with chronic diseases in urban areas of Punjab than in India. Life-style and dietary patterns in urban areas might have led to such a situation. The average duration of illness for communicable and acute illnesses in rural Punjab for both males and females was higher than in rural India. The duration in urban areas was somewhat same for Punjab and India (Table 12.11). It seems to indicate that the rural people of Punjab are not getting proper treatment for their illnesses as compared to their counterparts in other rural areas of the country and the urban areas of the state.

Table 12.11 Prevalence Rate of Illness Classified by Type and Duration of Illness (per 1000 persons)

Type and Duration of illness	*Rural*		*Urban*	
	Punjab	*India*	*Punjab*	*India*
Type of illness				
Serious communicable diseases	12.9	15.6	18.1	14.0
Acute illnesses	111.1	77.9	105.6	70.6
Chronic diseases	7.9	13.2	22.2	18.4
Total	132.0	106.7	145.8	103.0
Average duration of illness (in days) (for communicable and acute illness only)				
Male	14.0	11.4	9.2	10.4
Female	12.2	10.1	9.5	9.8
Total	13.2	10.8	9.3	10.1

Source: NCAER, *Household Survey of Health Care Utilization and Expenditure*, March 1995.

The 52nd round of NSS on morbidity and treatment of ailments also showed that the prevalence of morbidity was higher in Punjab than in India. For instance, prevalence of acute illness was 56 per 1000 in rural areas of Punjab against 42 per 1000 in rural areas of India; figures for chronic illness were 20 per 1,000 as against 13 per 1,000 respectively. Similarly, prevalence of acute and chronic illnesses was higher in urban areas of Punjab than in India. It also revealed that the number of persons reporting ailments usually increases with the increase in age in Punjab as well as in India. Chronic illnesses are generally prevalent among persons who are 40 years or older.

Further, data on incidence of morbidity in rural Punjab showed that, on the whole, 127 persons per 1000 population suffered from one or other types of illness during the first half of 2004. Incidence of morbidity was found to be higher in rural areas (136 persons per 1000 population) compared to that of in urban areas (107 persons per 1000 population). Further, morbidity incidence was significantly higher among females both in rural and urban areas. It was quite high as compared to all India average incidence of morbidity. In fact, Punjab was ranked as the second highest morbidity state after Kerala in the country (NSSO 2006). An analysis of estimated number of persons reporting ailment(s) in Punjab over two and half decades (1973-74, 1995-96 and 2004) revealed that number of ailing persons in the state grew at the rate of 3.8 percent per annum during 1973-74 to 1995-96. Between 1995-96 and 2004, growth in number of ailing persons rose to 7.1 percent.

The morbidity grew at a faster rate in rural Punjab, especially during the latter period of 1995-96 to 2004 (8.1 percent per annum) compared to the earlier period of 1973-74 to 1995-96 (3.0 percent per annum). However, in urban Punjab, growth rate in morbidity was 6.2 percent per annum between 1973-74 and 1995-96 compared to the growth rate of 4.8 percent per annum between 1995-96 and 2004 (Singh 2010).

Conclusion and Policy Implications

Punjab has recorded an impressive performance on reduction of birth rate, death rate, infant mortality rate and fertility rate, but rural-urban disparities in the health indicators are a feature of the existing health situation in Punjab. There is considerable difference in rural-urban health indicators. Rural areas still have a high birth rate, death rate, infant mortality rate and fertility rate as compared to those of the urban areas. The life expectancy in Punjab has also improved for both males and females, and in this case gender difference in health status is clearly noticeable.

The life expectancy of females has been observed to be higher than that of males. The immunization coverage has been uneven for infants, children and expectant mothers. The targets of immunization in case of infants and children have been met quite satisfactorily while in case of expectant mothers targets of immunization have not been fulfilling. The achievement rate of prophylaxies against nutritional anaemia was quite high during the eighties and the situation has deteriorated in recent years, as the achievement rates have been quite low for both children and expectant mothers. The incidence and prevalence rates of morbidity patterns in Punjab have been found to be higher than the all- India average in both rural and urban areas. The prevalence rate of illness has been higher among males and boys than among females or girls in both rural and urban areas of Punjab and all-India. Education did not have much impact on the morbidity patterns, except that the reporting of illness was less among the illiterates in both rural and urban areas of Punjab.

In order to improve the health scenario and to deal with health problems in the state the following policy interventions can be suggested:

The first priority for Punjab is to have a State Health Policy, clearly listing out future health care requirements. Punjab should take a long range view of the health sector. For better health care and family welfare services in future, the state must frame a health policy of its own. The government should take measures to improve the quality of health care and family welfare services in order to improve the health indicators in the state. Besides, health goals should be dovetailed with goals set in the areas of environmental sanitation, drinking water, elimination of maternal and child nutrition, education and health awareness. Safe drinking water, availability of drainage and sewage systems and waste disposal should be a priority. The state of Punjab requires a proper health management information system which is the backbone for immediate access to information on different health indicators such as birth rate, death rate, infant and child mortality rates, disease patterns etc. at the district level. New information technology can play a vital role in this regard. As the disease patterns have changed over the years, the growing incidence of life-style diseases such as cardiovascular diseases, diabetes, gastroenteritis, urology and newly emerging diseases such as cancer, HIV/AIDS, dengue and bird flu are posing new challenges for the state. The policy should examine the feasibility of setting up special clinics at the district hospitals to deal with some of these problems. The health policy should also consider suitable nutritional awareness programme, initially at the school and Anganwadi level. Agro-processing industrial units in the state should be encouraged to produce micronutrient-fortified food items. A number of primary studies should also be undertaken, through autonomous research institutions, to assess the health needs of the state.

A few concerns, which are outside the domain of this paper, but constitute an integral part of the healthy growth of the human mind and body are environment and occupational health, adequate availability of drinking water, hygienic living conditions, nutritious food, removal of drug addiction and other health hazards, therefore strategies must be set to deal with such problems.

References

Ahluwalia Isher Judge. (2010). "Social Sector Development: A Perspective from Punjab", available at http://www.icrier.org/pdf.

Government of Punjab. (2004). Punjab-- *Human Development Report 2004*, New Delhi: New Concept Information System.

Government of Punjab. *Statistical Abstract of Punjab*, Various Issues.

India Brand Equity Foundation. (2010). "Investment Climate in Punjab" available at http://www.ibef.org.

National Council of Applied Economic Research (NCAER), *Household Survey of Medical Care* New Delhi, *(May-June 1990)*, June 1992, 52 p.

National Council of Applied Economic Research (NCAER). (1995). *Household Survey of Health Care Utilization and Expenditure*, New Delhi, (March).

National Sample Survey Organisation (NSSO), Department of Statistics, Government of India, *Sarvekshana*, Volume IV, No. 1& 2, 1980.

National Sample Survey Organisation (NSSO), Department of Statistics, Government of India, *Morbidity and Treatment of Ailments* (52nd round),

July 1995-June 1996, Department of Statistics, Government of India, *Sarvekshana*, November 1998.

Sen, Amartya. (2000). "Health in Development", *Bulletin of World Health Organisation*, 77 (8).

Singh, Sukhwinder. (2010). "Rural Health in Punjab-Needs Reforms and Investment", Abstracts of Sikh Studies: July-Sept 2010.

World Health Organisation. (2003). *Health and Poverty, Health Financing: A Basic Guide*, Geneva, World Health Organization.